Law and the Great Plains

Recent Titles in
Contributions in Legal Studies

Questioning the Law in Corporate America: Agenda for Reform
Gerald L. Houseman

Reason Over Precedents: Origins of American Legal Thought
Craig Evan Klafter

The Iron Horse and the Constitution: The Railroads and the Transformation of the Fourteenth Amendment
Richard C. Cortner

Between Civil and Religious Law: The Plight of the *Agunah* in American Society
Irving A. Breitowitz

The Death Penalty and Racial Bias: Overturning Supreme Court Assumptions
Gregory D. Russell

The Rehnquist Court: In Pursuit of Judicial Conservatism
Stanley H. Friedelbaum

Parallel Importation in U.S. Trademark Law
Timothy H. Hiebert

John Marshall's Law: Interpretation, Ideology, and Interest
Thomas C. Shevory

Group Defamation and Freedom of Speech: The Relationship Between Language and Violence
Monroe H. Freedman and Eric M. Freedman, editors

Innovation, Reaction, and Atrophy: The Impact of Judicial-Selection Method on Policy in State Supreme Courts
Daniel R. Pinello

Controversy, Courts, and Community: The Rhetoric of Judge Miles Welton Lord
Verna C. Corgan

Constitutional Politics in the States: Contemporary Controversies and Historical Patterns
G. Alan Tarr, editor

LAW AND THE GREAT PLAINS

Essays on the Legal History of the Heartland

Edited by John R. Wunder

Contributions in Legal Studies, Number 82

GREENWOOD PRESS
Westport, Connecticut • London

Library of Congress Cataloging-in-Publication Data

Law and the Great Plains : essays on the legal history of the Heartland / edited by John R. Wunder.
p. cm.—(Contributions in legal studies, ISSN 0147–1074 : no. 82)
Includes bibliographical references and index.
ISBN 0–313–29680–4 (alk. paper)
1. Law—Middle West—History—Congresses. 2. Law—Great Plains—History—Congresses. I. Wunder, John R. II. Series.
KF352.L387 1996
349.77—dc20
[347.7] 95–37979

British Library Cataloguing in Publication Data is available.

Library of Congress Catalog Card Number: 95–37979

ISBN: 0–313–29680–4
ISSN: 0147–1074

First published in 1996

Greenwood Press, 88 Post Road West, Westport, CT 06881
An imprint of Greenwood Publishing Group, Inc.

Printed in the United States of America

The paper used in this book complies with the Permanent Paper Standard issued by the National Information Standards Organization (Z39.48–1984).

10 9 8 7 6 5 4 3 2 1

Copyright Acknowledgments

Chapters 2, 5, and 9 have been published in substantially similar form in the following journals:

Chapter 2

Kermit L. Hall, "The Legal Culture of the Great Plains," *Great Plains Quarterly* 12 (Spring 1992): 86–98. Reprinted with permission.

Chapter 5

James W. Ely, Jr., "The Railroad Question Revisited: *Chicago, Milwaukee & St. Paul Railway v. Minnesota* and Constitutional Limits on State Regulations," *Great Plains Quarterly* 12 (Spring 1992): 121–134. Reprinted with permission.

Chapter 9

Frank Pommersheim, "A Path Near the Clearing: An Essay on Constitutional Adjudication in Tribal Courts," *Gonzaga Law Review* 27, no. 3 (1991–1992): 393–421. Reprinted with permission.

Contents

Preface

This volume would not have been possible had it not been for the many participants in the first ever conference on law and the Great Plains held at the University of Nebraska and sponsored by the Center for Great Plains Studies in March 1991. They took a risk. They were willing to consider topics within a regional interdisciplinary context that had not previously been contemplated.

Sessions ranged from "Rights and the Great Plains: An International Dimension," "*Meyer v. Nebraska,*" "*Brown v. Board of Education of Topeka*," and "Economic and Environmental Regulation on the Great Plains," to "Image and Word of the Law: Architecture and Literature on the Great Plains," "Divorce, Great Plains Style," "Water Law and the Great Plains," "Law Enforcement on the Great Plains," "Extralegal Activity and the Great Plains," and "Native Americans and the Law."

In addition to the authors of the following essays, other noteworthy participants included Richard T. Harrison (University of Alberta), Thomas Baker (Texas Tech University), Lucius Barker (Stanford University), Jesse H. Choper (University of California, Berkeley), Arthur McEvoy (University of Wisconsin–Madison), H. Hamner Hill (Southeast Missouri State University), William G. Ross (Samford University), Nina Totenberg (National Public Radio), Andrew Eisenberg (Brown University), Emilia Gonzalez Clements (University of Kentucky), Yasuhide Kawashima (University of Texas at El

Paso), Robert S. Haller (University of Nebraska–Lincoln), Daniel E. Wueste (Clemson University), James E. Sherow (Kansas State University), Otis W. Templer (Texas Tech University), Peter Longo (University of Nebraska at Kearney), Larry D. Ball (Arkansas State University), Robert Thacker (St. Lawrence University), Frederick Luebke (University of Nebraska–Lincoln), Linda Grathwohl (University of Iowa), Barbara Jones (Minnesota State Historical Society), Stephen Wasby (State University of New York at Albany), C. Robert Haywood (Washburn University), John Findlay (University of Washington), Paula Petrik (University of Maine at Orono), Donald P. Lay (U.S. Court of Appeals, Eighth Circuit), Russell E. Lovell II (Drake University), Michael R. Hill (Lincoln, NE), Kathryn A. Bellman (University of Nebraska–Lincoln), Joan R. Gunderson (University of California, San Marcos), James Hewitt (Attorney, Lincoln, NE), James N. Gilbert (University of Nebraska at Kearney), George D. Watson, Jr. (Chadron State College), Carl Ubbelohde (Case Western Reserve University), Diana Abu-Jaber (University of Oregon), Harold S. Herd (Supreme Court of Kansas), William C. Hastings (Supreme Court of Nebraska), Michael Grossberg (Indiana University), Donald D. Landon (Southwest Missouri State University), Charles Ballard (University of Nebraska–Lincoln), Kurt D. Siedschlaw (University of Nebraska at Kearney), Kenneth Leyton-Brown (University of Regina), Anna Shavers (University of Nebraska–Lincoln), Elizabeth Grobsmith (University of Nebraska–Lincoln), Beth Ritter Knoche (University of Nebraska–Lincoln), Clare V. McKanna, Jr. (San Diego State University), and Walter Echo-Hawk (Native American Rights Fund).

Some of the essays produced at the conference appeared in the two journals published by the Center for Great Plains Studies: *Great Plains Quarterly* and *Great Plains Research*. Two special issues devoted to law and the Great Plains were *Great Plains Quarterly* 12 (Spring 1992) and *Great Plains Research* 2 (February 1992).

This volume benefitted from the assistance of the Center for Great Plains Studies staff, especially Gretchen Walker and Linda Ratcliffe; Clare McKanna, Jr. and Todd Kerstetter; the editing by Frances W. Kaye of *Quarterly* articles; the typing of Margaret Cullinane; and the strong support of John Peters, then Dean of the University of Nebraska–Lincoln College of Arts and Sciences and now at the University of Tennessee; Harvey Perlman, Dean of the University of Nebraska–Lincoln College of Law, and Susan Wunder of the University of Nebraska–Lincoln Teachers College.

I owe all of these people a tremendous debt of gratitude.

John R. Wunder
Lincoln, NE

Part I

Regional Legal History and the Great Plains

1

Toward a Legal History of the Great Plains

John R. Wunder

Regional history as a methodological concept is strong in the American history tradition. Some would date its origin with Frederick Jackson Turner's famous frontier thesis essay and his ideas about section and region. In the modern period after World War II historians of early America were the first to embrace model case studies to understand the notion of community in British colonial America, and these concepts have since been applied by other historians to other times, regions, and topical frameworks.

Similarly, the history of American law has undergone a transformation away from rote listings and analyses of statutory law and legislative debate. Modern legal historiography is instead methodologically derived from quantitative and qualitative case studies and synopses of regional and national legal cultures. Social, economic, and political history are viewed within the history of law and region in an attempt to understand how law was perceived and how it functioned.

While the study of American legal history in a modern sense is only about fifty years old, New Western History is even more youthful, being in existence for only two decades. According to Richard White, New Western History "is simply the aggregation of studies of race, gender, class, community, economic dependency, and the environment in the West."[1] New

Western historians prefer to view the West as a region rather than as a process as characterized by Turner's frontier.

Even though New Western historians have changed the dialogue in studies of the American West, they have been slow to pick up on legal constructs. White, for example, in his pathbreaking text, *"It's Your Misfortune and None of My Own": A New History of the American West*, rarely addresses law directly, and when he does it is as a tool of the federal government used against minorities and in favor of corporate exploitation of the land.[2] Similarly, William Cronon, in his award-winning environmental study of the Great Lakes hinterland, *Nature's Metropolis: Chicago and the Great West*, does not embrace the ideas of legal historians who have dealt with environmental law, economic growth, and urban expansion.[3] Patricia Limerick, however, addresses the relationship of law, the economy, race, and the West in more direct ways than do White and Cronon. She has written in *The Legacy of Conquest* that the relationship of law in the West has been oversimplified and propagandized. Says Limerick, "The West was once the Wild West, the old image held, and then heroically, law and order were introduced and the wilderness was mastered."[4] Limerick does not offer specifics here, and it is not her intent to do so. Thus, New Western History awaits a melding with the New Legal History.

Ironically, the New Legal historians have had a longer experience with concepts of "region" than have Western historians. Modern studies of American law have been formulated on case studies and regional legal histories. They have become standards in the field. Although much attention has been paid to regional legal culture by American legal historians, this has led to imbalances. Some areas are saturated; others are neglected. Happenstance, more often than not, has contributed to the building of knowledge.

Leading scholars in New Legal History include J. Willard Hurst, Harry N. Scheiber, Lawrence M. Friedman, Morton J. Horwitz, William E. Nelson, and John Phillip Reid. Hurst used Wisconsin as a model of law working in the Progressive tradition. Law acted as a stimulus to release the human and capital energy necessary for economic growth and development.[5] Friedman, too, began his scholarship in Wisconsin with a historic analysis of contract law, but he moved to California where he staked out regional concepts of criminal justice.[6] Scheiber's study of canals in Ohio is a classic example of law and economic growth building upon each other to effect major changes in a region's identity. Like Friedman, Scheiber moved his studies to California to take up twentieth-century legal economic concerns, and through his students at the University of California, both at San Diego and Berkeley, further significant new legal history studies of law, the economy, and the environment have been produced.[7]

Horwitz and Nelson teach in the East and primarily study New England through their emphases on time, the British colonial era, and the antebellum era. Criminal justice and economic growth are prominently featured in their regional studies.[8] Reid has connections to both New York and California, but his more recent work concerns law in the North American West. Indeed, combining New Legal History with certain aspects of New Western History is perhaps best personified in the breadth and evolution of the works of John Phillip Reid.[9]

What if J. Willard Hurst had taught law at the University of Oklahoma, Scheiber and Friedman were colleagues at the University of Colorado, and Horwitz, Nelson, and Reid divided their careers between the University of Wyoming and Yale University? Legal scholars would no doubt debate the merits of the legal cultures of the Great Plains and the interior West rather than point to Wisconsin, California, Ohio, or New England for verification of key concepts and generalities.

During the 1960s and 1970s this regional approach to legal development shifted to the American South. There, combined with New Southern historians who were discovering the world of African Americans and yeoman white farmers, New Legal historians addressed concepts of race and law on a regional level, in both pre– and post–Civil War periods. In many ways this was the first systematic attempt to understand the racial cleavages of the American past, and the works produced in the 1970s and 1980s were extremely influential in addressing this important issue.[10]

What if the modern scholarship of law and race had not initially considered slavery and African Americans and instead had evolved out of concepts of conquest or considerations of genocide and Native Americans or community property, civil law traditions, and the treatment of Mexican Americans and other Latinos? Instead of debating various aspects of the history of law, the economy, and slavery, legal historians would be considering the role law played in the displacement of Plains Indians or the development of water and mining law. Again regional happenstance dictated the direction of scholarship.

With the evolution of region as a methodological concept tried and tested by American historians, with the experience of American legal historians who have investigated questions of economics, environment, and race in case studies of a regional nature, and with the recent changes in the study of the American West, it is not surprising to see New Western History and

New Legal History meet to beget new areas of investigation. And the legal history of the Great Plains has never been written.

Modern legal history will inevitably lead scholars to new areas of investigation, such as the legal culture of the Great Plains, which has been completely ignored prior to this volume. There is no need to belabor this point for it is masterfully discussed by Kermit L. Hall in the following essay. What should be conceded at the outset, there having been little or no legal history written about the Great Plains, is the uneven nature of the initial scholarship. It does not focus on regional legal development per se because such a focus is premature. It merely represents a beginning, a testing of the concept of a regional Great Plains law.

The diverse essays are grouped into three sections: landmark cases originating on the Great Plains, legal theorists and practitioners of the Great Plains, and judges of the Great Plains. The first section considers specific historical precedents derived from three Great Plains disputes: *Meyer v. Nebraska* (1923), *Brown v. Board of Education of Topeka* (1954), and *Chicago, Milwaukee & St. Paul Railway Company v. Minnesota* (1890). The second section offers glimpses into the work of two legal thinkers of the Plains: Karl Llewellyn and William Jennings Bryan. And the third section considers two varieties of Plains courts: federal district courts and Indian tribal courts. Obviously, none of these essays offers the final word; rather, they are introductory in scope and designed hopefully to pique the reader's scholarly interests.

Great Plains legal history represents truly virgin territory. Encompassing the midsection of the United States from Montana and North Dakota on the Canadian border south to New Mexico and Texas on the Mexican border, the region is united environmentally as a place where aridity, treelessness, and flatlands confront Plains peoples. Indeed, the Great Plains is international in scope because it also includes three Canadian provinces.

Of course the basic question to be answered is whether the Great Plains as a region is legally distinctive. Previously, historians have considered the area to be unique environmentally and culturally. It is possible that environment, the relative lateness of non-Indian settlement, and the diverse native cultures and European heritage preserved in Plains life are factors that have influenced the spread of legal institutions on the Plains. Whether this geopolity presents a legal culture remains to be discovered, as Kermit Hall suggests. Much needs to be done. Particularly promising are the topics of Great Plains family law, economic regulation, water law, Native American law, environmental law, property law, violence, criminal justice, law enforcement, and religious freedoms.[11] The Great Plains offers scholarly challenges and opportunities to legal historians unlike any other region in North America. Like the dynamic stories of so many of the peoples of the Plains, the region holds promise as a meeting point where the New Legal History and the New Western History can converge.

NOTES

1. Richard White, " 'Far West. See also frontier': The 'New Western History,' Textbooks, and the U.S. History Survey Course," *Perspectives* 30 (September 1992): 10.

2. Ibid., *"It's Your Misfortune and None of My Own": A New History of the American West* (Norman: University of Oklahoma Press, 1991), pp. 117, 322–23, 402.

3. William Cronon, *Nature's Metropolis: Chicago and the Great West* (New York: W.W. Norton & Company, 1991). Law is primarily discussed in terms of doctrinal geographical concepts. See pp. 38–39. For a variety of essays featuring New Western History approaches, see William Cronon, George Miles, and Jay Gitlin, eds., *Under an Open Sky: Rethinking America's Western Past* (New York: W.W. Norton & Company, 1992).

4. Patricia Nelson Limerick, *The Legacy of Conquest: The Unbroken Past of the American West* (New York: W. W. Norton & Company, 1987), p. 173.

5. See J. Willard Hurst, *Law and Economic Growth: The Legal History of the Lumber Industry in Wisconsin, 1836–1915* (Cambridge, MA: Harvard University Press, 1964) and *Law and the Conditions of Freedom* (Madison: University of Wisconsin Press, 1956) among others.

6. Lawrence M. Friedman, *Contract Law in America: A Social and Economic Case Study* (Madison: University of Wisconsin Press, 1965) and with Robert V. Percival, *The Roots of Justice: Crime and Punishment in Alameda County, California, 1870–1910* (Chapel Hill: University of North Carolina Press, 1981). See also Friedman's text, the first text of the New Legal History era, *A History of American Law* (New York: Simon and Schuster, 1973).

7. Harry N. Scheiber, *Ohio Canal Era: A Case Study of Government and the Economy, 1820–1861* (Athens: Ohio University Press, 1969); and as editor, *The Old Northwest: Studies in Regional History, 1787–1910* (Lincoln: University of Nebraska Press, 1969), and as co-editor with Lawrence M. Friedman, *American Law and the Constitutional Order: Historical Perspectives* (Cambridge, MA: Harvard University Press, 1978). See also the works of Scheiber's students Arthur F. McEvoy, *The Fisherman's Problem: Ecology and Law in the California Fisheries, 1850–1980* (New York: Cambridge University Press, 1986) and M. Catherine Miller, *Flooding the Courtrooms: Law and Water in the Far West* (Lincoln: University of Nebraska Press, 1993).

8. Morton J. Horwitz, *The Transformation of American Law, 1780–1860* (Cambridge, MA: Harvard University Press, 1977) and *The Transformation of*

American Law, 1870–1960: The Crisis of Legal Orthodoxy (New York: Oxford University Press, 1992); William E. Nelson, *Americanization of the Common Law: The Impact of Legal Change on Massachusetts Society, 1760–1830* (Cambridge, MA: Harvard University Press, 1975) and *Dispute and Conflict Resolution in Plymouth Colony, Massachusetts, 1725–1825* (Chapel Hill: University of North Carolina Press).

9. See, for example, John Phillip Reid, *A Law of Blood: The Primitive Law of the Cherokee Nation* (New York: New York University Press, 1970); *A Better Kind of Hatchet: Law, Trade, and Diplomacy in the Cherokee Nation During the Early Years of European Contact* (University Park: Pennsylvania State University Press, 1976); *Chief Justice: The Judicial World of Charles Doe* (Cambridge, MA: Harvard University Press, 1967); *In a Defiant Stance: The Conditions of Law in Massachusetts Bay, the Irish Comparison, and the Coming of the American Revolution* (University Park: Pennsylvania State University Press, 1977); and *Law for the Elephant: Property and Social Behavior on the Overland Trail* (San Marino, CA: The Huntington Library, 1980).

10. For example, see Mark V. Tushnet, *The American Law of Slavery, 1810–1860: Consideration of Humanity and Interest* (Princeton, NJ: Princeton University Press, 1981); Don E. Fehrenbacher, *Slavery, Law, and Politics: The Dred Scott Case in Historical Perspective* (New York: Oxford University Press, 1981); and Paul Finkelman, *An Imperfect Union: Slavery, Federalism, and Comity* (Chapel Hill: University of North Carolina Press, 1981), among others. The body of literature has resulted in two important collections, David J. Bodenhamer and James W. Ely, Jr., eds., *Ambivalent Legacy: A Legal History of the South* (Jackson: University Press of Mississippi, 1984) and Kermit L. Hall and James W. Ely, Jr., eds., *An Uncertain Tradition: Constitutionalism and the History of the South* (Athens: University of Georgia Press, 1989).

11. For a recent collection featuring for the first time New Legal History approaches to the American West from both a Canadian and U.S. perspective, see John McLaren, Hamar Foster, and Chet Orloff, eds., *Law for the Elephant, Law for the Beaver: Essays in the Legal History of the North American West* (Regina, Sask.: Canadian Plains Research Center, University of Regina, 1992).

2

The Legal Culture of the Great Plains

Kermit L. Hall

The great prairie lawyer Abraham Lincoln once said of an opposing legal counsel's argument, "He caught on to something, but only by the hind leg."[1] Lincoln's observation applies with equal force to our current understanding of the legal culture of the Great Plains, and even that characterization is generous. Take, for example, the literature on the region's history of public and private law and legal institutions. It is pitifully small. Bits and pieces are scattered through specialized journals and state history periodicals, but there is nothing like a systematic body of scholarship.[2] The major bibliographic guide to the literature in American constitutional and legal history lists, during the past twenty years, only six articles dealing with the subject and no books. These numbers stand in sharp contrast to the more than sixty entries and two major books on southern legal history and the more than twenty articles devoted to the legal culture of the Rocky Mountain and Pacific states.[3] Our ignorance about the legal culture of the Great Plains is even more sobering when we realize that in the past century scholars of American constitutional and legal history have produced more than twenty thousand books and articles, with more than four thousand of those published in the 1980s. While the Great Plains economies have regularly gone through cycles of boom and bust, scholarship about the region's legal culture has never even taken off. Indeed, there is not even an agenda for such scholarship.

So an important threshold question is why this neglect? In part, it is an accident of location. The major centers of learning about legal history have not been in the Plains states; there has been no Willard Hurst or Lawrence Friedman to make the region a historical laboratory for testing various hypotheses about legal culture. Instead the nation's legal history has been drawn, at least until quite recently, from the East and from New England, especially. If Willard Hurst, perhaps the greatest American legal historian, had lived in Nebraska instead of Wisconsin, chances are good that we would know more today about its legal culture than we do. Even native Nebraskan Roscoe Pound, who had strong historical interests, drew his examples from England and New England rather than the Plains.[4]

Second, while scholars have churned out an impressive body of literature about the Great Plains, they have seldom thought to analyze law and legal institutions as reflections of the region's assumptions about society, culture, and economy. When they have turned to the law, historians of the Great Plains have usually taken climate and geography as both the beginning and the ending point of analysis, failing to probe the ways in which modes of economic production and social organization on the Plains have shaped and been shaped by the law. Historians of the Great Plains have not approached law as a social and cultural artifact; instead, they have typically viewed it as a closed system chained by environmental determinism.[5]

There is a third reason for the slight attention paid to the region's legal history. For the national community of jurists, the Great Plains has been a legal backwater. Judges and treatise writers in the nation's other regions have paid slight attention to legal developments on the Plains. Studies by Peter Harris, Lawrence Friedman, and Rodney Mott on the reputations of state supreme courts over the past century and a half leave little doubt about this matter.[6] Peter Harris measured citations by sixteen state supreme courts of cases from other state supreme courts for the period 1870–1970. The two Great Plains states included in his study—Kansas and South Dakota—have persistently lacked citation power. Indeed, the states of the Great Plains ranked even lower than the often maligned state courts of the South, including Alabama, North Carolina, and Virginia. In Harris's study, nobody cited two state supreme courts as authority—Delaware and South Dakota.[7] Of course, citation is not the same as influence, and there is reason to believe, according to the studies of Rodney Mott, that the high courts of Kansas and Nebraska in the early twentieth century achieved some distinction. But no appellate court on the Great Plains has ever achieved the reputation enjoyed by its counterparts in California, New York, and Massachusetts.[8]

This status reflects the fact that the states with the richest and most complex economic, social, and cultural settings are also likely to produce the richest legal environment.[9] But it is also true that the Great Plains states have been net importers of legal talent. A collective survey of the 420 judges who served on the highest courts of appeal in the ten states between 1870 and 1970 reveals as much.[10] Until the mid-1930s a majority of Plains state judges received their legal educations outside the region, a condition that suggests that legal education there lagged behind developments elsewhere. Only in the last fifty years have the Great Plains states developed a high proportion of judges trained within the region.

There is a fourth and final reason why legal historians have showered so little attention on the Great Plains. Lincoln, once again, captured the spirit of things. In describing an especially spirited wrestling match, he observed that the opponents had struggled so fiercely that they got inside one another's coats. More often than not, legal historians have simply swallowed up the Great Plains as part of the general legal history of the West.[11]

That the legal culture of the Great Plains has been ignored does not mean, of course, that it should be ignored or that it is unimportant. We should also recognize that our lack of attention to law and legal institutions on the Great Plains only abets the skewed vision that we have of American legal development as an emanation exclusively of New England.[12]

Having said all of this, we arrive at the central question. Has the Great Plains had and does it now have a distinctive legal culture? By legal culture we mean the ideas, attitudes, values, and opinions about law held by people in a society.[13] The assumption is that these ideas and attitudes influence legal behavior, especially the kind and level of demands placed on the legal system. In raising the question of legal culture, we are asking when and why and where people have turned to law and government. The assumption is that if we understand legal culture we can, in turn, better appreciate the role of law in society.

We can grasp the implications of this relationship between social change and the law by resorting to a somewhat stereotypical perspective. As one sage has observed:

> In Germany, under the law, everything is prohibited except that which is permitted.
>
> In France, under the law, everything is permitted, except that which is prohibited.

In the Soviet Union, under the law, everything is prohibited, *including* that which is permitted.

In Italy, under the law, everything is permitted, *especially* that which is *prohibited.*

And in the United States, under the law, everything is *both* permitted *and* prohibited, because Americans are forever deciding the law but nothing ever seems to get decided.[14]

We should remember, however, that particularity is not the same thing as legal culture. The Great Plains, like all regions of the nation, has certainly generated unique demands that have, in turn, produced laws and legal institutions different from those of other areas of the country. How different these changes really have been, both as a matter of inter- and intraregional comparison, is something worth paying attention to, but we should remember that uniqueness and adaptation of older legal forms to newer circumstances do not necessarily herald a new legal culture. It is the attitudes, values, ideas, and opinions behind those changes that really count, and they can, of course, be exactly the same even if they are expressed in different ways. The other important point is that legal culture is not static; it evolves over time as the nature of social demands and expectations change. As Roscoe Pound once observed: "The law must be stable, but it must not stand still."[15]

REGIONALISM AND LAW

Our interest in the legal culture of the Great Plains is further evidence of the renewed vigor of regional history generally, especially in legal history.[16] After more than forty years of neglect, regional studies of all stripes are once again on the rise, in part because they appear to offer certain comparative advantages not found in local, state, or national studies. Legal historians have in fact shown increasing sympathy toward regional studies over the past decade. David Bodenhamer, Gordon Bakken, James W. Ely, Jr., Paul Finkelman, John Reid, and David Langum, to name but a few, have argued that generalizations drawn from regional patterns of legal organization and behavior are of greater comparative significance than generalizations drawn from community or national studies alone.[17] Regional studies, they contend, have allowed scholars to identify more precisely that which is merely local and to control for its effects. Similarly, proponents of regional studies insist that their findings offer the best test of attitudes and behavior that purport to be truly national.

In order to have a regional legal history, however, one must first have a region. In the case of the Great Plains, the matter of definition is a good deal more complex than might first appear. The simplest and most commonly used definition is environmental. Its leading proponent was Walter Prescott Webb, who believed that physical geography and climate unified the region. Webb's book, *The Great Plains*, first published in 1931, remains today the single most widely read history of the region. In it he approached the Great Plains as an environment unified by its flatness, lack of trees, and semiaridity. For our purposes, this Plains environment can be narrowed to what constitutes the heart of the region—portions of the ten states of Montana, Wyoming, Colorado, New Mexico, North and South Dakota, Nebraska, Kansas, Oklahoma, and Texas. Webb argued that once immigrants crossed the eastern boundary of the Great Plains at the ninety-eighth meridian, all of the institutions they had known in the East were, in his words, "either broken or remade or else greatly altered."[18]

This environment, Webb insisted, produced not only a unique body of law but a legal culture entirely distinct from that in the East. "The Easterner, with his background of forest and farm," Webb observed, "could not always understand the man of the cattle kingdom."

> One went on foot, the other went on horseback; one carried his law in books, the other carried it strapped round his waist. One represented tradition, the other represented innovation; one responded to convention, the other responded to necessity and evolved his own conventions. Yet the man of the timber and the town made the law for the man of the plain; the plainsman, finding this law unsuited to his needs, broke it and was called lawless.[19]

Webb also pointed to the democratic nature of the Great Plains, giving special attention to the development of women's suffrage. In short, according to Webb, the legal culture of the Great Plains resonated to the values of innovation, individualism, democracy, and lawlessness present in the region's general culture. The great open skies of the Plains, it seems, provided almost boundless opportunities for individuals, so much so that individuals often took the law into their own hands.

Historians, geographers, and anthropologists have subjected Webb's environmental determinism to often withering criticism but it retains considerable vitality, as any reader of Ian Frazier's similarly titled recent book on the region will appreciate.[20] Moreover, of all the historians who have written on the Great Plains, Webb provides by far the most coherent, if ultimately clipped, assessment of the law and legal institutions. Thus, both as a way of assessing the region's legal culture and as a means of dealing with the coherence of the Great Plains as other than a geographic fact of life, Webb's thesis of individualism, innovation, and violence seems an appropriate place for the infant field of Great Plains legal history to begin.

TESTING WEBB'S THESIS

Much of Webb's argument about the inventiveness and individualism of the Great Plains rested on his analysis of property law in three important areas: land, livestock, and water. But how well do his arguments hold up?

Take, for example, the open-range cattle industry in the Great Plains. The fact that fencing materials were scarce in the treeless plain led cattlemen to demand that the English common-law requirement to fence livestock be abrogated and the burden of fencing be placed upon crop farmers. Plains legislators passed open-range statutes that placed the burden to fence on the farmer. If damage to crops by livestock were litigated, then the farmer had to prove he had maintained a legal fence around his crops to collect money damages from the cattle owner. Yet there was considerable borrowing; fencing-out statutes were hardly unique to the Plains. Borrowing legal doctrine from the East was one of the common features of the Great Plains, and even in an area so seemingly unique as the cattle industry, cultural memories about law were often long. John Reid has made the same point about migrants crossing the Great Plains in the 1850s.[21]

What gave visibility to the fencing statutes on the Great Plains was not their novelty but the fact that they sought to resolve conflicts among farmers, free-grass cattlemen, and barbed-wire ranchers. Hence the legal culture of the Great Plains resonated far more to the economic pressures associated with a shift on the Plains from the nineteenth-century economics of pastoral stockraising to the twentieth-century practice of farming. In short, the law as it affected cattle and fencing had more to do with competing modes of economic production than it did with innovation as a paramount value.[22]

There seems little doubt that the law of property rights in the West was highly instrumental where issues of economic development were involved. Initially land on the Great Plains was not a scarce resource although it eventually became so. For much of the 1860s and 1870s "squatter sovereignty" was sufficient for settling land ownership questions.[23] The range was open and there was little in the way of an exclusive right to own and use it. Cattlemen did not own the land; they exercised instead "range rights" that neighbors recognized but that the law did not enforce. To secure these accustomed rights, ranchers ran claim advertisements in local newspapers.

By the 1880s, however, competing agricultural groups on the Plains often had conflicting claims to the same land without any enforceable mechanism to settle them. The result was a prolonged struggle among different kinds of land users. Cattlemen, for example, organized an effort to persuade state and territorial legislators to pass statutes that punished those who drove their stock from the accustomed range, but by the 1880s stock growers' associations had persuaded several state legislatures to enact statutes that restricted entry onto the range through control of access to the limited water supplies. The entire movement in land law in the Great Plains at the end of the nineteenth century was from communal to exclusive ownership, a development that had long been under way in the East and that has continued unabated even today as more and more of Great Plains land and productive capacity has been placed in fewer and fewer hands.[24] While often advertised as protecting individual property rights, these developments have actually produced a consolidation of landholding that mocks the notion of the small, self-reliant farmer. Once again, the generally inefficient small livestock and farming enterprises yielded before large, well-capitalized agricultural businesses.

Much the same has happened with water law, an area to which Webb pointed to underscore the inventiveness of Great Plains legal culture. As with land and livestock, however, water regulation on the Plains seems less innovative and distinctive than Webb imagined.[25] From the outset, access to and control of water was the most crucial economic consideration on the Plains. Initially western settlers adopted the riparian system of water rights, which meant that the right to use water accrued to the one who owned the bank of the stream. That such riparian water rights, whether implicit or explicit, were adopted by the frontiersman is not difficult to understand. Indeed, it was not until settlement was well under way, as Donald J. Pisani has shown, that water law began to change significantly, granting to the first appropriator of it an exclusive right and to later appropriators rights conditioned upon the prior rights of those who had gone before them.[26] The new rules also permitted the diversion of waters to nonriparian lands, the extinguishment of rights in water if not used, and the transfer of water rights from one person to another.

As with land and livestock, the pattern in the development of water law on the Great Plains was from common to exclusive rights. Yet even in this seemingly most unique area, the states of the Great Plains were borrowers, as Robert G. Dunbar has observed. The states did not build their own system of water law *de novo*; instead they borrowed lavishly from the California legislature and Supreme Court, whose decisions in *Irwin v.*

Phillips, *Lux v. Haggin*, and *Katz v. Walkinshaw* became models adopted in the Plains states.[27] Colorado, for example, which led the states of the Great Plains in dealing with the issues of multiple uses of water, drew heavily from the California experience to fashion what became known as the Colorado Doctrine—a doctrine that protected vested users in their rights to water.[28]

Moreover, there were significant differences within the Great Plains. Much like Lincoln's wrestlers, Webb often let the statutes of water law in the Great Plains get swallowed up in his description of the West as a whole. The trend toward exclusivity was strongest in those states—Montana, Wyoming, Colorado, and New Mexico—where rainfall averaged less than fifteen inches a year, while in states with somewhat greater amounts of rainfall—North and South Dakota, Nebraska, Kansas, Oklahoma, and Texas—the common law was retained in a modified form, one that followed the lead of California in recognizing *both* riparian *and* appropriative rights. Furthermore, the long-term pattern has not been to serve the individual small water user but to reward the heavily capitalized businesses that make modern agribusiness work.

There is no doubt that innovation was an important feature of the Great Plains legal culture, but it was neither unique nor determinative. Property rights were sometimes treated in different ways than they were in the East, but that did not mean that easterners, in other areas of economic development, such as the fellow servant rule, assumption of risk, and contributory negligence, were incapable of innovating on their own. The reasonable use doctrine, which became an important part of water law on the Great Plains, was also applied to stream courses and water power in the East as a way of expediting the development of manufacturing.[29] In the end, felt economic needs, not geography and climate, were the real inducements to legal innovation—in the Great Plains or elsewhere.

LAWLESSNESS AND VIOLENCE

Interregional differences in legal culture and the habit of borrowing were evident in two other areas: lawlessness and violence and the legal/political status of women. The Great Plains, according to commentators as different in outlook as Webb and Patricia Nelson Limerick, was a rough and tumble place, in which violence and extralegal behavior figured prominently in the underlying culture. Truman Capote, of course, crystallized the notion of the violent Plains in his book *In Cold Blood*. Capote captured the essence of what frightens us most about violence on the Plains—it was random, remorseless, methodical, and suffered in a remote Kansas farm house. There were, of course, other kinds of violence on the Plains; some of it, like that associated with Bat Masterson and Wyatt Earp, involved conflict resolution, while other violence, such as that associated with ecotage and the Earth First! movement, was directed at authority itself.[30]

Let us, however, concentrate only on one kind of crime—homicide. One of the reasons that Capote's book so shocks our conscience is that it is the exception and not the rule. Every recent study of violence and crime finds the Great Plains states lagging far behind the national leader—the South. The white male homicide rates from the late nineteenth century up to today reveal that no Great Plains state, including that seeming bastion of violence—Texas—, ranks in the top twenty, with most of the states of the Plains scattered over the middle or lower end of the spectrum.[31] In more recent times, Texas and New Mexico have shown a higher rate of homicide, but even they lag behind Louisiana, Mississippi, Alabama, Georgia, South Carolina, and Florida. The other Great Plains states rank very low.[32]

These figures also caution us against thinking about the Great Plains in an exclusively North-South fashion. Cultural interpreters of the Plains, such as Earl Pomeroy and Robert Berkhofer, have argued that in many instances such an alignment does not make sense.[33] Homicide rates suggest as much. The culture of North Dakota, for example, more closely resembles that of Minnesota than that of Nebraska and Kansas. The southern Plains, on the other hand, have much more in common with Arkansas and Tennessee than with the northern Plains. According to many geographers, folklorists, and linguists, it is the East-West patterns of settlement and interregional migration flows rather than environmental attributes that define the Plains.[34]

In the case of homicide and suicide that was certainly true. Where the influx of southern immigrants was greatest—Texas, New Mexico, and Oklahoma—the incidence of violence was the highest. Where the flow of population included more Scandinavian and Yankee stock, as was true in the northern tier of the Great Plains states, homicide has been less frequent. In short, as Raymond D. Gastil's study of cultural regionalism reveals, the presence of *southerners* on the Great Plains has historically been the best predictor of violence. At the same time, the incidence of suicide has been highest in the northern Plains, with its strong Scandinavian origins.[35] Any characterization of the Great Plains as violent always has to be framed comparatively, since there are fairly significant inter- and intraregional variations.

LEGAL AND POLITICAL STATUS OF WOMEN

The same can be said of the legal and political status of women. We are only beginning to have some idea of the historical development of family law on the Plains. There is a working hypothesis that marital matters in farming communities tend to be conservative, with little room for women to escape. Yet if we look beneath this relationship, as Paula Petrik is doing in her on-going study of divorce law in the West, we find a mixture of morality and economic expediency. Here as elsewhere, Great Plains lawmakers seemed sensitive to economic necessity, crafting the law in instrumental ways so as to protect the integrity and earning power of the family. Take, for example, the case of Nebraska. Its divorce law included grounds of desertion, adultery, extreme cruelty, intemperance, and an omnibus provision of other but less utilized causes, including impotency, conviction for a felony, and the like. In this regard Nebraska divorce law mimicked developments elsewhere in the country.[36] But in those Plains states with large numbers of homesteaders, Petrik has also discovered that a "dower" clause was attached to most divorce statutes. It entitled a wronged wife to her dower right (one-third of the property) should her spouse be blamed for the dissolution of the marriage. The dower clause, in short, complicated divorce in late nineteenth-century Nebraska and demonstrated the influence of homestead-based land ownership on divorce in the upper Great Plains. The dower clause probably helped to account for the higher number of matrimonial and alimony cases that came to the highest appellate courts of the northern Plains, which were faced with the task of constantly refining the boundaries of spousal support.

The dower clause also apparently influenced husbands. We know, for example, that more men than women filed for divorce in Nebraska, employing a preemptive strike strategy to shift blame to their wives and protect their farms from division. There is also evidence, according to Petrik, that the highest appellate courts of the northern tier of the Great Plains states were increasingly pressed to give clearer and clearer definitions of extreme cruelty and desertion—normally "women's" charges in a divorce proceeding. The Montana Supreme Court in *Albert v. Albert* in 1885 defined extreme cruelty as a single incident of physical abuse and set the stage for the lower courts' use of mental cruelty. The Wyoming legislature in 1899, however, threw in the towel and simply provided that divorces could be granted as a result of any "indignities" that rendered the marriage "intolerable."[37] For a short period in the 1870s and 1880s the lenient divorce and residency laws in North and South Dakota made them havens for migratory divorces. The pattern, however, was much different in the southern Plains, where Texas, Oklahoma, and New Mexico made divorce harder.[38]

There were also differences in the legal provisions governing property rights of married women. While Texas and New Mexico adopted the civil law system of community property, the other Great Plains states embraced the common law system. Several of these states also wrote some degree of protection for married women's property rights into their constitutions, with Texas in 1845 and Kansas in 1859 leading the way. The expansion of land ownership by women gave these acts special significance, with Wyoming giving married women separate control over their earnings during marriage and equal custody of their children.[39]

Wyoming, of course, also led the way in granting women suffrage. In 1869 the territory granted women the right to vote, which also gave them access to the jury box and service in other positions formerly reserved for men. Esther Morris, a Wyoming suffragist, served as the first female justice of the peace in the United States. Yet by 1900 only one other Great Plains state—Colorado—had followed Wyoming's lead. By 1914 Montana and Kansas had extended the franchise, but the other states in the region did not follow until shortly before passage of the Nineteenth Amendment in 1920.[40]

These developments underscore the problems of thinking of the Great Plains as a legal unity. It is clear, of course, that a change in women's status was far more welcome there than in the East, but the motives were mixed at best. Where married women's property rights were involved, the pattern seems to have been more uniform, since giving women access to the economic mainstream was beneficial to economic growth. Why this was so in the Plains rather than the East is a question that, if answered, would tell us as much about developments there as on the Great Plains.

In the case of suffrage, the motives behind the legal and constitutional reforms were more varied. In the East, entrenched political structures prevented broader social change; in lonely Wyoming there were no established political machines and accordingly there was no established opposition to the idea of women's suffrage.[41] In Colorado there is some evidence—though far from conclusive—that its radical labor movement and strong populist roots led to acceptance of the related movement for female equality.[42] In Kansas, women's rights were tied to women's religiosity and the hope that the women's vote would promote temperance other moral causes. There were, once again, important intraregional as well as interregional variations.[43]

ECONOMICS AND LAW

For all of its seeming democratic and individualistic tendencies, the Great Plains legal culture reflects back to us strong tendencies toward regulation of that most important of all areas of human endeavors—the creation of wealth. While seemingly professing the cowboy ideal of "don't fence me in," Great Plains lawmakers were more than willing to regulate and redistribute wealth.

While geography and climate may well have shaped the agriculture practiced on the Plains, it was distant eastern and world markets that most influenced the wealth that residents of the Plains could generate from crops and livestock. Even so adamant an environmentalist as the sociologist Carl Kraenzel concluded that the Great Plains had been exploited by eastern manufacturers and railroads in such a way as to turn it into a kind of third-world economy that depended on agricultural exports in order to attain eastern credit and technology.[44] These developments, Kraenzel and others argue, accelerated in the last quarter of the nineteenth century and gave birth to first the Granger and then the Populist political movements.

With the exception of a brief boom during the 1880s, the prices of agricultural commodities grown on the Plains plunged, with wheat, for example, falling by more than half its value, to $63 a bushel in 1897. Great Plains farmers attributed this collapse to the monopolistic practices of grain elevator and railroad operators, who in turn charged that the farmers had brought it on themselves by overproduction. Whatever the truth of the matter, the Plains farmers concluded that they were badly abused, cheated by elevator owners, robbed by railroad barons, and overcharged by eastern manufacturers.[45] Thus political action became the means to redress these woes, first in individual states, which passed antitrust and regulatory legislation involving railroads and elevators, and later in the movement for similar legislation in Washington. The Granger movement of the 1870s was especially strong in Kansas and Nebraska where small town merchants and businessmen, who also suffered from predatory pricing policies, joined with farmers. Yet even on these important issues of economic regulation and redistribution, the states of the Great Plains were not pioneers. The four upper Mississippi Valley states—Illinois, Iowa, Wisconsin, and Minnesota—were models of regulation, in large measure because the Republican and Democratic parties were evenly balanced there and hence vulnerable to political pressure from the Grange.[46]

Eventually, however, the political activism of these states spilled over into the Plains. In the 1880s the boom in demand for Plains foodstuffs brought an enormous infusion of speculative capital. Land values skyrocketed; speculation was rampant; every tiny hamlet began to think itself a metropolis. Fifteen Kansas towns installed streetcar systems during the boom, all paid for by speculative eastern capital. Farmers committed the fatal sin of overmortgaging their property, and when the weather turned dry at the end of the 1880s the farm economies of the Plains collapsed.[47]

The depression of the late 1880s was so sweeping in its destruction that it forced many Plains farmers, at least those who stayed, to rethink their relationship to the political and legal system. Between 1888 and 1892 half the population of western Kansas moved out, most of it back to the East. The farmers that remained were not only overmortgaged, but they quickly fell into a vicious cycle of going deeper into debt each year in order to sell more goods at lower prices. This sweeping economic disaster brought new attention to the rights of debtors and the power of creditors to seize and hold property in default, issues that deserve far closer attention among legal historians than they have received. This cumulative economic frustration eventually ignited the Populist revolt.

THE POPULIST REVOLT

Populism on the Plains was not so much a political movement, although it was certainly that, as it was a quasi-religious revival, in which the farmers rallied to seek legal solutions to the crushing debt and the burdensome taxes that they faced. The agrarian revolt in 1890 produced startling legal results on the Plains.

The Populist revolt also ushered in the most important period of legal innovation on the Plains, and these developments came at a time when the Plains had, in turn, the greatest impact on national law. While the Populist revolt spread far beyond the boundaries of the Great Plains, its farmers nonetheless symbolized its strength. At the 1892 convention of the People's Party in Omaha, Nebraska, the delegates agreed on what became for the next third of a century the major elements of reform politics in America: the creation of a flexible currency; honesty, economy, and greater openness in government; a graduated income tax; postal savings banks; government ownership of railroads and telegraph lines; abolition of alien land holdings; and reclamation of all lands held by railroads and other corporations in excess of their needs. The Populists insisted in the preamble to their 1892 Omaha platform that "wealth belongs to him who creates it."[48]

The Populist program looks mild by today's standards, but it was thoroughly radical in its own day. The legal and economic readjustments called for by the Populists had class conflict overtones, so much so that employers retaliated against many members by threatening them with wage cuts and layoffs if they voted for William Jennings Bryan in 1896. Bryan, of course, lost to the Republican William McKinley, although Bryan did carry all the Great Plains states except North Dakota.

In defeat the Populists were ultimately vindicated. They succeeded in securing from Plains state legislatures debt relief legislation that became a model for agricultural states outside the region. They wanted progressive constitutional and governmental reforms: the conservative Theodore Roosevelt gave them railroad regulation, the reactionary William Howard Taft postal savings banks, and the liberal Woodrow Wilson a more flexible currency through the Federal Reserve System. The initiative and referendum the Populists desired, and the recall they considered too radical to ask for, were in general used not only in the Plains but throughout the nation by 1912. The Seventeenth Amendment, allowing a federal income tax, came shortly afterward.

THE FEDERAL IMPACT

These developments also help place the Plains within American federalism. The Populist revolt sought through the power of the federal government to restore a semblance of balance between producers and consumers, one in which the exporting states of the Plains would have an opportunity to compete effectively in the national marketplace. Hence in the twentieth century, the Great Plains states have been the beneficiaries of enormous government largess. In 1974 Governor Richard Lamm of Colorado echoed sentiments a century old when he endorsed an OPEC-like organization of energy-rich western states against proposed federal controls. "We're saying," Lamm asserted, "that there are certain things that happen to colonies—whether they are in Colorado or the Congo—if there is not some assertiveness on the part of their leaders. And we are not going to be colonized."[49]

Beneath such rhetoric lurks a profound reality: On a per capita basis, no other region of the country in this century has been better supported by the federal government than the Great Plains, through massive agricultural subsidies, land and water reclamation projects, military bases, and most recently a futile effort to develop coal gasification and synthetic fuels projects. Between 1850 and 1950, the federal government poured more than $150 billion into the region, and it has long since been the largest single employer in two of the Plains states: North Dakota and New Mexico.[50] The distribution of this federal largess was neither simple nor automatic, depending as it has on a complicated network of federal, state, and local administrative agencies staffed by thousands of bureaucrats. The relationship between the federal administrative process and administrative law, on the one hand, and the economic development of the Great Plains, on the other, is certainly one of the least understood aspects of the region's legal culture. Many of the Plains states have resisted this federal involvement at the same time that they have benefited from it. Indeed, many residents of the Great Plains seem to love to hate the federal dollars that they love to receive.

CONCLUSION

While the general drift in twentieth-century legal culture has been to secure individual rights through government-sponsored social welfare and economic opportunity programs, most of the region's states, especially in the upper Plains, have resisted. Moreover, for a region that prides itself on individualism and autonomy, its lawmakers have, like those in other sections of the nation, displayed a nasty tendency to strike out against those it fears. Thus, as Paul Finkelman explains in his study of *Meyer v. Nebraska*, powerful nativist tendencies have frequently shaped the culture of rights on the Plains.[51] Surely legal historians can do much to understand the interplay of economic imperative and racial and ethnic prejudice on the Plains. Much work remains to be done, as well, on what rights meant on the Great Plains in the context of white and Native American relations, although we have made a beginning of sorts.[52]

At least on first impression, those qualities that seem to set the Great Plains apart—individualism, innovation, democracy, and lawlessness—appear on closer inspection to be more dimly reflected in the region's legal culture than Webb and other environmentalists believed. It may well be, as Patricia Nelson Limerick has argued, that as often as not these frontier qualities dissolved into surface-skimming waste, brash overconfidence, and reckless speculation.[53] She may well be right: The inhabitants of the Great Plains have been too absorbed in their own pursuit of wealth to pay much attention to the needs of society. The Plains states have been, throughout their history, strongholds of political conservatism, despite outraged cries of easterners about Plains radicalism. The periodic protests raised on the Plains have usually been leveled against change, with the region's residents preferring the maintenance of an agrarian social order against an increasingly industrialized and interdependent world economy. Ironically this seems to have been the motivation of farmers who in the 1930s shifted the center of conservative Republicanism to the upper Plains in their vain effort to check a "New Deal" that held forth the best promise for farm supports, relief to the victims of the Dust Bowl, and programs to address the cataclysmic effects of massive land erosion. More recently, the Plains have given support to Richard Nixon and Ronald Reagan, doing so in the apparent belief that private enterprise and individual effort alone would solve national problems.

Taken together, these developments warn us about the elusive nature of our quest for the legal culture of the Great Plains. It may exist, but more as a paradox than as a bundle of values and attitudes associated with a clear geographical area. Scholars disagree about whether there is—or was—a Great Plains and whether the widely accepted environmental definition of region gains coherence at the expense of distorting the East-West cultural similarities that sing through the Plains.

As is true with all regional approaches to legal culture, we must be careful not to confuse the description of an area with the motive forces that bring about legal change in the first place. Even if we find, in the end, a strong correlation among geography, climate, and law, we may not be much further along in understanding the region's legal culture, because to grasp the values and attitudes that shape law on the Great Plains or elsewhere we must necessarily look at those issues of law and society where they are most likely to appear—in the ways in which law mediates among competing modes of production and in the role it has played in defining and sustaining gender, class, and race relations. My suspicion is that when we approach the issue of legal culture in this way we are likely to find that the Great Plains was far more like the rest of American legal culture than it was different from it. Differences between the Plains and other regions tended to be those of timing, pace, and manner, not differences in fundamental social attitudes.

There is, of course, no such thing as the legal culture of the Great Plains, or of the South or the West for that matter. In an area as diverse as the Plains, there are all sorts of attitudes and opinions about law, and we should be prepared to understand them. But on a broad scale the standard shibboleths about individualism, innovation, democracy, and lawlessness seem overwrought. We may be skillful—and yes, lucky—enough to be able to divine certain broad tendencies, ones that would help, if identified, to shape our understanding of not just the law—the statutes, the judicial pronouncements, the organizational schemes—but of the connection between it and social change. If we understand such connections, then we will certainly have a much better idea about whether what goes on through the legal process in this region can actually be analyzed as a coherent legal culture.

These are of necessity only surface impressions about the legal culture of the Great Plains. Perhaps there is more that is distinctive to it than seems to be the case. There may well be some yawning gulf that separates attitudes and values about the law in, say, South Dakota, from those in California or New Jersey. To find out we simply must learn more about law on the Great Plains.

NOTES

1. As quoted in David Hackett Fischer, "Models of Intellectual Change in the Antebellum South and North: A Comparative Perspective," paper presented at the Southern Intellectual History Circle Conference, Gainesville, FL, February 21, 1991, p. 4.

2. See Kermit L. Hall, *Comprehensive Bibliography of American Constitutional and Legal History*, 5 vols. (Millwood, NY: Kraus International Publications, 1984); and Hall, *Comprehensive Bibliography of American Constitutional and Legal History Supplement 1980–1987*, 2 vols. (Millwood, NY: Kraus International Publications, 1991).

3. See, for example, Kermit L. Hall and James W. Ely, Jr., eds., *Constitutionalism and the History of the South* (Athens: The University of Georgia Press, 1989) and David J. Bodenhamer and James W. Ely, Jr., *Ambivalent Legacy: A Legal History of the South* (Jackson: University Press of Mississippi, 1984). A good introduction to most of the recent writing on the legal history of the Rocky Mountain region and the Far West is Gordon Bakken, *The Development of the Law on the Rocky Mountain Frontier: Civil Law and Society, 1850–1912* (Westport, CT: Greenwood Press, 1983); and Bakken, *Rocky Mountain Constitution Making, 1850–1912* (Westport, CT: Greenwood Press, 1987). Suggestive of some of the work on the Pacific states is Arthur F. McEvoy, *The Fisherman's Problem: Ecology and Law in the California Fisheries, 1850–1980* (Berkeley: University of California Press, 1986). There are no comparable volumes for the Great Plains.

4. Kermit L. Hall, "The Magic Mirror: American Constitutional and Legal History," *The International Journal of Social Education* 1 (Autumn, 1986): 22–48; James Willard Hurst, *Law and Economic Growth: The Legal History of the Lumber Industry in Wisconsin, 1836–1915* (Cambridge, MA: Harvard University Press, 1964); Roscoe Pound, *The Formative Era of American Law* (Boston: Little, Brown, 1938).

5. The best example is Walter Prescott Webb, *The Great Plains* (New York: Grosset & Dunlap, 1931), pp. 385, 398–431, 496–502. More recent studies give only slight attention to legal and constitutional developments and most often they emphasize the lawless nature of the region. See, for example, Ray Allen Billington

and Martin Ridge, *Westward Expansion: A History of the American Frontier*, 5th ed. (New York: Macmillan, 1982); and Patricia Nelson Limerick, *The Legacy of Conquest: The Unbroken Past of the American West* (New York: Norton, 1987).

6. Peter Harris, "Ecology and Culture in the Communication of Precedent Among State Supreme Courts, 1870–1970," *Law & Society Review* 19 (Number 3, 1985): 449–86; Lawrence M. Friedman, Robert Kagan, Bliss Cartwright, and Stanton Wheeler, "State Supreme Courts: A Century of Style and Citation," *Stanford Law Review* 33 (May, 1981): 787; Rodney Mott, "Judicial Influence," *American Political Science Review* 30 (March, 1936): 295–322.

7. Harris, "Communication of Precedent," pp. 476–77.

8. "Mott, "Judicial Influence," pp. 300–302.

9. Harris, "Communication of Precedent," p. 470.

10. Robert A. Kagan, Bobby D. Infelise, and Robert R. Detlefsen, "American State Supreme Court Justices, 1900–1970," *American Bar Foundation Research Journal* (Spring, 1984): 371–408. This conclusion is supported, moreover, by studies such as John D. W. Guice, *The Rocky Mountain Bench: The Territorial Supreme Courts of Colorado, Montana, and Wyoming, 1861–1890* (New Haven, CT: Yale University Press, 1972); Michael W. Homer, "The Territorial Judiciary: An Overview of the Nebraska Experience, 1854–1867," *Nebraska History* 63 (Fall, 1982): 349–80; and Robert A. Heiberg, "Social Backgrounds of the Minnesota Supreme Court Justices: 1858–1968," *Minnesota Law Review* 53 (April, 1969): 901–76. The same pattern was observed in Washington Territory by John R. Wunder in *Inferior Courts, Superior Justice: A History of the Justices of the Peace on the Northwest Frontier, 1853–1889* (Westport, CT: Greenwood Press, 1979).

11. See for example, the excellent articles edited by David Langum in the special issue of *Journal of the West* 24 (January, 1985) devoted to legal history.

12. James W. Ely, Jr., and David J. Bodenhamer, "Regionalism and American Legal History: The Southern Experience," *Vanderbilt Law Review* 39 (April, 1986): 540–48.

13. Lawrence M. Friedman, *Total Justice* (New York: Russell Sage Foundation, 1985), pp. 30–34.

14. Newton Minnow, quoted in *National Law Journal* (February 4, 1985), p. 4.

15. Roscoe Pound, *Introduction to the Philosophy of Law*, rev. ed. (New Haven, CT: Yale University Press, 1954), p. 10.

16. Ely and Bodenhamer, "Regionalism and American Legal History," pp. 539–40.

17. See, for example, Ely and Bodenhamer, "Regionalism and American Legal History"; Bakken, *Rocky Mountain Constitution Making*; Paul Finkelman, "Exploring Southern Legal History," 64 *North Carolina Law Review* (November, 1985): 77–116; John P. Reid, *Law for the Elephant: Property and Social Behavior on the Overland Trail* (San Marino, CA: The Huntington Library, 1980); and

David J. Langum, *Law and Community on the Mexican California Frontier: Anglo-American Expatriates and the Clash of Legal Traditions, 1821–1846* (Norman: University of Oklahoma Press, 1987).

18. Webb, *The Great Plains*, p. 8.

19. Ibid., p. 206.

20. Ian Frazier, *Great Plains* (New York: Penguin Books, 1989).

21. Terry L. Anderson and P. J. Hill, "The Evolution of Property Rights: A Study of the American West," *Journal of Law and Economics* 18 (April, 1975): 172–76; Kermit L. Hall, *The Magic Mirror: Law in American History* (New York: Oxford University Press, 1989), p. 46; Reid, *Law for the Elephant*, pp. 9–11.

22. This argument is also treated in Kermit L. Hall, "The 'Magic Mirror' and the Promise of Western Legal History at the Bicentennial of the Constitution," *Western Historical Quarterly* 18 (October, 1987): 429–36 and Donald Worster, "New West, True West: Interpreting the Region's History," *Western Historical Quarterly* 18 (April, 1987): 141–56.

23. Anderson and Hill, "Evolution of Property Rights," pp. 169–72.

24. Frazier, *Great Plains*, pp. 121–25.

25. Anderson and Hill, "Evolution of Property Rights," pp. 176–78.

26. Donald J. Pisani, "Enterprise and Equity: A Critique of Western Water Law in the Nineteenth Century," *Western Historical Quarterly* 18 (January, 1987): 15–21.

27. Robert G. Dunbar, *Forging New Rights in Western Waters* (Lincoln: University of Nebraska Press, 1983); *Irwin v. Phillips*, 5 Cal 140 (1855); *Lux v. Haggin*, 69 Cal 255 (1886); and *Katz v. Walkinshaw*, 141 Cal 116 (1903).

28. Robert G. Dunbar, "The Adaptability of Water Law to the Aridity of the West," *Journal of the West* 24 (January, 1985): 60–62.

29. Morton J. Horwitz, *The Transformation of American Law, 1780–1860* (Cambridge, MA: Harvard University Press, 1977), pp. 34–42.

30. Webb, *The Great Plains*, pp. 496–502; Limerick, *The Legacy of Conquest*, pp. 169–75; Truman Capote, *In Cold Blood: A True Account of a Multiple Murder and Its Consequences* (New York: Random House, 1965).

31. Raymond D. Gastil, *Cultural Regions of the United States* (Seattle: University of Washington Press, 1975), pp. 97–116.

32. Hugh Davis Graham and Ted Robert Gurr, *Violence in America: Historical and Comparative Perspectives*, 2 vols. (Washington, DC: U.S. Government Printing Office, 1969), 2: 392–93.

33. Earl Pomeroy, "Toward a Reorientation of Western History: Continuity and Environment," *Mississippi Valley Historical Review* 41 (March, 1955): 581 and Robert Berkhofer, Jr., "Space, Time, Culture, and the New Frontier," *Agricultural History* 38 (January, 1964): 24–30.

34. Frederick C. Luebke, "Introduction," in Brian W. Blouet and Frederick C. Luebke, eds., *The Great Plains: Environment and Culture* (Lincoln: University of Nebraska Press, 1979), pp. ix–xxv.

35. Gastil, *Cultural Regions*, pp. 108–37, 293.

36. Paula Petrik, "Women and the Law on the Great Plains," paper presented at the Center for Great Plains Studies Symposium, "Law, the Bill of Rights, and the Great Plains," Lincoln, NE, March 6–9, 1991, pp. 10, 7.

37. Ibid., and Lawrence M. Friedman and Robert J. Percival, "Who Sues for Divorce? From Fault through Fiction to Freedom," *Journal of Legal Studies* 5 (January, 1976): 63–65.

38. Robert L. Griswold, *Family and Divorce in California, 1850–1890: Victorian Illusions and Everyday Realities* (Albany: State University of New York Press, 1980), p. 25.

39. Mari J. Matsuda, "The West and the Legal Status of Women: Explanations of Frontier Feminism," *Journal of the West* 24 (January, 1985): 50–51.

40. Ibid., pp. 51–54.

41. Ibid., p. 53.

42. Billie Barnes Jensen, "Colorado Woman Suffrage Campaigns of the 1870s," *Journal of the West* 12 (June, 1978): 182–90.

43. Eleanor Flexner, *Century of Struggle: The Women's Rights Movement in the United States*, 7th ed. (Cambridge, MA: Belknap Press, 1982), pp. 178–80.

44. Carl F. Kraenzel, *The Great Plains in Transition* (Norman: University of Oklahoma Press, 1955), p. 283. See also the discussion of Kraenzel's work in Luebke, "Introduction," pp. xiv–xvi.

45. Berkhofer, "Space, Time, Culture," p. 24.

46. Billington and Ridge, *Westward Expansion*, pp. 669, 680–81.

47. Ibid., p. 671.

48. Ibid., p. 677.

49. Quoted in Harry N. Scheiber, "Xenophobia and Parochialism in the History of American Legal Process: From the Jacksonian Era to the Sagebrush Rebellion," *William & Mary Law Review* 23 (Summer, 1982): 660.

50. Gerald D. Nash, "Bureaucracy and Reform in the West: Notes on the Influence of a Neglected Interest Group," *Western Historical Quarterly* 2 (July, 1971): 295–305.

51. Paul L. Finkelman, "German Victims and American Oppressors: The Background and Legacy of *Meyer v. Nebraska*," paper presented at the Center for Great Plains Studies Symposium, "Law, the Bill of Rights, and the Great Plains," p. 10, and Chapter 3 of this volume.

52. See, for example, John R. Wunder, *"Retained by The People": A History of American Indians and the Bill of Rights* (New York: Oxford University Press, 1994).

53. Limerick, *Legacy of Conquest*, pp. 17–32.

Part II

Landmark Cases of the Great Plains

Through the years the Great Plains has spawned a number of landmark cases in American law. It is not yet clear whether the region itself offers a favorable climate for testing American law, but it cannot be denied that important legal distinctions have been discovered as a result of Great Plains disputes.

One of the most important legal areas, perhaps unique to the Great Plains, where significant litigation has occurred is in Indian law. Numerous landmark opinions have been written about disputes involving Native Americans of the Great Plains. Topics have ranged from water law, termination policy, family law, and Bill of Rights designations to federal jurisdiction and Indian self-determination. Two of the most important decisions involved a murder and the taking of lands from a reservation.

Spotted Tail, a respected Brulé Sioux, was murdered by Crow Dog on the Rosebud Reservation in 1881. Spotted Tail's assassination marked the beginning of a series of murders, such as that of Crazy Horse and Sitting Bull, which drained the Sioux of their leadership. A United States attorney in Dakota Territory tried Crow Dog for the murder. Upon reaching a guilty verdict, the decision was appealed to the U.S. Supreme Court. In *Ex parte Crow Dog* (1883)[1] the Supreme Court found that there was no federal jurisdiction involved when one Indian committed a crime against another

Indian on a reservation unless Congress legislated differently. The result was a significant attack upon Indian sovereignty by Congress, which passed the Major Crimes Act of 1885[2] that with numerous amendments over time has established federal jurisdiction in select felonies and misdemeanors, thereby overriding Native American legal systems.[3]

The General Allotment Act of 1887[4] has been recognized as one of the worst pieces of legislation ever passed for Indians. Native Americans lost more land as a result of this law than from any war. By carving up reservations and selling "surplus lands," the federal government hoped to assimilate Indians. Instead, it led to poverty and despair among Native Americans. The validity of the General Allotment Act was challenged by the Kiowas, Comanches, and Apaches in *Lone Wolf v. Hitchcock* (1903).[5] In this opinion, viewed by some historians as the *Plessy v. Ferguson*[6] of Indian law, the Supreme Court ruled that treaties can be abolished by federal statute and that Congress has plenary power over Indian tribes. Whatever Congress passes will stand because issues dealing with Indian law are political issues.[7]

Great Plains landmark cases also reach other areas of American law. Civil liberties and civil rights have been the subject of considerable debate. For example, in *Wolf v. Colorado* (1949)[8] evidence taken without a warrant from a doctor's office about his abortion patients that was inadmissible in federal court was allowed for use in a state court criminal proceeding. This holding was later overruled by the U.S. Supreme Court. Another example is *McLaurin v. Oklahoma State Regents* (1950).[9] In this case the University of Oklahoma tried to prevent an African American from pursuing a doctorate because of his race, and the university was prevented from doing so by the Supreme Court.

In the three essays to follow, three Great Plains landmark cases are explored in detail. They consider whether a state can forbid the teaching of a particular foreign language, the impact of Great Plains leadership on integration, and the issues involved in economic development of the region.

Paul Finkleman first explores the background and ramifications of *Meyer v. Nebraska* (1923).[10] In his essay Finkleman explains how states responded to the hysteria provided by the experience of World War I. Anti-German legislation was widespread, but nowhere was it more forceful than on the Great Plains, the home of many ethnic immigrants. Nebraska, in addition to amending its constitution to certify English as its official language, passed a law in 1919 prohibiting teaching in any language other than English. Languages other than English could only be officially spoken in high school foreign language courses. These restrictions were aimed at instruction in German. Robert Meyer, a teacher in a Lutheran parochial school, used a German Bible as a text for teaching the German language and religion, and he was charged with violating the Nebraska statute. The dispute went to the U.S. Supreme Court, which reversed Meyer's conviction and held that Nebraska's statute violated the Fourteenth Amendment. The case was a forerunner to the activation of the Fourteenth Amendment for other civil rights issues.

The essay by Michael S. Mayer looks at *Brown v. Board of Education of Topeka* (1954),[11] a seminal decision involving African Americans and the successful integration of public schools. The setting involves many Great Plains participants, such as third grader Linda Brown, who wanted to attend an all-white school in Topeka near her home;[12] Herbert Brownell, native Nebraskan who served as Attorney General for a new Republican administration; and Dwight Eisenhower, favorite son of Kansas and newly elected President of the United States. Mayer chronicles how Eisenhower dealt with this issue, how he tried to weigh his sense of racial justice against his perception of how things had been done in the past and the disruption that the Supreme Court's decisions in *Brown* and *Brown II*[13] most assuredly would cause.

The last essay in this section by James W. Ely, Jr. tackles an important nineteenth-century Supreme Court decision, *Chicago, Milwaukee & St. Paul Railway Company v. Minnesota* (1890).[14] The farmers of many Great Plains states suffered significant economic hardships in the 1870s and 1880s. In addition to the fluctuations in markets and weather conditions, railroads continued to raise rates. The result was a Granger and then a Populist movement of some significance, and many states passed legislation designed to regulate railroad rates. Minnesota did so by setting up a commission to determine the reasonableness of railroad charges. In the inevitable challenge, the U.S. Supreme Court ruled the Minnesota statute unconstitutional, finding that it violated the railroad's right to economic due process. This case solidified the beginnings of the incorporation of laissez-faire economic policy into the federal law of the land. But as Ely points out, there was room to maneuver, and Minnesota and other states continued to pass legislation within more restricted boundaries.

Meyer v. Nebraska, *Brown v. Board of Education*, and *Chicago, Milwaukee & St. Paul Railway Company v. Minnesota* are just three of the landmark cases that began as Great Plains disputes.

NOTES

1. *Ex parte Crow Dog*, 109 US 556 (1883).

2. U.S., "An Act making appropriations for the current and contingent expenses of the Indian Department, and for fulfilling treaty stipulations with various

Indian tribes, for the year ending June thirtieth, eighteen hundred and eighty-six, and for other purposes [Major Crimes Act of 1885]," *Statutes at Large* 23 (March 3, 1885): 362–85.

3. See Sidney L. Harring, "Crow Dog's Case: A Chapter in the Legal History of Tribal Sovereignty," *American Indian Law Review* 14 (November, 1989): 191–239, and *Crow Dog's Case: American Indian Sovereignty, Tribal Law, and United States Law in the Nineteenth Century* (New York: Cambridge University Press, 1994).

4. U.S., "An Act to provide for the allotment of lands in severalty to Indians on the various reservations, and to extend the protection of the laws of the United States and the Territories over the Indians, and for other purposes [General Allotment Act or Dawes Severalty Act], *Statutes at Large* 24 (February 8, 1887): 388–91.

5. *Lone Wolf v. Hitchcock*, 187 US 553 (1903).

6. *Plessy v. Ferguson*, 163 US 537 (1896).

7. See Ann Laquer Estin, "*Lone Wolf v. Hitchcock*: The Long Shadow," in Sandra L. Cadwalader and Vine Deloria, Jr., eds., *The Aggressions of Civilization: Federal Indian Policy Since the 1880s* (Philadelphia: Temple University Press, 1984), pp. 215–45, and Blue Clark, *Lone Wolf v. Hitchcock: Treaty Rights and Indian Law at the End of the Nineteenth Century* (Lincoln: University of Nebraska Press, 1994).

8. *Wolf v. Colorado*, 338 US 25 (1949).

9. *McLaurin v. Oklahoma State Regents*, 339 US 637 (1950).

10. *Meyer v. Nebraska*, 262 US 390 (1923).

11. *Brown v. Board of Education of Topeka*, 347 US 483 (1954).

12. See Richard Kluger, *Simple Justice: The History of Brown v. Board of Education and Black Americans Struggle for Equality* (New York: Alfred A. Knopf, 1976), especially pp. 401–24.

13. *Brown v. Board of Education of Topeka* [*Brown II*], 349 US 294 (1955).

14. *Chicago, Milwaukee & St. Paul Railway Company v. Minnesota*, 134 US 418 (1890).

3

German Victims and American Oppressors: The Cultural Background and Legacy of *Meyer v. Nebraska*

Paul Finkelman

In a post-holocaust age it seems odd to talk about Germans as victims. Yet, during and after World War I German Americans were the targets of official harassment, political suppression, police brutality, and mob violence. These actions led to a number of cases that helped shape the meaning of the Fourteenth Amendment and the Bill of Rights. In this early history *Meyer v. Nebraska*[1] looms large for two reasons. First, it was the immediate prelude to the beginning of the incorporation of the Bill of Rights through the Fourteenth Amendment.[2] Second, in an age when civil liberties were under assault from all sides, *Meyer* stands out as the most significant civil liberties victory of the World War I period. To understand this case, we must first examine the repression of German Americans and other immigrants in the United States from the late nineteenth century until the mid-1920s.

GERMANS AND RADICALISM: PRELUDE TO REPRESSION

The repression was rooted in the hostility to foreigners that reemerged in the late nineteenth century as nativist organizations, such as the American Protective Association, began agitating for an end to non-Anglo-Saxon immigration.[3] Part of this hostility was tied to the rise of the prohibitionist movement. Most immigrants, and especially Germans, were "wet." Moreover, Germans celebrated Sunday by drinking beer—not something that fit with emerging American white Anglo-Saxon Protestant (WASP) notions of propriety.

Compounding Anglo-American Protestant opposition to German beer gardens was the emerging identification of Germans with radicalism. Even before the rise of this new xenophobia, conservative Americans had been appalled by the labor radicalism and socialism espoused by many immigrants.

Long before World War I German immigrants and their children gained a reputation for radicalism, anarchism, and violence. After being expelled from Germany and imprisoned in England, Johann Most brought his brand of anarchism to America in 1882. He soon "pulled the scattered fragments of the social revolutionary movement together, giving it new energy and a more sharply defined sense of purpose."[4] His German language periodical, *Freiheit*, published in New York City, symbolized the importance of German immigrants to the new labor and social radicalism of the era.

Johann Most was the first of a number of Germans who became publicly associated with radicalism. Rev. Robert Reitzel left his position as a pastor in the German Reformed Church and in 1884 founded the newspaper *Arme Teufel* in Detroit. Carl Nold, a young German immigrant, spent five years in prison after the Homestead steel strike.[5] Six of the eight men tried for the Haymarket riot were German-American anarchists.[6] William Trautmann, a brewery union organizer, became the secretary-treasurer of the radical Industrial Workers of the World (IWW) and translated the works of Karl Marx from German into English.[7] Thus, by the time the United States entered World War I there was already a climate favorable to repression based on the assumption that German radicals threatened American society. The position of German Americans was further undermined by the fact that the vast majority of people within the German American community, while not supporters of the Kaiser, nevertheless wanted the United States to continue its policy of neutrality, and not enter the war against Germany.

GERMAN AMERICAN OPPOSITION TO THE WAR

German American opposition to the American entrance into World War I came from three different sources. Unfortunately, most Americans, blinded by their war fever, were incapable of understanding what were not even mildly subtle differences between these groups of German Americans.

Superpatriots lumped all German Americans together, concluding that every German American opposed the war and sympathized with the enemy.

In 1914 most German Americans "were either indifferent to the war in Europe or actually hostile to the German government and its goals."[8] German Americans, after all, had abandoned Germany for the United States. They may have respected their cultural heritage and loved their mother tongue, but by voting with their feet as immigrants, they had clearly rejected German militarism and the Kaiser's imperialism. Most "thought of themselves as Americans totally loyal to American democratic ideals. . . . In the German American's view, his cultural heritage created no special loyalty for the German Imperial Government, nor did it inhibit his capacity for patriotic citizenship in his adopted homeland."[9] Indeed, "German Americans believed that they had earned their American political spurs in the Civil War" and that their service "on behalf of the Union was conclusive proof that they could retain their German culture and yet be unswervingly loyal to the United States."[10] This feeling was true even for recent German immigrants, who could immediately lay claim to an American heritage through the glory of Carl Shurz and company.

However, this did not mean they were anxious to fight against their friends and relatives in their former homeland. Few German Americans faced the family crisis of the singer Ernestine Schumann-Heinck "who had sons in both the German and American armies,"[11] but since the vast majority of German Americans were either immigrants or the children of immigrants, the prospect of fighting against their relatives was disturbing. Even the Chicago *Tribune* thought that German Americans should not be sent to the front "to drive bayonets into the breast of [their] blood brother unless that brother is invading the country."[12]

Not surprisingly, before 1917 German Americans strongly supported America's non-interventionist policy. After the United States entered the war most Germans agreed with the *Cincinnati Volksblatt* that "to support the United States is a duty."[13] But many Americans could not forgive their prewar support for peace and their continuing hostility to supporting Great Britain.

After 1917 the overwhelming majority of German Americans accepted the war and cooperated with conscription.[14] However, two groups of German Americans did not. A small number of German Americans opposed conscription on religious grounds. These were mostly members of pacifist Protestant sects, and most were descendants of seventeenth- and eighteenth-century immigrants. A smaller group of German Americans, mostly recent immigrants, opposed the draft on political grounds.

Mennonites, Amish, Dunkards, Hutterite Brethren, and other pietists retained their pacifist values.[15] Their rejection of modern garb and technology, as well their continued use of the German language, made them particularly vulnerable in their opposition to military service. Some Mennonite conscientious objectors were drafted and then purposely denied adequate food, beaten, or tortured at Army camps. The government jailed over 130 German American conscientious objectors, mostly in Fort Leavenworth, where some died from their poor treatment. By contrast, Canada granted Mennonites conscientious objector status, although that nation lacked a bill of rights or a guarantee of religious freedom and separation of church and state. Where the government failed to act, the mob took over. Mobs forced some Amish in Ohio to buy Liberty bonds; in South Dakota Liberty Loan committee members confiscated farm animals from Hutterites and sold them in order to purchase bonds; in Illinois "patriots" desecrated Mennonite churches; in Kansas members of a mob forcibly cut off the beards of some Mennonites while other German Americans were whipped and tarred and feathered.[16]

German radicals, along with socialists and anarchists from other backgrounds, wanted nothing to do with the war because they believed it was a capitalist plot, in which working men would die to further the imperial goals of England and Germany. The prominence of German socialists, like Victor Berger of Milwaukee, led many Americans to believe that most Germans were socialists, and that the socialists were allied with the Kaiser in an attempt to undermine the American war effort. Socialist opposition to the war, tied to the visibility of many German Americans and other immigrants in labor and socialist organizations, gave conservative forces an excuse for a general crackdown on the American left. This helped lead to the eventual destruction of the American left as a viable political option.[17]

People of German ancestry were not the only Americans to oppose the war. Woodrow Wilson, after all, had been reelected in 1916 on a slogan of "he kept us out of war." In April 1917 six Senators and 50 members of the House opposed the declaration of war. This contrasts sharply with the unanimous Senate support for World War II and the single symbolic dissent in the House. Perhaps an even greater contrast is with the 98-to-2 vote in the Senate in favor of the Gulf of Tonkin Resolution in 1964.

THE AMERICAN DOMESTIC PROPAGANDA CAMPAIGN FOR WAR SUPPORT

The divided sentiments about the conflict in Europe help to explain the wartime domestic crusade against German culture. Americans had to be convinced that the war was just and necessary. Part of that effort was a massive propaganda campaign against Germany, Germans, and German culture. The need to switch from neutrality to support for the war led to excessive patriotic attacks on Germans. In this context hyperbolic denunciations of the German government and the Kaiser are perhaps understandable. Thus, a reference to Kaiser Wilhelm as "Bill the Butcher" seems little more than a cute bit of wartime propaganda. But, if the Kaiser was a "butcher," what did that make those who carried out his orders? One article explained, "The Satanic Kaiser stalks gloomily among his hordes of Satan-whelps, calls upon God to help him in his nameless crimes, and urges his faithful imps to still greater deeds of brutality."[18] Such propaganda made the German people into, at best, unwitting servants of the devil. This propaganda at least had the virtue of allowing that Germans might cease to be "Satan-whelps" or "faithful imps" if they were educated to appreciate democratic values and taught to reject the Kaiser. "Whelps" and "imps," after all, might grow up to be better adults. In the United States, at least in Nebraska, Iowa, and Ohio, turning "imps" into citizens would require prohibiting them from learning the language of their parents or ancestors.[19]

But many commentators were not satisfied with simply attacking the Kaiser and the German political system. To justify the carnage of World War I, propagandists on both sides of the Western Front painted their enemies as hopelessly less than human. Thus, calling Germans "whelps" implied they were in fact animals; calling them "imps" implied they were otherworldly creatures. Other propaganda followed this line, referring to the Kaiser as "the beast of Berlin" or the "werewolf of Potsdam." In the 1890s the American Protective Association and other nativist groups had begun referring to German immigrants as "huns."[20] During the war propagandists revived this epithet, which conjured up images of bloodthirsty, anarchistic, and heathen barbarians. The evangelist Billy Sunday said of Germany that "no nation so infamous, vile, greedy, sensuous, bloodthirsty ever disgraced the pages of history."[21]

America entered the war late but quickly made up for lost time with articles that argued that Americans had to reject their "good-natured and somewhat sentimental" attitudes in order to fight Germany. It was "not only foolish but positively dangerous" to make a distinction between the German government and the German people because "if it is a perilous thing to underestimate one's opponent physically, it is at least equally hazardous to overestimate him morally. And this is precisely what we are doing when we sentimentalize over the poor deluded, naturally sweet tempered and generally angelic Hun and weep about the way his Government forces him to do things entirely out of keeping with his kindly disposition." After detailing the alleged atrocities of the German Army, this article concluded, "It is time we stop sentimentalizing over the Hun, and realize . . . [it is] congenial to him to perform such barbarous cruelties that beside his deeds those of the Huns of old appear white and shining. . . . We are at war, not with a mere government, but with a nation of moral perverts, a nation which exalts in torture, admires murder, and has no faintest conception of the meaning of the word of honor."[22]

THE DOMESTIC WAR ON GERMANS AND GERMAN CULTURE

If the German people were "moral perverts" and "barbarians" who had no sense of honor, then it was logical to assume that German Americans could not easily overcome their propensities for evil. Assuming Americanization might make Germans into better people, this could be accomplished only by destroying the vestiges of German culture present in the United States. Indeed, the logical result of this thinking was the conclusion, reached by many Americans during the war, that German culture was evil and dangerous. It was the culture of barbarians and huns. The military war abroad led to the repression of Germans and things German in a cultural war at home.

"The Prussian," Professor Louis Gray of the University of Nebraska declared, "is a moral imbecile, an arrested development, a savage in civilization's garb, and even the garb he has stolen. Like the savage he is boastful and cunning. Among the nations he is precisely what the type of moral imbecile but intellectually educated criminal is among individuals. . . . The war is but an episode in the age-long struggle between good and evil, between God and the Devil." Professor Vernon Kellogg at Stanford declared the Germans "unclean, unclean."[23]

With nearly three quarters of a century of hindsight, the American response to World War I seems almost incomprehensible. On the home front hostilities were directed, not so much at the Kaiser's Germany, as at people of German ancestry and German culture.

Some of the responses are truly horrifying. The lynching of Robert Prager in Collinsville, Illinois, in April, 1918, leads any list of wartime attacks on Germans. There were countless examples of Germans being beaten, tarred and feathered, and humiliated or intimidated. In Detroit a mob dragged a German American from his home in the middle of the night, cut his hair, and threatened to throw him into the Detroit River. In San Jose, California, a German American was tarred and feathered and then chained all night to a cannon in a park. The numerous burnings of German books, including Bibles, did not physically harm anyone, but the intimidation factor must have been great.[24]

Many individuals lost their jobs, or their freedom, because of their ancestry or their unwillingness to placate superpatriots. The violinist Fritz Kreisler was barred from many concert halls because he was allegedly an officer in the Austrian army. He went into temporary retirement for the last year of the war. Dr. Karl Muck, the conductor of the Boston Symphony Orchestra, a Swiss citizen of German birth, nearly lost his position because he refused, on aesthetic grounds, to begin his concerts with the "Star Spangled Banner" and because he insisted, also on aesthetic grounds, on playing music by German composers. The trustees of the symphony backed Muck but may have felt some sense of relief when federal authorities arrested him as an enemy alien, despite his Swiss citizenship. Muck's Cincinnati counterpart, who was in fact a German citizen, suffered a similar fate, although unlike Muck who was interned, he was soon paroled as a "non-vicious" alien enemy.[25]

The litany of silly things that Americans did to de-Germanify the nation seems almost endless. Hamburgers became "liberty steak," frankfurters became "victory sausage," and sauerkraut became "victory cabbage." Berlin, Iowa changed its name to Lincoln while East Germantown, Indiana became Pershing. Banks, hotels, and other businesses with "German" in their name soon found new identities. Vigilantes, meanwhile, defaced statues of Schiller, Beethoven, Heine, and other icons of German culture. More serious was the defacement of numerous Lutheran and Mennonite churches and the physical assaults and intimidation on German clergymen.[26]

The American Defense Society declared that German music was "one of the most dangerous forms of German propaganda, because it appeals to the emotions and has power to sway an audience as nothing else can." With attitudes like this it is not surprising that German music quickly fell out of favor. The city of Pittsburgh prohibited the playing of Beethoven's music. Operas in New York and Chicago stopped performing works in German.[27]

LANGUAGE AND AMERICANIZATION

Authorities were especially concerned with protecting young children from the contamination of things German. In Columbus, Ohio public school teachers pasted "in school music books blank sheets of paper covering 'The

Watch on the Rhine' and 'The Lorelei.' " The superintendent of schools in New Jersey banned all German songs, and "in California, the state board of education directed that all pages in music textbooks that contained German folk songs be cut out."[28]

The most important aspect of the control of culture and the protection of children concerned attempts to limit the teaching of foreign languages, particularly German, in the nation's schools. Tied to this was a desire to eliminate private schools, especially those connected to churches.

Such goals were of course not new in American history. Conflict over foreign language education and parochial schools emerged in the 1880s—at precisely the same time that immigration from Central, Eastern, and Southern Europe began to rise dramatically and that "foreign" doctrines like socialism and anarchism began to capture the minds of some American workers. In 1889 Illinois passed the Edwards Law, which required mandatory education in English. That year in Wisconsin the Bennett Law required that children attend a school in "the city, town or district" where they lived, and that all "reading, writing, arithmetic and United States history" be taught "in the English language." This undermined Catholic and Lutheran schools in the state, which often drew students from more than one school district. It also undermined the many German language schools in Wisconsin.[29]

The Wisconsin law, and similar laws in Illinois and Michigan,[30] reflected the larger movement to "Americanize" foreigners. This movement did not catch on quickly. Moreover, "the anti-foreign nativist movement had the effect of creating a renewed ethnic awareness among Germans in America"[31] which had important political ramifications. In Wisconsin, German Lutherans rejected the Republican party because of its support for English language education. A Democratic landslide in the 1890 election led to the repeal of the Bennett Law in 1891. In Illinois opposition to the Edwards Law led to massive statewide Democratic victories, including the election of the German-born John Peter Altgeld as the state's governor.[32] By 1903 only fourteen states required education in English. Some of these states still allowed education in foreign languages beyond the primary grades.[33]

Not all states joined the anti-foreign language bandwagon. Nebraska, for instance, went in the opposite direction. In 1913, "under pressure from the National German-American Alliance,"[34] the state adopted the Mocket Law,[35] which required that school districts provide elective courses in "modern European languages" beginning in the fourth grade if parents of fifty children in a district petitioned for such classes. In *State, ex rel. Thayer v. School District* (1916)[36] the Nebraska Supreme Court upheld a writ of mandamus ordering that German be taught in a school district.

The defeat of this early English-language movement, as well as statutes like the Mocket Law, showed the voting power of German Americans, especially in the Midwest. But, whether successful or not, the assault on foreign language education also revealed the desire of many Americans to force immigrants to conform to the language and customs of their new home. When the war made the German American community more vulnerable to political demagoguery, and at the same time less politically potent, nativists would be able to achieve a hegemony in education and language that they had been striving for since the late 1880s.

THE WAR AND FOREIGN LANGUAGE EDUCATION

The superpatriotism of World War I stimulated the attack on education in foreign languages, and more importantly, on the teaching of foreign languages. The end of the war did not end the linguistic xenophobia. The American Legion, organized in 1919, made English-only instruction one of its major goals. In 1921 the American Bar Association joined the crusade. That year former Secretary of War John H. Weeks, writing in the *American Legion Weekly*, argued that "ignorance of the English language, of American ideals and the history of our country and its form of government, is America's most powerful enemy." Weeks noted in his article that during the recent war 24 percent of all prospective draftees had been unable to read English.[37]

Immigration, not foreign language education, was the main reason for "ignorance of the English language." But this reality mattered little to state legislators still caught up in postwar patriotism and fearful of bolshevism, socialism, and increased labor militancy. Thus, the crusade against foreign language education was enormously successful. On the eve of World War I only seventeen states required instruction in English. By 1923, thirty-five states had adopted this policy.[38]

While foreign languages in general were under assault, German was the major target during and after the war. The National Security League urged a total ban on teaching either German language or German literature.[39] Former President Theodore Roosevelt, a scholar in his own right who had also been president of the American Historical Association, supported a ban on teaching German, and a professor at Johns Hopkins University declared that German was "a barbarous tongue" with no cultural or commercial value.[40] During or immediately after the war at least twenty-two states regulated or prohibited the teaching of foreign languages in elementary schools.[41] In South Dakota the legislature prohibited all foreign language education before ninth grade. Meanwhile, the State Council of Defense unilaterally ordered an end to the teaching of German.[42] The governor of Montana likewise prohibited the German language in his state's schools, while in Iowa the governor banned the use of German in any public place.[43]

Louisiana led the nation in paranoia of the enemy's language. Its wartime prohibition on teaching German in any public or private school in the state, at all levels from elementary schools to universities, was the most extreme in the nation.[44] A second Louisiana statute prohibited the display or use of any "sign, insignia, name, designation, title, phrase, circular, or other form of advertisement or description, written, printed or appearing in the German language or that of any of its allies, or derived from such any language." Furthermore, the law prohibited "the sale or disposal in any manner of books, magazines, and papers printed or appearing in the German language or the language of any of its allies."[45]

The legislature of Louisiana, however paranoid, might at least be excused as acting during wartime. Nebraska, Indiana, and Ohio waited until after the war was over to crush foreign language education. Indiana, which had had state supported German language primary schools earlier in the century, declared that "the German language shall not be taught in any of the elementary schools in this state." Ohio similarly adopted a postwar statute that prohibited the teaching of German in elementary schools.[46] Anti-German hysteria, once ignited during the war, did not quickly recede in the strange peace that followed. The Red Scare, the rise of the Soviet Union, and the failure of America to bring democracy and peace to the world made it seem as if the war had not ended. Once the anti-foreign language bias was legitimized by the war, midwesterners apparently had a difficult time breaking the habit of persecuting foreigners.

Where states did not act, localities and students did. Throughout the country high school students stopped studying German when the war began. School districts throughout the nation eliminated German from their curricula. In Seattle a newspaper indicated the tone of the movement with the headline, "Speech of Hated Hun Forbidden."[47] This movement was astonishingly successful, and like the legislation against teaching German, continued after the war. In 1915 an astounding 24 percent of all high school students in America studied German. During World War I thousands of school districts dropped German from their curricula, never to return to it.[48] By 1922 less than 1 percent of all American high school students studied German.[49]

Not all Americans reacted to the study of German with such hostility. The *New York Globe* argued that "ignorance of the language and customs of our enemies harms us, not them." But such an intelligent view was rare. In Baltimore the editors of *The Manufacturers' Record* agreed that studying German might be useful, "provided there is no ulterior motive behind such teaching." However, the paper believed that supporters of teaching German had done so, not because of "its intrinsic value, but rather as part of a persistent political propaganda intended to wean the people of this country away from their Anglo-Saxon and Anglo-Celtic origins and ideals and divide the national interest and national sympathy."[50]

Even if all school administrators had agreed with the practical and enlightened views of the *New York Globe*, it seems unlikely that German would have retained its dominance as the most studied foreign language in the nation. Where schools did not drop the language from their curricula, students simply stopped studying it. The story "American Students Boycotting German" in the *Literary Digest* carried the revealing subtitle: "French and Spanish are Crowding out the Enemy Tongue."[51]

With no one studying German, it took little effort to remove German books from the schools and libraries. During the war book burnings became common, as schools disposed of their German language texts. The public library in Columbus, Ohio sold its German collection for scrap paper. The Cincinnati library canceled its German language newspapers and removed all German books from its shelves.[52] If this could occur in Cincinnati, with its large and established German American community, it is hardly surprising that libraries across the nation took similar actions.

MEYER V. NEBRASKA: A BIT OF SANITY IN A CRAZY WORLD

With American entrance into World War I, Nebraskans, like other Americans, began to have second thoughts about their support for foreign language teaching and also for the use of any foreign languages at all. Throughout the war and its aftermath, the Nebraska State Council of Defense pressured people to stop using German and other foreign languages. An attempt to prohibit the use of German on all telephones was unsuccessful, although many German-speaking Nebraskans were frightened into giving up telephone service.

The council also pressured clergymen to preach and pray in English. While aimed at German-speaking Catholics and Lutherans, this pressure also affected many other immigrants in the state. Bohemians complained that no one questioned their loyalty and their opposition to Germany, but nevertheless, the growing xenophobia in the state made their clergymen afraid not to conduct services in English. One Danish American, who spoke fluent English, told the council that after his church ended foreign language services his elderly mother was "entirely cut off" from religious succor. This man pointed out that in 1864 Germany prohibited the use of Danish in territories seized from Denmark. He reminded the council that the same "Iron hand" that suppressed Danish was now America's enemy. He implored the Nebraska patriots, "Let us not do as they did for if we give just a little time all people will be glad to talk American."[53]

Such ironies were lost on most authorities in Nebraska, who saw the war as an opportunity to end the use of foreign languages in the state. In 1918 the legislature repealed the Mocket Law, which had required school districts to provide courses at the elementary level in "modern European languages" if parents of fifty children petitioned for them. In 1919 the Nebraska legislature considered, but rejected, two bills that would have destroyed the parochial schools in the state.[54] However, that year Nebraska did adopt the Siman Act, which prohibited instruction in any "private, denominational, parochial or public school," except in English, and also prohibited the teaching of any modern foreign language, until "after a pupil shall have attained and successfully passed the eighth grade." The Siman Act provided for a fine of $25 to $100 or up to thirty days in jail for offending teachers.[55]

A year later Nebraska added a twenty-seventh section to its bill of rights, making English "the official language of the state" and providing that it be the language of instruction in "the common school branches . . . in public, private, denominational, and parochial schools."[56] The following year the legislature repealed the Siman Act and adopted the Norval Act. This law declared English "to be the official language of" the state. The Norval Act contained all of the basic provisions of the Siman Act, but also prohibited the teaching of foreign languages at all times and places, except in houses of worship on the Sabbath.[57]

In 1920 authorities charged Robert T. Meyer, a teacher in a Lutheran school, with violating the Siman Act by teaching biblical studies, in German, to ten-year-old children during a special hour and a half recess period that the school had instituted after Nebraska enacted this law.[58] This arrest underscores that the law, although aimed at "Americanizing" foreigners, had important religious overtones. Meyer understood that it was impossible to teach children to read the Bible in German if their education was limited to churches on Sunday.

Although this law proscribed all foreign language education, it was aimed at the large German American population in the state. The law's purpose was clearly described by the Nebraska Supreme Court, which upheld its constitutionality:

> The salutary purpose of the statute is clear. The legislature had seen the baneful effects of permitting foreigners who had taken up residence in this country, to rear and educate their children in the language of their native land. The result of that condition was found to be inimical to our own safety. To allow the children of foreigners . . . to be taught from early childhood the language of the country of their parents, . . . was to educate them so that they must always think in that language, and, as a consequence, naturally inculcate in them the ideas and sentiments foreign to the best interests of this country.[59]

By a seven-to-two vote an odd coalition of justices on the United States Supreme Court rejected and overturned Meyer's conviction under this law. In the minority were the relatively liberal Justice Oliver Wendell Holmes, Jr. and the extremely conservative George Sutherland. The majority opinion was written by James C. McReynolds—"the most reactionary" member of the court[60]—but was supported by the very liberal Louis D. Brandeis. In a companion case, the Supreme Court also struck down Nebraska's Norval Act, as well as similar acts from Iowa and Ohio. The Ohio law flatly prohibited the teaching of German. On this last point, even Justices Holmes and Sutherland concurred.[61]

McReynolds was notorious for his bigotry and anti-Semitism. *Time Magazine*, never a bastion of liberalism, called McReynolds "Puritanical," "intolerably rude," "savagely sarcastic," "incredibly reactionary," and "anti-Semitic."[62] The magazine might have also added that the justice from Tennessee was incredibly racist and ethnocentric as well. Nevertheless, his opinion for the Court in *Meyer* showed a remarkable sensitivity to minorities. He was also able to defend minority rights on grounds that were also compatible to economic and social conservatives.

McReynolds conceded the inherent value of all Americans speaking the same language. He appeared to agree with the "desire of the [Nebraska] legislature to foster a homogeneous people with American ideals, prepared readily to understand current discussions of civic matters." He also agreed that the "unfortunate experiences of the late war . . . were certainly enough to quicken that aspiration."[63] For McReynolds the goals of the legislature seemed laudable enough. The question was the constitutionality of the methods.

McReynolds found three problems with the Nebraska law. First, it seemed overly broad. It prohibited the teaching of all modern foreign languages before the eighth grade. But, was this reasonable? The justice noted that the "mere knowledge of the German language cannot reasonably be regarded as harmful. Heretofore it has been commonly looked upon as helpful and desirable."[64] Therefore, was it reasonable to now proscribe it? McReynolds did not directly confront this question because he had an easier route to striking down the law.

The justice found that the Nebraska law unconstitutionally deprived foreign language teachers of their liberty to make a living, in violation of the Fourteenth Amendment. McReynolds wrote that the Fourteenth Amendment guaranteed "the right of the individual to contract, to engage in any of the common occupations of life."[65] McReynolds noted that in banning the teaching of all modern foreign languages "the legislature has attempted materially to interfere with the calling of modern language teachers" as well as "with the opportunities of pupils to acquire knowledge, and with the power of parents to control the education of their own."[66] Both Meyer and the parents who hired him had a contract and property interest: "His right thus to teach and the right of parents to engage him so to instruct their children, we think, are within the liberty of the Amendment."[67] In a sense this was simply an application of the substantive due process and freedom of contract doctrines that had been used to strike down protective labor legislation in earlier cases, such as *Lochner v. New York*.[68] The economic aspects of *Meyer* dovetailed perfectly with McReynolds's concurring opinion in *Adkins v. Children's Hospital*, striking down a minimum wage law, which he delivered earlier that term.[69]

However, McReynolds also hinted that the Fourteenth Amendment might protect non-economic substantive rights as well. Indeed, he placed the right to contract in a much broader context:

> While this court has not attempted to define with exactness the liberty thus guaranteed [by the Fourteenth Amendment], the term has received much consideration, and some of the included things have been definitely stated. Without doubt, it denotes not merely freedom from bodily restraint, but also the right of the individual to contract, to engage in any of the common occupations of life, to acquire useful knowledge, to marry, establish a home and bring up children, to worship God according to the dictates of his own conscience, and, generally, to enjoy those privileges long recognized at common law as essential to the orderly pursuit of happiness by free men.[70]

McReynolds further found that "it is the natural duty of the parent to give his children education suitable to their station in life."[71] He thus concluded that the Fourteenth Amendment protected the parents' right to educate their children, subject to the "reasonable" police power of the state. Prohibiting the teaching of a foreign language was, in this context, unreasonable.

The unreasonableness of the statute did not stem solely from the inherent value of learning a foreign language. It also reflected the dangers that could result from the overregulation of education. McReynolds, of course, had consistently opposed excessive regulation in other areas of the law. *Meyer* was thus consistent with McReynolds's jurisprudential philosophy. Quoting from Plato's *Republic* and describing education in ancient Sparta, McReynolds showed how a society might undermine the parent-child relationship in order to ensure the proper education of all children. The ancient Greek models, he conceded, would "submerge the individual and develop ideal citizens," but such a system was also "wholly different from" the "ideas touching the relation between individual and state" in the United States.[72] In essence, McReynolds saw the Nebraska law as leading to a totalitarian state that could undermine basic American liberties.

McReynolds's position on this point was completely in accordance with the conservative views of parenting championed by midwestern Lutherans. In Iowa the Missouri Synod Lutherans made similar arguments when trying to defeat the Dean Bill, Iowa's equivalent of Nebraska's Siman Act. The Iowa Lutherans had argued in ways that McReynolds would have appreciated.

> It is of the utmost importance for the welfare of the family and the State that the children should honor their father and mother, serve and obey them and hold them in love and esteem. Will the children do this if they do not understand the language of their parents? Will they not rather despise them as foreigners? A law that undermines parental authority is certainly not beneficial.[73]

Justice Holmes's dissent rested on his concept that the states were free to experiment in new forms of legislation. He accepted as uncontrovertible "that it is desirable that all the citizens of the United States should speak a common tongue" and thus accepted that the Nebraska act might be a "reasonable or even necessary method of reaching the desired result."[74] Holmes's one page dissent ignored the fact that the goal—teaching all children to speak and read English—was hardly undermined by simultaneously teaching them to read and speak a foreign language. The restrictive laws were not reasonably calculated to achieve an English-speaking population; on the contrary, they were only reasonably calculated to create a population that could speak *only* English.

Indeed, McReynolds noted in his *Meyer* opinion that the Court did not question the power of the state to require school attendance or "that they shall give instructions in English."[75] Holmes, for whatever reasons, chose to cast the law as doing something it did not do and similarly chose to misrepresent the McReynolds opinion as prohibiting the states from requiring English language education at all. In fact, all *Meyer* did was prevent the states from prohibiting all modern foreign language education.

It seems logical that Holmes would not accept McReynolds's economic arguments that the law denied the teacher his property right in teaching. Holmes did not like substantive due process at all, especially when it was applied to economic rights. But Holmes might easily have concurred with the majority on the claims of freedom of speech and freedom of religion that were inherent in *Meyer*. After all, only a few years later Holmes would make strong arguments in favor of restricting state action in the area of free speech.[76] Perhaps Holmes's hostility to economic due process and his commitment to judicial deference to legislatures may have simply blinded him to the individual liberty issues at stake in the cases.

Two years after *Meyer*, in *Pierce v. Society of Sisters*, the Court struck down an Oregon law banning private schools. Again, the Court relied on economic, property, and substantive due process arguments to find the law in violation of the Fourteenth Amendment.[77] A revived Ku Klux Klan, which focused its hate against Catholics, Jews, and immigrants, as well as blacks, had actively supported this law. Governor Walter Pierce, who signed the bill, had been elected with strong Klan support. Opposition to the law predictably came, not only from Catholics, Jews, and blacks, but also from German Lutherans, who "bristled at the bill not only because they had parochial schools to defend but also because they knew that their way of life was threatened."[78]

By 1925 German Americans had retained the right to educate their children in their own schools and to teach them to read and speak their mother tongue. However, by this time the repression of the war period and the push for Americanization had taken their toll. Most German churches now conducted their services in English; the readership of German newspapers diminished; German theater was virtually destroyed; and many German Lutheran and Catholic schools closed their doors or cut back their programs. Most important of all, for nearly a decade neither significant numbers of German Americans nor other school children had been educated to speak German.

SHORT-TERM SUCCESSES AND LONG-TERM FAILURES

The short- and long-term results of this repression are ironic. In the short run most of the actions and measures aimed at individual Germans were successful. They stifled labor radicals, muffled opposition to World War I, and in general made life more difficult for German Americans. This hostility led to the decimation of the American socialist movement and the nearly total destruction of the IWW, the lynching of one unfortunate German immigrant, and the terrorizing of thousands of German Americans during the "war to make the world safe for democracy."

In the long run this repression affected American culture in unexpected ways. By mid-century American labor had achieved many of the early twentieth-century goals, such as the eight-hour work day. At the same time, German American labor leaders, such as Walter Reuther, became models of respectability on the national scene. Similarly, Americans remembered the repression of World War I with embarrassment. During World War II there was little hostility to German Americans and often great sympathy for German nationals who were usually seen as refugees from oppression, rather than potential spies. With leaders of the Army and Navy named Eisenhower and Nimitz, it was hard to conceive of German Americans as a group threatening the war effort.

Nor was vigilantism a threat to Americans of German or Italian descent during World War II. Americans learned from their mistakes in World War I and were, generally, able to distinguish between nationality and national loyalty when it came to people of European ancestry. Japanese Americans were another story. The energies that created the dehumanizing propaganda of Germans during the First World War were now directed, for the most part, against the Japanese. Yet, even in this case, the response was different. In what might be called the application of the federal preemption power to bigotry, the national government assumed responsibility for the suppression of this new "alien" enemy within the country. The internment differed from the local vigilantism of World War I. Internment was not random and terrorizing. Rather, it was bureaucratic, systematic, and efficient. Perversely, the official explanation for the internment reflected the World War I experience, as the national government justified removing Japanese Americans from the West Coast in order to protect them from vigilantes and mobs.

The massive suppression of freedom of speech and the press, so common in World War I, was not repeated during World War II. In more recent times the Supreme Court has rejected the repressive free speech precedents of World War I.[79] While the suppression of free speech was successful during World War I, only to be repudiated in a later age, the suppression of German culture during World War I had a more twisted history and a more lasting effect. The failure of most modern Americans to study German, or indeed, any foreign language, is in part a legacy of World War I. During and after the war the study of German almost disappeared from American schools. Before the war one in four high school students studied German; five years after the armistice less than one in a hundred studied the language. More than half a century after the First World War the study of the German language had not regained its place in American high schools or universities.

This long-term result is ironic because the only major civil liberties victories before the Supreme Court in this period concerned the right of parents to educate their children in private schools and in foreign languages. The first modern Supreme Court civil liberties victory, *Meyer v. Nebraska*, involved a prohibition on the teaching of German to children. The second major civil liberties victory centered on Oregon's statute prohibiting parochial and private education. Although this law affected many different Americans, it was especially aimed at foreigners in general and German Americans in particular.[80]

While these court victories insured that German Americans might continue to teach their children their mother tongue in their own schools, in the long run the war on German culture in America was successful. Fearful of repression, German churches and schools began to switch to English during the war. After the successful appeal in *Meyer v. Nebraska* German Americans knew they had the right to teach their children German, but the incentive was already disappearing. As Marion L. Huffines has argued, "The trends toward English were well in place before 1917; the war served only to accelerate them."[81] This may be true, but the acceleration was extraordinarily, almost catastrophically, rapid. Moreover, even if most ethnic Germans had abandoned speaking German on their own, this shift would not have dramatically affected the teaching of German in schools nationwide.

Beyond the German American communities, the hysteria of the war seriously undermined the traditional connections between American and German scholars. The ties to German universities that had developed in the late nineteenth century had begun to break down before the war; the war rapidly finished this process.

The war also undermined the even stronger tradition of German and other foreign language training in America. Schools across America teach foreign languages poorly, in part because World War I ushered in an era of intellectual isolationism that was followed after World War II by a long period of cultural imperialism.[82] But, even if American schools taught languages well, it is unlikely very many Americans of today would be able to read or speak German. Today American students are more likely to have the opportunity to study Spanish or French, than German. The gap, however, between the first two languages and German is enormous. In 1982, more than 1.5 million students studied Spanish, over 800,000 studied French, but only 266,000 studied German. This is true, despite the importance of Germany to American foreign policy from 1954 to 1992, the vast post–World War II American military presence in Germany, and the strong economic ties between the United States and Germany. Until 1965 German ranked fourth, behind Latin, as the language of choice among students in public schools.[83] It probably remains fourth among all students today, and may in the future drop further, as the teaching of other languages, such as Japanese, Korean, Chinese, and Hebrew, continues to grow rapidly. This may be the greatest legacy of the repression of World War I.

NOTES

I wish to thank research assistants Marni Schlissel and Philip Presby at Brooklyn Law School for their help on this project. An earlier version of this article was read at the Drittes Krefelder Deutsch-Amerikanisches Historisches Symposium, Kerfeld, Germany, 1990.

1. *Meyer v. Nebraska*, 262 U.S. 390 (1923).

2. For a useful discussion of the jurisprudential issues in this case, see William G. Ross, "A Judicial Janus: *Meyer v. Nebraska* in Historical Perspective," *Cincinnati Law Review* 57 (1988): 125. See also idem, *Forging New Freedoms: Nativism, Education, and the Constitution, 1917–1927* (Lincoln: University of Nebraska Press, 1994).

3. David H. Bennett, *The Party of Fear: From Nativist Movements to the New Right in American History* (Chapel Hill: University of North Carolina Press, 1988), pp. 171–82.

4. William 0. Reichert, *Partisans of Freedom: A Study in American Anarchism* (Bowling Green, Ohio: Bowling Green University Press, 1976), p. 375.

5. Ibid., pp. 367–73.

6. Defendants August Spies, Adolph Fischer, George Engle, Michael Schwab, and Louis Lingg were born in Germany. Oscar Neebe was born to German immigrant parents in New York City but was sent to Hesse Cassel for his primary education and did not return to the United States until he was fourteen years old. Samuel Fielden, the seventh defendant, was an English immigrant. Only Albert R. Parsons was born in the United States. See generally Philip S. Foner, ed.,

The Autobiographies of the Haymarket Rioters (New York: American Institute for Marxist Studies, 1969). All eight were convicted of killing seven policemen and wounding more than seventy others in the riot.

7. Melvyn Dubofsky, *We Shall Be All: The History of the Industrial Workers of the World* (Chicago: Quadrangle Books, 1969), p. 108.

8. Frederick C. Luebke, *Bonds of Loyalty: German Americans and World War I* (DeKalb: Northern Illinois University Press, 1974), p. 88.

9. Ibid., pp. 50–51.

10. David W. Dejen, *The Germans in Missouri, 1900–1910* (Columbia: University of Missouri Press, 1985), p. 24.

11. Carl Wittke, *German-Americans and the World War* (Columbus: Ohio State Archaeological and Historical Society, 1936), p. 184.

12. Quoted in ibid., p. 160.

13. Quoted in Luebke, *Bonds of Loyalty*, p. 229.

14. Ibid., pp. 228–31; Wittke, *German-Americans and the World War*, pp. 160–61.

15. Many suffered tremendously for their pacifist beliefs. They were harassed and beaten by mobs and often jailed for refusing to serve. See generally, Luebke, *Bonds of Loyalty*, pp. 256–59, 289–90; Wittke, *German-Americans and the World War*, pp. 159–60.

16. Wittke, *German-Americans and the World War*, pp. 159–60, 191; Luebke, *Bonds of Loyalty*, pp. 257–59, 274, 289; H. C. Peterson and Gilbert C. Fite, *Opponents of War, 1917–1918* (Madison: University of Wisconsin Press, 1957), pp. 121–38, 262–64.

17. In 1912, for example, Eugene V. Debs, the socialist candidate for president, won almost 900,000 votes. By 1918 he would be in jail for his opposition to the war and the draft. *Debs v. United States*, 249 U.S. 211 (1919).

18. *The Liberty Bell*, quoted in Luebke, *Bonds of Loyalty*, p. 244.

19. Sean Dennis Cashman, *America in the Age of the Titans: The Progressive Era and World War I* (New York: New York University Press, 1988), pp. 503–4.

20. Bennett, *The Party of Fear*, pp. 174–75.

21. Cashman, *America in the Age of the Titans*, p. 504. Many nativists, like Sunday, were also prohibitionists, and this further made them hostile to German Americans who were usually "wets."

22. Louise Maunsell Field, "Sentimentalizing the Hun," *Forum* 58 (1917): 307–12, reprinted in David F. Trask, ed., *World War I at Home: Readings on American Life, 1914–1920* (New York: John Wiley & Sons, 1970), pp. 83–86.

23. George Sylvester Viereck, *Spreading the Germs of Hate* (New York: Horace Liveright, 1930), pp. 189–90.

24. These events are described in Paul Murphy, *World War I and the Origins of Civil Liberties in the United States* (New York: W. W. Norton, 1979), pp. 128–32, and Luebke, *Bonds of Loyalty*.

25. Wittke, *German-Americans and the World War*, pp. 159, 183; Luebke, *Bonds of Loyalty*, pp. 244–45, 248–49; Murphy, *Origin of Civil Liberties*, pp. 128–32.

26. Murphy, *Origin of Civil Liberties*, pp. 128–32; Luebke, *Bonds of Loyalty*, pp. 248–49; Wittke, *German-Americans and the World War*, pp. 183–93. Some German clergymen were publicly whipped, although the usual intimidation was to make them publicly kiss a flag or perform some other "patriotic" act.

27. Murphy, *Origin of Civil Liberties*, pp. 128–32; Luebke, *Bonds of Loyalty*, pp. 248–49; Wittke, *German-Americans and the World War*, p. 183.

28. Murphy, *Origin of Civil Liberties*, pp. 128–32; Luebke, *Bonds of Loyalty*, pp. 248–49; Wittke, *German-Americans and the World War*, p. 183.

29. Paul Kleppner, *The Cross of Culture: A Social Analysis of Midwestern Politics, 1850–1900* (New York: The Free Press, 1970), p. 158. The Irish Catholic hierarchy in the Midwest supported such laws as a way of undermining German Catholic priests. Sidney E. Ahlstrom, *A Religious History of the American People* (New Haven and London: Yale University Press, 1972), p. 562.

30. Richard Jensen, *The Winning of the Midwest: Social and Political Conflict, 1888–1896* (Chicago: University of Chicago Press, 1971), p. 123; David Tyack, Thomas James, and Aaron Bennett, *Law and the Shaping of Public Education, 1785–1954* (Madison: University of Wisconsin Press, 1987), p. 68.

31. Marion L. Huffines, "Language Maintenance Efforts Among German Immigrants and Their Descendants in the United States," in Frank Trommler and Joseph McVeigh, eds., *Immigration, Language, Ethnicity* (Philadelphia: University of Pennsylvania Press, 1985), 1:247.

32. Jensen, *Winning of the Midwest*, pp. 220–21.

33. Tyack, et al., *Law and the Shaping of Public Education*, pp. 171, 68.

34. Orville H. Zable, *God and Caesar in Nebraska* (Lincoln: University of Nebraska Press, 1955), p. 139.

35. *Nebraska Laws, 1913*, Chap. 31; *Nebraska Revised Statutes 1913*, Sec. 6941.

36. *State, ex rel. Thayer v. School District of Nebraska City*, 99 Neb. 338, 156 N. W. Rep. 641 (1916).

37. Tyack, et al., *Law and the Shaping of Public Education*, pp. 171–73. Weeks, quoted in "Brief of the Defendants [the State of Nebraska]," pp. 31–32, in *Nebraska District of Evangelical Lutheran Synod v. McKelvie*, 262 U.S. 404 (1923).

38. Tyack, et al., *Law and the Shaping of Public Education*, pp. 171–73.

39. Ibid., p. 174.

40. Peterson and Fite, *Opponents of War*, p. 195.

41. "Brief of the Defendants [the State of Nebraska]," p. 25, in *Nebraska District of Evangelical Lutheran Synod v. McKelvie*, 262 U.S. 404 (1923). These states are listed on pages 25–31 of the brief. This list also includes excerpts from some of the statutes. *Lutheran Synod* was a companion case to *Meyer* that challenged the Norval Act, the successor statute to the Siman Act. On this act, see Ross, "Judicial Janus," pp. 148–51.

42. *South Dakota Laws, 1918*, Chaps. 41, 42, excerpted in U.S. Judge Advocate General's Department (Army) *Compilation of War Laws of the Various States and Insular Possessions* (Washington, DC: U.S. Government Publishing Office, 1919), p. 147; Peterson and Fite, *Opponents of War*, pp. 195–96.

43. Peterson and Fite, *Opponents of War*, pp. 195–96.

44. *Louisiana Acts, 1918*, No. 114, p. 188, excerpted in U.S. Judge Advocate General's Department (Army) *Compilation of War Laws*, 47.

45. *Louisiana Acts, 1918*, No. 177, p. 333, quoted from U.S. Judge Advocate General's Department (Army) *Compilation of War Laws, p. 39.*

46. "Brief of the Defendants [the State of Nebraska]," pp. 26, 29–30, in *Nebraska District of Evangelical Lutheran Synod v. McKelvie*, 26 U.S. 404 (1923). *Meyer v. Nebraska, Brief and Argument of State of Nebraska*, 25, 28, 24, reprinted in Philip B. Kurland and Gerhard Casper, eds., *Landmark Briefs and Arguments of the Supreme Court of the United States: Constitutional Law* (Arlington, Va.: University Publications of America, 1975), 21:725, 728, 724. See also Wittke, *German-Americans and the World War*, p. 179.

47. Peterson and Fite, *Opponents of War*, p. 196.

48. Patricia Dandonoli, "Report on Foreign Language Enrollment in Public Secondary Schools," *Foreign Language Annals* 20 (October 1987).

49. Tyack, et al., *Law and the Shaping of Public Education*, p. 170.

50. *Globe* and *Manufacturers' Record* quoted in "American Students Boycotting German," *Literary Digest* 56 (March 30, 1918): 29.

51. Peterson and Fite, *Opponents of War*, 196, citing "American Students Boycotting German," *Literary Digest* 56 (March 30, 1918): 9, 44, 46–50, 52, 54–55, 58, 61–64, 70, 72–74.

52. Wittke, *German–Americans and the World War*, p. 182; Luebke, *Bonds of Loyalty*, p. 253.

53. Quoted in Ross, *Forging New Freedoms*, p. 85.

54. Ibid., Chap. 4; Zable, *God and Caesar in Nebraska*, pp. 139–40, 135.

55. "An Act Relating to the Teaching of Foreign Language in the State of Nebraska," Act of April 9, 1919, *Laws of Nebraska, 1919*, Ch. 249.

56. Legislative Drafting Research Fund of Columbia University, *Constitutions of the United States: National and State* (Dobbs Ferry, N.Y.: Oceana Publications, 1990), Binder 3. At the same time, Nebraska changed its constitutional provisions on the ownership of property. Both the 1866 and 1875 Constitutions provided "No distinction shall ever be made by law between resident aliens and citizens in reference to possession, enjoyment, or descent of property." In 1920 this provision was amended to read: "There shall be no discrimination between citizens of the United States in respect to acquisition, ownership, possession, enjoyment, of descent of property. The right of aliens in respect to acquisition, enjoyment, and descent of property may be regulated by law."

57. "An act to declare the English language the official language of this State, and to require all official proceedings, records and publications to be in such

language and all school branches to be taught in said language in public, private, denominational and parochial schools," Act of May 14, 1921, *Nebraska Laws, 1921*, c. 61. See Ross, "Judicial Janus," pp. 148–51, for further discussion of this law.

58. *Mever v. Nebraska, Brief and Argument for the Plaintiff in Error*, 1–2, reprinted in Kurland and Casper, *Landmark Briefs*, pp. 675–76.

59. *Meyer v. State*, 107 Neb. 657, 187 N.W. 100, at 102 (1922) Significantly, the author of this decision, Judge Flansburg, was the member of the court with the most "German" name. For a detailed discussion of the state litigation, see Ross, "Judicial Janus," pp. 141–48, 151–55.

60. David Burner, "James C. McReynolds," in Leon Friedman and Fred L. Israel, *The Justices of the United States Supreme Court*, 5 vols. (New York: Chelsea House, 1980), 3:2023.

61. *Bartles v. Iowa*; *Bohning v. Ohio*; *Pohl v. Ohio*, 262 U.S. 404 (1923).

62. Burner, "James C. McReynolds," p. 2024.

63. *Meyer v. Nebraska*, 262 U.S. 390, at 402 (1923). He did not, however, indicate what those "unfortunate experiences" were.

64. Ibid., at 400.

65. Ibid., at 399.

66. Ibid., at 401.

67. Ibid., at 400.

68. *Lochner v. New York*, 198 U.S. 45 (1905).

69. *Adkins v. Children's Hospital*, 261 U.S. 525 (1905).

70. *Meyer v. Nebraska*, at 399.

71. Ibid., at 400.

72. Ibid., at 401–02.

73. *Lutheran Witness* 38 (March 18, 1919): 87–88, quoted in Neil M. Johnson, "The Missouri Synod Lutherans and the War Against the German Language, 1917–1923," *Nebraska History* 56 (1975): 141.

74. *Bartles v. State of Iowa*, 262 U.S. 404, at 412.

75. *Meyer v. Nebraska*, at 402.

76. See *Gitlow v. New York*, 268 U.S. 652 (1925) and *Whitney v. California*, 274 U.S. 357 (1927).

77. *Pierce v. Society of Sisters*, 268 U.S. 510 (1925).

78. Tyack, et al., *Law and the Shaping of Public Education*, p. 184.

79. The first three Supreme Court decisions on free speech were *Schenck v. United States, Frowerk v. United States*, 249 U.S. 204 (1919) and *Debs v. United States*, 249 U.S. 211. The first involved an Eastern European Jewish immigrant who was the secretary of the Socialist party in Philadelphia. The second was the prosecution, under the Espionage Act of 1917, of the persons associated with the *Missouri Staats of Zeitung*, a German paper published in Kansas City, Missouri. Only after the Supreme Court upheld these two convictions did it review, and uphold, the conviction of the leader of the Socialist party, Eugene Victor Debs. The precedents in these cases were overturned in *Bradenberg v. Ohio*, 398 U.S. 444 (1969).

80. *Meyer v. Nebraska*, at 390; *Pierce v. Society of Sisters*, at 510.

81. Huffines, "Language Maintenance Efforts Among German Immigrants and Their Descendants in the United States," p. 249.

82. In 1982 only 21.3 percent of American public secondary school students studied a modern foreign language. This contrasts with the 35.9 percent rate in 1915. In 1982 only 2.1 percent of public secondary school children studied German, while in 1915 24.4 percent studied that language. Patricia Dandonoli, "Report on Foreign Language Enrollment."

83. Statistics for 1960 and 1965 show German ranking a far distant fourth behind Spanish, French, and Latin in numbers of American students enrolled in all schools.

Foreign Language Enrollment for Public and Private Students, 1960, 1965

	1960	1965
TSE	11,847,783	16,400,985
TFLE	2,775,152	4,494,212
Spanish	1,037,320	1,833,960
French	853,342	1,586,852
Latin	678,928	626,199
German	162,130	373,771
Russian	10,051	32,027
TSE = Total Student Enrollment		
TFLE = Total Foreign Language Enrollment		

Source: ACTFL, *Foreign Language Education: Volume I, An Overview* (Skokie, IL: National Textbook Co., 1973): 417.

Foreign Language Enrollment for Public School Students

	1960	1965	1982
TPSSE	8,649,495	11,611,197	12,879,254
TPSFLE	1,867,358	3,067,613	2,740,198
Spanish	933,409	1,426,822	1,562,984
French	744,404	1,251,373	857,984
Latin	654,670	591,445	169,580
German	150,764	328,028	266,901
Russian	9,722	26,716	5,702
TPSS = Total Public School Student Enrollment			
TPSFLE = Total Public Foreign Language Enrollment			

Source: Patricia Dandonoli, "Report on Foreign Language Enrollment in Public Secondary Schools," *Foreign Language Annals* 20 (October, 1987): 459.

4

A Kansan Looks at *Brown*

Michael S. Mayer

This essay examines the school segregation cases of 1954 as a means of gaining an insight into the legal and political culture of the Great Plains. Not only did the lead case originate on the Great Plains, but people from the Great Plains played key roles at the national level in shaping the decision known as *Brown v. Board of Education*. Both Herbert Brownell, Dwight Eisenhower's attorney general, and Assistant Attorney General J. Lee Rankin, who argued *Brown I* before the Supreme Court, came from Nebraska. More important still, the president himself grew up in Kansas. The point is not so much that Eisenhower was representative, but his racial attitudes and his approach to government, formed in part on the Kansas plains, shaped his response to the school segregation cases. Thus, an examination of Eisenhower's response provides a glimpse into the prevalent racial attitudes as well as the legal and constitutional culture of the Great Plains.

EISENHOWER AND AFRICAN AMERICANS

In his memoirs, Eisenhower recalled that "since boyhood I had accepted without qualification the right to equality before the law of all citizens of this country, whatever their race or color or creed."[1] One might well question, however, the degree to which he actually confronted the issue of racial discrimination.

It is fair to say that Eisenhower's upbringing left him with no personal animosity towards blacks. Indeed, individual acts of bigotry revolted him. When the future president attended high school in Abilene, Kansas, he was a fine athlete, and baseball was a passion. A coach harassed and eventually dismissed a black player from the baseball team. In response, Eisenhower, the team captain, threatened to quit and, with support first from his brother Edgar and then from other members of the team, forced the coach to reinstate the black player.[2] Throughout his life, Eisenhower retained the same sense of horror when confronted with overt discrimination. General Lucius Clay recalled that the Eisenhowers and the Clays were vacationing off the coast of Florida and were about to check into a hotel when Eisenhower saw a sign that read: "Negroes and Jews not welcome." Eisenhower told Clay that he would never stay at such a place, and the two couples returned to Miami.[3]

On the other hand, Eisenhower reflected the racist mores of the time and environment that produced him. Few black families lived in Abilene, and there were no blacks enrolled at West Point when Eisenhower attended. Eisenhower's career in the Army provided no greater opportunity to establish contacts with black people, except those in menial or personal service roles. A number of his early assignments took him to posts in the South, and southerners were over-represented among the Army's professional officer corps. Eisenhower's tour of duty in the Philippines served only to reinforce stereotypes of racial servility and inferiority.[4] In addition, many of Eisenhower's friends were southerners, and their attitudes influenced him.[5] Family as well as friends exposed Eisenhower to racial prejudice. Lucy Eisenhower, the wife of Dwight's older brother, Edgar, held particularly virulent racist attitudes.[6] All of these influences went into shaping Eisenhower's response to *Brown v. Board of Education*.

THE EISENHOWER ADMINISTRATION PREPARES FOR A CONTROVERSIAL CASE

When Dwight D. Eisenhower became president, the government had already entered the school segregation cases on behalf of the black children seeking admission to all-white schools. The Supreme Court had already heard arguments and announced that it wished to hear reargument on the intention of the framers of the Fourteenth Amendment, the power of

Congress and the courts to abolish segregation, and whether or not the Supreme Court had power to grant gradual relief.[7]

The new Eisenhower administration had not yet appointed a solicitor general, so Attorney General Herbert Brownell brought the case into his own office, placing it under the supervision of Assistant Attorney General J. Lee Rankin.[8] The Court's request that the government submit an opinion of fact and an opinion concerning the intention of the Fourteenth Amendment made Eisenhower uncomfortable. He thought that such an "opinion" by the attorney general would encroach on the authority of the Supreme Court. On August 19, 1953, he telephoned the attorney general to express this view.[9] Brownell, whose political judgment and legal abilities Eisenhower admired greatly, persuaded him that answering such a question in no way violated the Court's integrity or authority; and then government's brief contained an opinion on the Fourteenth Amendment.[10]

Eisenhower's reluctance to have his Justice Department file a brief revealed much about his approach towards civil rights in general. While he strove to make sure that the federal government in no way supported segregation, he rejected the use of federal coercive power to achieve desegregation on two grounds: it would usurp powers that properly belonged to the states, and it would be ineffective. At the same time, however, Eisenhower urged his friend James F. Byrnes, the governor of South Carolina, to cooperate with desegregation.[11]

Perhaps Eisenhower's most significant contribution to the outcome of the *Brown* decision came indirectly, through his appointment of Earl Warren to the chief justiceship. While the president did not have the school segregation cases specifically in mind when he appointed Warren, Eisenhower chose the Californian because of his "middle of the road philosophy," his political skills, and his leadership abilities. Warren's political dexterity proved crucial in obtaining a unanimous decision overturning segregation.[12]

Between the oral arguments before the Supreme Court (in which Assistant Attorney General J. Lee Rankin took the position that "segregation in public schools cannot be maintained under the Fourteenth Amendment") and the Court's decision, Eisenhower maintained a close watch over the case through his attorney general. On January 26, 1954, Brownell informed the president that the Court might decide the constitutionality of segregation that spring but postpone the problem of a remedy until fall. Obviously struggling with the issue, Eisenhower replied vaguely, "I don't know where I stand, but I think that the best interests of the U.S. demand an answer in keeping with past decisions." When the attorney general suggested that the

Court wanted to defer the matter as long as possible, the president joked that perhaps they would defer the matter until the next administration.[13]

EISENHOWER'S REACTION TO *BROWN V. BOARD OF EDUCATION*

If Eisenhower entertained any serious hopes along those lines, the Court shattered them on May 17. As Brownell had predicted, the Court found segregation to be unconstitutional but held off on the question of relief.[14]

In spite of the assertion in his memoirs that "I definitely agreed with the unanimous decision," Eisenhower harbored serious misgivings about the Court's ruling in *Brown*.[15] While he believed in the morality, necessity, and inevitability of ending segregation, he thought it best accomplished through a gradual process. He advocated beginning with graduate and professional schools and working down slowly, perhaps at the rate of one grade per year. He also believed that a process of education and public acceptance had to precede other gains, and he rejected the idea that segregation should end by a summary court order or federal statute.[16] Then, too, the president worried that southern states would abolish public education systems and replace them with "private" schools supported by state aid. Such a result, he believed, would most severely handicap blacks and "poor white" children.[17]

Like it or not, however, Eisenhower had to deal with *Brown*. Immediately after the decision, Eisenhower determined not to comment on it. He would state publicly only that the Supreme Court was the law of the land, that he was sworn to uphold the Constitution, and that he would do so. He adopted the position that once he expressed an opinion on a Supreme Court decision, he would be obliged to do so in other cases. Eventually, he would be drawn into a statement disagreeing with the Court, and that would create doubt as to the vigor with which he would enforce that decision.[18]

Although Eisenhower made it a point not to make public his discomfort with the Court's decision, hints of his displeasure emerged. At a press conference, he pointedly reminded a reporter who asked him how he felt about *Brown* coming under a Republican administration that the "Supreme Court, as I understand it, is not in my administration."[19] At every opportunity, the president reiterated his belief that one could not change the "hearts of men with laws or decisions."[20] Not once in the summer following the *Brown* decision did the president lend his public support to the Court or to the decision. Not only did this deny the benefit of his tremendous personal popularity to the Court, it gave encouragement to southerners preparing to argue for the slowest possible implementation when the Court reconvened in the fall.

Not all of the signals emanating from the White House during this period were hostile, however. Immediately after the decision, Eisenhower declared that there was no need for a judicial order to make the federal government recognize its responsibilities and that the District of Columbia would serve as a model for the nation by desegregating its schools voluntarily and immediately. Actions lent weight to his rhetoric; he called in the D.C. Commissioners and told them that he expected them to take the lead in desegregating Washington's schools. Under continuing pressure from the White House, the District government complied. If complete desegregation was not achieved during his administration (or during the next several administrations, for that matter), the process began immediately and it did so under the auspices of the Eisenhower administration.[21]

BROWN II

President Eisenhower played a significant, and mixed, role in the administration's preparation of its brief on the implementation of the Court's ruling in *Brown*. On the one hand, he reined in more activist subordinates such as Simon Sobeloff, the solicitor general, and Philip Elman, a career attorney in the Justice Department. Indeed, the president struck out a paragraph of the brief in which Sobeloff and Elman had argued for the immediate commencement of desegregation. The paragraph contended that contacts between whites and blacks eased the process of desegregation and supported that contention by citing the success of desegregation in the armed forces. Eisenhower also added a passage in which he argued that in declaring segregation unconstitutional, the Court had struck down a social system that had existed for generations. In doing so, Eisenhower asserted, the Court had recognized the psychological and emotional impact of segregation, and it should recognize such factors in fashioning the transformation that would take place.[22]

On the other hand, even after Eisenhower's alterations, the government's brief argued for a slightly more forceful position than that which the Court adopted in *Brown II*. The administration argued for an order requiring school boards to submit a satisfactory plan (defined as one which began the process of desegregation immediately) within ninety days. If they failed to do so, the lower courts were to order that desegregation begin the next school term.[23] Although the Court's ruling in *Brown II* generally adopted the government's proposals, it eliminated the ninety-day time limit for school boards to present a satisfactory plan.

Aside from Eisenhower's own personal views towards blacks, which tended toward the paternalistic, his convictions regarding the proper role of the federal government helped shape his response to civil rights issues. The president honestly believed that there were some areas in which state government should retain authority. His concerns over federalism were no mere sophistic justification for his reluctance to act forcefully on civil rights. Nor was he alone in his disquietude over the relationship between state and federal governments. Even an activist such as Brownell had his doubts about federal authority to act in certain instances.[24]

Eisenhower's personal views about race relations were also balanced by his perception of his duty as president and his conviction that every citizen, irrespective of race, deserved equal treatment at the hands of the government. Whatever his own prejudices and his sympathy for the desires of southerners to remain apart from blacks (particularly in social situations), he believed that legally mandated segregation was wrong. He also considered it his duty as president to make sure that the government treated all its citizens equally.[25]

Following through on that conviction, he attempted to end segregation in federal employment, in the armed forces, and in Washington D.C., even before the Court spoke in *Brown*.[26] Similarly, once the Court had ruled that segregation was unconstitutional, he had no doubts as to his duty. He would enforce the decision. However, just what that meant and the extent to which he would act were determined at least in part by his personal feelings about desegregation and by his conceptions of the proper role of the federal government.

While he had been willing to act forcefully whenever he considered federal and executive authority unquestioned, *Brown* constituted another matter entirely. It affected public schools, run by state and local authorities; and the president was not at all certain that the federal government, including the courts, had any business telling them how to conduct their affairs. In addition, he was convinced that a court order was the wrong way to undertake desegregation. Forcing southern whites to accept blacks through a court order or coercive legislation, he believed, would only generate a hostile reaction and set back the cause of racial justice. Finally, he sympathized with southerners who objected to forced and immediate contact with unacculturated blacks.

Even after the Court ruled on implementation, Eisenhower never lent his public support to desegregation and often urged patience.[27] Yet he made efforts to shape desegregation along lines with which he could be comfortable. He urged the evangelist Billy Graham to influence southern ministers to counsel calm rather than to inflame public opinion. Eisenhower believed that ministers had a significant role to play because "success through conciliation will be more lasting and stronger than could be attained through force and conflict." He then asked Graham to consider the possibility of electing "a few qualified Negroes" to school boards and to city and county commissions, and admitting qualified blacks into graduate schools solely on the basis of merit.[28]

When, however, in the course of meeting with other ministers, Graham used the president's name to support his plea for moderation, Eisenhower acted immediately to prevent himself from being drawn into the controversy. In a chilly letter to the evangelist, he made it clear to Graham that he considered their correspondence to be private. At the same time, he stated his own position: "I shall always, as a matter of conviction and as a champion of real, as opposed to spurious, progress, remain a moderate in this regard."[29]

Eisenhower resisted with equal ardor the efforts of the press to get him to go on record with his own views. He repeatedly reiterated that it was his job to carry out decisions of the Supreme Court, not to pass judgment on them.[30] Eisenhower honestly considered it improper to express his approval of a Supreme Court decision; he was even more certain that his doubts about the *Brown* decision should not be made public. Thus, in June 1957, he became distressed over reports that he was at odds with Warren over the *Brown* decision. He dashed off a quick note to Warren assuring the chief justice that he had not, as reported in one story, expressed anger at the Supreme Court. "I have no doubt," he explained, "that in private conversation someone did hear me express amazement about one decision, but I have never even hinted at a feeling such as anger. To do so would imply not only that I knew the law but questioned motives. Neither of these things is true." He concluded, however, by resolving that "even in private conversations I shall be more careful of my language."[31]

EISENHOWER'S CONTINUED AMBIVALENCE

In spite of his protestations to the contrary, Eisenhower was uncomfortable with the *Brown* decision. In July 1957, he unburdened his thoughts on the matter to his boyhood friend and lifelong confidant, Swede Hazlett. "I think," Eisenhower reflected, "that no other single event has so disturbed the domestic scene in many years as did the Supreme Court's decision of

1954 in the school segregation case." He observed that *Brown* and other decisions placed a heavier responsibility on the federal government to insure each citizen's constitutional rights. Moreover, he believed that laws were "rarely effective unless they represent the will of the majority" and cited the failure of prohibition as evidence to support his position. In addition, the Court had upheld segregation for almost sixty years, during which time southerners had come to regard their system as legal and ethical. Therefore it was unrealistic to expect a "complete and instant reversal of conduct" on the part of southerners. The Court itself recognized this by ordering gradual implementation.[32]

Not only was Eisenhower concerned about *Brown's* implications for race relations, but the decision challenged his constitutional world view. During a pre-press conference briefing in 1956, James Hagerty, Eisenhower's press secretary, reminded the president of a recent Supreme Court decision barring segregation on intrastate buses. The president remarked that "in some of these things he was more of a 'States Righter' than the Supreme Court." Eisenhower then expressed fear that if steps were taken too quickly, the cause of blacks would be set back rather than advanced. His thoughts shifted to *Brown*, and once again his disquietude over the issue of federalism emerged. How, he asked, could the federal government enforce a ruling that applied to schools supported by state funds? Practical considerations troubled him as well; he worried about a general strike in the South. Eisenhower commented prophetically that one day a district court would cite someone for contempt, "and then we are going to be up against it."[33]

The president revealed himself yet again when Bernard Shanley, his secretary, in a speech praising the administration's record on civil rights, told an audience in New Jersey that, although he personally agreed with the Court's ruling, "the immediate result caused [some] harm." To some it appeared that the administration, and by extension the president, had expressed disapproval of the decision through Shanley. Eisenhower told Shanley that he was right but that he never should have said it in public. The president decided that, if asked about Shanley's comment, he would simply state that he had no quarrel with the Supreme Court.[34]

In spite of his reservations about *Brown*, he did not, as is often charged, come to regret his appointment of Warren because of it. On the contrary, he continued to show great respect for Warren as a justice. In December 1955, Hagerty and Eisenhower discussed possible Republican candidates for the presidency in 1956, assuming that Eisenhower would not run. Hagerty suggested Warren. "Not a chance," responded Eisenhower, "and I'll tell you why. I know that the Chief Justice is very happy right where he is. He wants to go down in history as a great Chief Justice, and he certainly is becoming one."[35] This was, of course, after *Brown* and *Brown II*.

The oft-repeated story that Eisenhower considered Warren's appointment to be the biggest mistake of his administration has no basis in fact. Repeated attempts to trace the original source of the quotation all lead back to a Columbia Oral History interview with Ralph Cake, a reactionary Republican leader from Oregon and a longtime enemy of Warren.[36]

JUDICIAL APPOINTMENTS AND THE *BROWN* IMPACT

Whatever reluctance Eisenhower felt about the Brown decision, his appointments to the Supreme Court and the courts of appeals for the Fourth and Fifth Circuits indicated at the very least a tacit acceptance of the principles enunciated in *Brown*. After the Court's initial ruling in May 1954, he appointed John Marshall Harlan to the Supreme Court over the strenuous objections of southern senators. Eisenhower's first appointment after the ruling on implementation was William Brennan, a confirmed liberal. Even after the incident at Little Rock, Eisenhower considered appointing both Brownell and Elbert Parr Tuttle, whom he had appointed to the Fifth Circuit and who had become the leader of the liberals on that court.[37]

Moreover, his first appointment to the Fourth Circuit was Simon Sobeloff, the solicitor general who had argued *Brown II*. Southern senators held up that nomination for over a year. Eisenhower followed that appointment with Clement Haynsworth, whose nomination was opposed by Strom Thurmond because Haynsworth was not a segregationist. As chief judge after 1958, Sobeloff led the Fourth Circuit to a reputation as one of the most liberal appellate courts, and Haynsworth voted consistently to end segregation. Only later when the issue became integration did Haynsworth's voting take on a more conservative cast. Sobeloff continued to represent an advanced liberal position until his death in 1973.[38]

Eisenhower also appointed John Minor Wisdom, John R. Brown, and Warren Jones to the Fifth Circuit. Along with Tuttle and Robert Taylor Rives, they became Jack Bass's "unlikely heroes." The lone exception among Eisenhower's appellate judges was Ben Cameron, and political necessity accounted for his appointment.

Eisenhower's appointments to federal appellate courts in the South constituted his greatest contribution to civil rights. The liberals and moderates he appointed to the areas most affected by the *Brown* decision guaranteed an ongoing process of desegregation. Compared to the appointments of his predecessor and successor, they stand out in dramatic relief. The judges Eisenhower appointed would enforce the Court's ruling, and that meant an end to legal segregation; but, by the very nature of the legal system, the process would be a gradual one.[39]

These appointments shed considerable light on Eisenhower's approach to *Brown*. Eisenhower could agree in principle with the decision's intent, but he had qualms about the exercise of judicial power it represented and even more serious doubts about the extension of federal power it implied. Moreover, he believed that a court ruling (or compulsory, immediate legislation for that matter) would fail to bring about equality for blacks. Indeed, he worried that such action would create a backlash that would wipe out advances that had already been made. His quarrel, however, remained with the Court's methods, not its intent.

CONCLUSION

Eisenhower's response to *Brown v. Board of Education of Topeka* in many ways reflects the ideas Eisenhower developed as a boy in Kansas and later at West Point. He had a high school civics class regard for the separation of powers and for the federal system. Yet he also believed in the fundamental equality of all citizens before the law. The boy who threatened to quit a baseball team to win reinstatement for a black teammate grew up to hate discrimination and bigotry. Yet his conception of constitutional government limited his willingness to respond to discrimination as a national issue. Nothing in his background enabled him to project his horror at individual acts of discrimination onto the larger canvas of national policy.

NOTES

1. Dwight D. Eisenhower, *The White House Years: Waging Peace, 1956–1961* (New York: Doubleday, 1965), p. 148.

2. Virgil Pinkley, *Eisenhower Declassified* (Old Tappan, N.J.: Fleming H. Revell, 1979), pp. 47–48. Stephen E. Ambrose, in *Eisenhower Soldier, General of the Army, President-Elect, 1890–1952* (New York: Simon and Schuster, 1983), tells a different story, but one with a similar gist. A football team from Abilene on which Eisenhower played discovered that the opposition had a black player. None of the players from Abilene would play across the line from the black player, who was the other team's center. Eisenhower declared that he would play center that day, even though he normally played end and had never played center before. He shook hands with the black player both before and after the game (pp. 34–35). Ambrose's source is Bela Kornitzer, *The Great American Heritage: The Story of*

the Five Eisenhower Brothers (New York: Farrar, Straus and Cidahay, 1955), p. 52.

3. Pinkley, *Eisenhower Declassified*, pp. 47–48.

4. Peter Lyon, *Eisenhower: Portrait of a Hero* (Boston: Little, Brown, 1974), p. 556; Steve Neal, *The Eisenhowers: Reluctant Dynasty* (Garden City, N.Y.: Doubleday, 1978), pp. 106–7; Elmo Richardson, *The Presidency of Dwight D. Eisenhower* (Lawrence: Regents Press of Kansas, 1979), p. 105.

5. Michael S. Mayer, "Eisenhower's Conditional Crusade: The Eisenhower Administration and Civil Rights, 1953–1957," Ph.D. Diss. Princeton University, 1984, pp. 197–98; E. Frederic Morrow, *Forty Years a Guinea Pig* (New York: Pilgrim Press, 1980), p. 212; Interview with E. Frederic Morrow, March 6, 1978; Stephen Ambrose, *Eisenhower: The President* (New York: Simon and Schuster, 1984), p. 125; interview with E. Frederic Morrow conducted by the Columbia Oral History Project, Columbia University Library, New York, New York (hereafter cited as Morrow, COH), pp. 29–30.

6. Lucy Eisenhower to Dwight Eisenhower, August 26, 1958, Whitman File, Name Series, Eisenhower, Edgar (1957–1958), Dwight D. Eisenhower Library (hereafter cited as DDEL), Abilene, Kansas.

7. Richard Kluger, *Simple Justice: The History of Brown v. Board of Education and Black America's Struggle for Equality* (New York: Knopf, 1976), p. 558; Daniel M. Berman, *It Is So Ordered: The Supreme Court Rules on School Desegregation* (New York: Norton, 1966), pp. 60–61; Michael S. Mayer, "With Much Deliberation and Some Speed: Eisenhower and the *Brown* Decision," *Journal of Southern History* 52 (February, 1986): 46–48; *Brown v. Board of Education*, 345 US 972 (1953); Dennis J. Hutchinson, "Unanimity and Desegregation: Decision-making and the Supreme Court, 1948–1958," *Georgetown Law Journal* 68 (1979): 31–32.

8. Kluger, *Simple Justice*, pp. 650–51.

9. Memorandum for the Record, August 19, 1953, Eisenhower Diary, August-September 1953, Whitman File, DDEL.

10. Eisenhower, *Waging Peace*, p. 150; brief filed by the United States government as *amicus curiae* in *Brown v. Board of Education*, papers of Simon E. Sobeloff, Segregation, Manuscript Division, Library of Congress, Washington, D.C.; Alfred H. Kelly, "The School Desegregation Case," in John A. Garraty, ed., *Quarrels That Have Shaped the Constitution*, (New York: Harper and Row, 1964), p. 265; Ambrose, *Eisenhower: The President*, p. 124.

11. Eisenhower Diary, July 20, 1953, Eisenhower Diary Series, 1953–1954 (2), Whitman File, DDEL; Eisenhower to Byrnes, August 14, 1953, Administration Series, Nixon, Richard (5), Whitman File, DDEL; Eisenhower to Byrnes, November 30, 1953, Official File (hereafter cited as OF), 142–A-4 (1); Mayer, "With Much Deliberation and Some Speed," pp. 49–50.

12. Leo Katcher, *Earl Warren: A Political Biography* (New York: McGraw-Hill, 1967), pp. 302–305; John D. Weaver, *Warren: The Man, the Court, the Era*

(Boston: Little, Brown, 1967), pp. 190–91; Earl Warren, *The Memoirs of Earl Warren* (Garden City, N.Y.: Doubleday, 1977), pp. 261, 269–71; Dwight D. Eisenhower, *The White House Years: Mandate for Change, 1953–1956* (Garden City, N.Y: Doubleday, 1963), pp. 226–28; Bernard Schwartz, *Super Chief: Earl Warren and His Supreme Court: A Judicial Biography* (New York: New York University Press, 1983), pp. 1–7; Diary of James C. Hagerty, June 16, 1954, Papers of James C. Hagerty, DDEL; Edgar Eisenhower to Dwight Eisenhower, September 11, 1953; Dwight Eisenhower to Edgar Eisenhower, September 14, 1953; Edgar Eisenhower to Dwight Eisenhower, September 16, 1953, Dwight Eisenhower to Edgar Eisenhower, September 22, 1953, all in Name Series, Eisenhower, Edgar, 1953 (1), Whitman File, DDEL; Milton Eisenhower to Dwight Eisenhower, September 15, 1953, Name Series, Eisenhower, Milton, 1953 (1), Whitman File, DDEL; COH Interview with Herbert Brownell, p. 128.

13. For the Rankin quote, see Berman, *It Is So Ordered*, p. 96. Transcript of telephone conversation, Brownell to Eisenhower, January 25, 1954, Eisenhower Diary Series, Phone Calls, January-May 1954, Whitman File, DDEL.

14. *Brown et al. v. Board of Education of Topeka et al.*, 347 US 483 (1954); *Bolling et al. v. Sharpe et al.*, 347 US 497 (1954).

15. Eisenhower, *Waging Peace*, p. 150; Arthur Larson, *Eisenhower: The President Nobody Knew* (New York: Scribner, 1968), p. 124; Emmet John Hughes, *The Ordeal of Power: A Political Memoir of the Eisenhower Years* (New York: Athenaeum, 1963), p. 201; Sherman Adams, *Firsthand Report: The Story of the Eisenhower Administration* (New York: Harper, 1961), pp. 331–32.

16. Eisenhower, *Waging Peace*, p. 151; Eisenhower, *Mandate for Change*, p. 230; William Bragg Ewald, *Eisenhower the President* (Englewood Cliffs, N.J.: Prentice-Hall, 1981), p. 205. Eisenhower also expressed his support for such a plan in a conversation with Ann Whitman, his personal secretary, Whitman Diary, August 14, 1956, Whitman Diary Series, August 1956, (1), Whitman File, DDEL. Maxwell Rabb, Eisenhower's advisor on minority issues, believes that Eisenhower "had his doubts" about *Brown* and forced desegregation but that once the Court settled the issue the president was "dead set" on enforcement. Interview with Maxwell Rabb by Fred Greenstein. The author is indebted to Professor Greenstein for permitting him to listen to the tape of the interview. Rabb expressed the same views in a conversation with the author in Gettysburg, Pennsylvania, on October 12, 1990.

17. Hagerty Diary, May 18, 1954, Hagerty Papers, DDEL.

18. Ibid.; Eisenhower, *Waging Peace*, p. 150; Richardson, *The Presidency of Dwight D. Eisenhower*, p. 110; *Public Papers of the Presidents of the United States: Dwight D. Eisenhower, 1958* (Washington, D.C.: U.S. Government Printing Office, 1959), p. 123.

19. *Public Papers, 1954*, pp. 491–92.

20. Anthony Lewis, *Portrait of a Decade: The Second American Revolution* (New York: Random House, 1964), p. 12; Charles C. Alexander, *Holding the*

Line: The Eisenhower Era, 1952–1961 (Bloomington: Indiana University Press, 1975), p. 119; J. W. Peltason, *Fifty-Eight Lonely Men: Southern Federal Judges and School Desegregation* (New York: Harcourt, Brace and World, 1961), p. 47.

21. Hobart M. Corning to D.C. Board of Education, May 25, 1954; Samuel Spencer to Eisenhower, May 26, 1954; Spencer to Eisenhower, June 5, 1954, all in OF 71–U, DDEL; Spencer to Eisenhower, September 20, 1954; OF 142–A, DDEL; Eisenhower, *Waging Peace*, p. 150; Robert J. Donovan, *Eisenhower: The Inside Story* (New York: Harper, 1956), p. 162; Adams, *Firsthand Report*, p. 334; Washington *Post*, June 18, 1954, September 17, 22, 23, 1954; Pittsburgh *Courier*, May 29, 1954; Robert Frederick Burk, *The Eisenhower Administration and Black Civil Rights* (Knoxville: University of Kentucky Press, 1984), pp. 54-61; Martha Derthick, *City Politics in Washington, D.C.* (Cambridge: Massachusetts Institute of Technology Press, 1962), pp. 214, 220–21, 223.

22. Draft of the Brief for the United States on further argument of the questions of relief (see especially pp. 6, 8), Papers of Simon E. Sobeloff, Manuscript Division, Library of Congress, Washington D.C.; Mayer, "With Much Deliberation and Some Speed," pp. 65–69.

23. Draft of Brief for the U.S. Government, pp. 28–29; Mayer, "With Much Deliberation and Some Speed," pp. 64–67.

24. Brownell to Whitman, September 20, 1957, Administration Series, Brownell, 1957 (1), Whitman File, DDEL; Brownell COH, pp. 230–231.

25. Mayer, "Eisenhower's Conditional Crusade," pp. 209–11.

26. Mayer, "With Much Deliberation and Some Speed," p. 45; Michael S. Mayer, "The Eisenhower Administration and the Desegregation of Washington, D.C.," *Journal of Policy History* 3 (No. 1, 1991): 24.

27. Richardson, *The Presidency of Dwight D. Eisenhower*, p. 111; New York *Times*, March 12, 1955; *Public Papers, 1954*, pp. 491–92; *Public Papers, 1958*, pp. 626, 647; *Public Papers, 1959*, p. 123; Lewis, *Portrait of a Decade*, p. 12; Peltason, *Fifty-Eight Lonely Men*, p. 47.

28. Whitman Diary, March 21, 1956, Whitman Diary Series, March 1956 (1), Whitman File, DDEL; Eisenhower to Graham, March 22, 1956, Eisenhower Diary Series, March 1956, Misc. (1), Whitman File, DDEL; Eisenhower, *Waging Peace*, pp. 151–52.

29. Eisenhower to Graham, March 30, 1956, Eisenhower Diary Series, March 1956, Misc. (1), Whitman File, DDEL. Ann Whitman recorded in her diary that the president was "slightly disturbed because Billy Graham has shown his first letter to some individuals." Whitman Diary, March 30, 1956, Whitman Diary Series, March 1956 (1), Whitman File, DDEL. Eisenhower was prompted to write to Graham after receiving a letter from C. C. Warren, president of the Southern Baptist Convention, in which Warren said that he had spoken to Graham about race relations and that he (Warren) supported Eisenhower's position. Eisenhower responded by restating his devotion to the twin principles of "moderation and progress." C. C. Warren to Eisenhower, March 28, 1956, OF 142, DDEL, Whit-

man Diary, March 30, 1956, Whitman Diary Series, 1956 (1), Whitman File, DDEL.

30. *Public Papers, 1956*, p. 737; *Public Papers, 1958*, pp. 626, 647. On September 5, 1956, he told reporters that it made "no difference whether I endorse it [the *Brown* decision]. The Constitution is as the Supreme Court interprets it; and I must conform to that and do my very best to see that it is carried out." *Public Papers, 1956*, p. 737. In 1958, responding to a question by Anthony Lewis, Eisenhower restated his commitment to enforce the Constitution as stated by the Supreme Court and said that "discussion of separate cases, where I might agree or might disagree, seems to me to be completely unwise." *Public Papers, 1958*, p. 626.

31. Eisenhower to Warren, June 21, 1957, Eisenhower Diary Series, June 1957 Misc. (1), Whitman File, DDEL; Neal, *The Eisenhowers: Reluctant Dynasty*, p. 384. Eisenhower had explained his position in an earlier letter to the chief justice:

> On several occasions, in press conferences and elsewhere, I have expressed my devotion to the twin principles of "moderation and progress" in the delicate but explosive problem of race relations. I take this stand as a matter of principle and conviction so that every bit of progress made may be real and lasting, because it will have the support of the vast majority of the individuals affected. (Eisenhower to Warren, March 30, 1956, OF 142, DDEL.)

32. Eisenhower to Hazlett, July 22, 1957, Name Series, Hazlett, Swede, January 1956–December 1958 (3), Whitman File, DDEL. Eisenhower told Ann Whitman that the troubles brought about by the Supreme Court's decision constituted the most important domestic problem facing the government. Whitman asked what alternative course the Court could have adopted. The president responded that the justices could have demanded the elimination of segregation first in graduate schools, then in colleges, next in high schools, and so on. He believed that such a system would provide a means for overcoming "the passionate and inbred attitudes" that had developed over generations. Whitman Diary, August 14, 1956, Whitman Diary Series, August 1956 (1), Whitman File, DDEL. On March 23, 1956, Eisenhower also told Ovetta Culp Hobby, the secretary of the Department of Health, Education, and Welfare, that graduate schools should desegregate immediately. Whitman Diary, March 21, 1956, Whitman Diary Series, March 1986 (1), Whitman File, DDEL.

33. Notes on Pre-Press Conference Briefing, November 14, 1956, Whitman Diary Series, November 1956 (1), Whitman File, DDEL.

34. Shanley to Hagerty, n.d., Presidential Press Conference, March 27, 1957, Hagerty Papers, DDEL; Pre-Press Conference Briefing, March 27, 1957, Press Conference Series, Whitman File, DDEL.

35. Hagerty Diary, December 14, 1955, Hagerty Papers, DDEL.

36. Ralph Cake, COH; Brownell, COH, pp. 26–28; Ambrose, *Eisenhower: The President*, p. 129.

37. Eisenhower Diary, February 5, 1957, Eisenhower Diary Series, February 1957, Diary, Whitman File, DDEL; Eisenhower to William P. Rogers, September

17, 1958, Eisenhower Diary Series, Staff Notes, September 1958, Whitman File DDEL.

38. Michael S. Mayer, "Eisenhower and the Southern Federal Judiciary: The Sobeloff Nomination," in Shirley Anne Warshaw, ed., *Re-examining the Eisenhower Presidency* (Westport, Conn.: Greenwood, 1993), pp. 57–75.

39. Mayer, "Eisenhower's Conditional Crusade," pp. 223–24, 495–501. In evaluating the civil rights records of federal judges, most historians give high marks to the judges Eisenhower appointed to the Fourth and Fifth Circuit Courts of Appeal. See Harold W. Chase, *Federal Judges: The Appointing Process* (Minneapolis: University of Minnesota Press, 1972); "Judicial Performance on the Fifth Circuit," *Yale Law Journal* 73 (1963): 90; Peltason, *Fifty-Eight Lonely Men*; Jack Bass, *Unlikely Heroes* (New York: Simon and Schuster, 1981); and Frank T. Read and Lucy S. McGough, *Let Them Be Judged: The Judicial Integration of the Deep South* (Metuchen, N.J.: Scarecrow Press, 1978). The one notable exception is Mary Curzan, "A Case Study in the Selection of Federal Judges: The Fifth Circuit, 1953–1963," Ph.D. Diss., Yale University, 1968. Curzan challenges the idea that Eisenhower's appointments had better records on civil rights than Kennedy's appointments. Aside from the fact that the dissertation is available only in summary form and without full scholarly apparatus, her quantative approach is grossly inadequate. She weighs all cases the same, despite the obvious fact that some decisions are clearly more important than others. She also fails to separate district judges from appellate judges, and Eisenhower's appointments to the appellate bench (which, of course, had greater impact on the development of law) established particularly impressive records in civil rights cases. Moreover, Curzan's peculiar method of categorizing cases leads her to the startling conclusion that Frank Johnson, one of Eisenhower's district court judges and a genuine civil rights hero of the bench, was a segregationist. For evidence to the contrary, see Tinsley E. Yarborough, *Judge Frank Johnson and Human Rights in Alabama* (University: University of Alabama Press, 1981) and Robert F. Kennedy, Jr., *Judge Frank M. Johnson, Jr.* (New York: Putnam, 1978). For an account of the Fourth Circuit's decisions, see Sanford Jay Rosen, "Judge Sobeloff's Public School Race Decisions," *Maryland Law Review* 34 (1974): 498.

5

The Railroad Question Revisited: *Chicago, Milwaukee & St. Paul Railway v. Minnesota* and Constitutional Limits on State Regulations

James W. Ely, Jr.

Few issues more vexed Americans during the Gilded Age than the regulation of railroads. America's first big business, the railroads, wielded enormous economic power and by the end of the nineteenth century represented 10 percent of national wealth.[1] Farmers and other local shippers often viewed railroads as an exploitative monopoly and blamed them for excessive and discriminatory charges. They repeatedly clamored for regulation of the freight and passenger rates fixed by railroad companies. Agricultural interests in the Great Plains states were particularly active in seeking regulatory legislation. Railroad investors and managers, on the other hand, opposed regulatory laws and defended their autonomy to determine rates. They feared that governmental control of rates would benefit shippers and farmers at the expense of the railroads by imposing unreasonably low charges. Moreover, they asserted that regulation of rates would likely impair capital investment and thus stifle railroad growth and economic development.

Sectional division was evident in the legislative response to the growth of railroads. The eastern states created advisory commissions that could make reports and recommend reforms but had no enforcement power or authority to set transportation rates.[2] Skeptical about the efficacy of competition, western farmers demanded more stringent governmental control of railroad operations. Their growing resentment was heightened when western railroads passed under the control of eastern investors. During the 1870s the Granger movement spearheaded the drive for the initial wave of more radical state railroad regulations. Many midwestern and southern state legislatures enacted so-called Granger laws to control the prices charged by railroads and related utilities, such as grain elevators and warehouses. They also established powerful commissions to supervise railroad operations and enforce regulatory laws.[3]

In *Munn v. Illinois* (1877) the Supreme Court adopted a deferential attitude toward legislative authority to regulate economic activity. Sustaining an Illinois law that set the rate for storing grain in Chicago elevators, Chief Justice Morrison R. Waite ruled that "when private property is devoted to a public use, it is subject to public regulation." Whether this public interest doctrine applied to a particular enterprise was considered a matter for legislative judgment. Although recognizing that the owner of property "clothed with a public interest" was entitled to reasonable compensation, Chief Justice Waite further declared that the determination of such compensation was a legislative, not a judicial, task. The only protection for property owners against legislative abuse was to resort to the political process. Justice Stephen J. Field vigorously dissented, warning that under the *Munn* rationale "all property and all business in the State are held at the mercy of a majority of its legislature." Asserting that grain storage was a private business, he maintained that the due process clause afforded substantive protection to owners in the use and income of their property.[4] In practice state legislatures rarely applied the *Munn* doctrine to control the charges of any major business other than railroads.

During the 1880s judicial attitudes began to change. The Supreme Court receded from the deferential approach of *Munn* and adopted a more skeptical posture toward state regulation of property and business. In *Stone v. Farmers' Loan and Trust Co.* (1886), for instance, the justices upheld a Mississippi statute that empowered a commission to regulate railroad rates, but they cautioned that such authority was not unlimited. Chief Justice Waite observed that "the State cannot require a railroad corporation to carry persons or property without reward; neither can it do that which in law amounts to a taking of private property for public use without just compensation, or without due process of law."[5] Simultaneously the Supreme Court began to formulate a substantive interpretation of the due process clause to safeguard fundamental property rights.[6] This laid the basis for the doctrine of economic due process. The Court took another step away from *Munn* in *Wabash, St. Louis & Pacific Railway v. Illinois* (1886), holding that state regulation of interstate railroad rates unconstitutionally invaded federal power under the commerce clause.[7]

State courts likewise moved toward increased scrutiny of rate regulations. In *Spring Valley Water Works v. San Francisco* (1890) the Supreme Court of California invalidated a municipal ordinance fixing the rates charged by a privately owned water company. Cautioning that "[r]egulation, as provided for in the constitution, does not mean confiscation, or a taking without just compensation," the court asserted judicial authority to review the reasonableness of regulated prices.[8]

Historians agree that *Chicago, Milwaukee & St. Paul Railway Company v. Minnesota* (1890) was a milestone in the evolution of economic due process.[9] The decision inaugurated an era of increased judicial scrutiny of railroad and utility rate fixing and enhanced the protection of property rights; yet this landmark ruling has received relatively little attention from scholars. In view of the renewed interest in economic rights,[10] it seems pertinent to examine the litigation that culminated in *Chicago, Milwaukee,*[11] and to assess the decision's place in constitutional history.

BACKGROUND OF THE CONTROVERSY

In the early 1870s Minnesota experimented briefly with railroad rate regulation but abandoned the system in 1875 amid fears that governmental controls discouraged capital investment. A decade later many western and southern states joined in a new wave of stringent railroad rate regulations.[12] Minnesota was no exception. Republicans dominated Minnesota politics throughout the Gilded Age, a fact that underscores the public consensus favoring regulation of railroad activities. In March of 1887 the Minnesota legislature enacted a comprehensive scheme to regulate the intrastate activities of common carriers.[13] Building upon 1885 legislation that established the Railroad and Warehouse Commission, lawmakers provided that all charges for railroad services "shall be equal and reasonable."

Carriers were required to file a schedule of rates with the commission, and the commissioners were empowered to review the reasonableness of charges. The commission could order a railroad to change any fare deemed unequal or unreasonable and could impose a recommended rate. If a railroad failed to comply with such a rate directive the commission could seek a writ of mandamus. The statute also prohibited unreasonable preferences to any shipper and outlawed rebates and the practice of charging more for transportation for a short distance than a long distance. Because at that time neither the Interstate Commerce Commission nor most state railroad commissions had the authority to fix charges, the Minnesota law went beyond the prevailing regulatory models.

Organized under Wisconsin law in 1874, the Chicago, Milwaukee & St. Paul Railway Company was the successor to numerous small railroads. By the late 1880s the company owned nearly 6,000 miles of completed track, more than 1,400 grain elevators, and numerous terminal facilities. The railroad's main line ran between Minneapolis and St. Paul and Chicago, and other lines extended into Iowa, Wisconsin, Nebraska, and the Dakotas. It was one of four major carriers that served the northern prairie states.[14] Operating in states strongly influenced by Granger agitation, the Chicago, Milwaukee & St. Paul Railway had long battled state fare regulations.

In June of 1887 local boards of trade complained to the Minnesota Railroad Commission that the rates charged by the Chicago, Milwaukee & St. Paul Railway for transporting milk from various points within Minnesota to St. Paul and Minneapolis were unreasonably high. The company countered that the milk rates were in fact low. After a hearing at which both the petitioners and the railroad were represented, the commission concluded that the charges for transporting milk from Owatonna and Faribault were unreasonable. The commission directed that a rate of 2 1/2 cents per gallon in ten gallon cans be substituted for the existing rate of 3 cents per gallon. When the railroad refused to carry out the recommended reduction in milk rates, the attorney general, acting for the commission, procured a writ of mandamus from the Supreme Court of Minnesota directing the railroad to obey the order or show cause why it should not be followed. The railroad challenged the constitutionality of the rate-fixing provision on three grounds: (1) that the legislative authority to set transportation rates could not be delegated to the commission; (2) that under its franchise the railroad was entitled to determine transportation rates; and (3) that the commission's order constituted "a pro tanto taking" of the railroad's property in violation of the due process clause of the Fourteenth Amendment. Counsel further argued that the statute did not provide for a hearing and that the reasonableness of rates was a judicial question.[15]

The Supreme Court of Minnesota unanimously upheld the commission's order in April of 1888. After disposing of jurisdictional issues, the court considered the nature of the commission's rate-setting powers. The court construed the statute to mean that rates recommended by the commission "should be not simply advisory, nor merely *prima facie* equal and reasonable, but final and conclusive as to what are lawful or equal and reasonable charges."[16] Consequently the court refused to review the reasonableness of rates set by the commission.

Turning to the constitutional objections, the court relied heavily on the *Munn* decision and stressed the need for legislative control of railroads. The court described railroads as "practically the public highway system of the country" and declared that "no modern civilized community could long endure that their public highway system should be in the uncontrolled, exclusive use of private owners. The only alternative was either governmental regulation or governmental ownership of the roads."[17] The court charged that railroads, "and even the eminent counsel for the respondent in this case," were reluctant to accept the legitimacy of legislative supervision. Nor were the judges sympathetic to the argument that the power to fix rates might be abused and in effect deprive the railroads of property without due process. Lastly the court rejected the contention that the act improperly delegated legislative power to the commission. The judges reasoned that the legislature had not conferred upon the commission power to make law but simply granted administrative discretion to carry out the regulatory purpose of the statute.

The Chicago, Milwaukee & St. Paul Railway petitioned for a reargument in part on the grounds that the court did not consider later rulings that limited the *Munn* decision. When this petition was denied the company obtained a writ of error to bring the case before the Supreme Court of the United States. Meanwhile, the order of the commission went into effect.

SUPREME COURT DECISION

The appeal was argued before the Supreme Court on 13 and 14 January 1890. The railroad was represented by its able general counsel John W. Cary. He was experienced in rate litigation before the Supreme Court, having previously appeared in several companion cases to *Munn*.[18] A proponent of laissez-faire constitutionalism, Cary labored to secure judicial protection for the rights of railroads against state regulation. He espoused the principle that property ownership encompassed the right to set the price for its use. Cary argued that in order to vindicate property rights the reasonableness of rates was a matter for judicial inquiry. In short, Cary was prominent among a group of attorneys who were instrumental in promoting laissez-faire values and advocating a strong role for the courts in limiting state regulatory power.[19]

This laissez-faire philosophy guided Cary's arguments on behalf of the Chicago, Milwaukee & St. Paul Railway. He first contended that the rate-setting provisions violated the corporate charter in which the Minnesota Territory granted the railroad directors power to fix "the rate of tolls."

Hence the Minnesota legislation unconstitutionally impaired the obligation of contract by interfering with the company's rights under its charter.[20]

More significantly, Cary then endeavored to restrict application of the *Munn* decision. Insisting that the right to receive value for use of one's property was an essential attribute of ownership, he charged that the Minnesota court judgment "violates the natural right which belongs to every one to fix the price of his services and of its property or its use." Cary conceded that *Munn* limited a railroad to charging reasonable rates, but he denied a legislature's "right to arbitrarily and finally fix or determine such charges by positive statutes." He agreed that a legislature, under its police power, could regulate railroad operations to protect the safety of persons. Cary maintained, however, that this power did not give lawmakers the right to fix transportation charges. In an impassioned plea, Cary argued that rate regulation was unprecedented and "destructive of the rights of property and more to be feared than the insane ravings of the advocates of socialism and the commune." He charged that railroads could be compelled to provide services at an unremunerative rate, effectively confiscating their property. Thus Cary sought to reopen the broad question of legislative control of railroad fares. Contending that "[i]nvestments in railroad property are entitled to the same protection and consideration as other investments," he maintained that a reasonable rate must include "a fair return on the value of the investment or plant of the railroad."[21] Cary finished by arguing that the Chicago, Milwaukee & St. Paul Railway was engaged in interstate commerce and was not subject to the Minnesota law since passage of the Interstate Commerce Act in 1887.

Attorney General Moses E. Clapp defended the Minnesota rate-fixing act. As might be expected, he emphasized that the "unbroken line" of Supreme Court decisions commencing with *Munn* sustained the power of legislatures to establish rates for common carriers. He recognized that a state could not use regulatory authority to confiscate property but disputed the company's allegations that the milk rate was unreasonable. Clapp concluded by emphasizing first that state legislatures could decide what constituted a reasonable transportation rate and second that "the question of the reasonableness of the rate is a question for legislative determination, and when so determined, ceases to be the subject of judicial inquiry."[22]

On 24 March the Supreme Court in a brief opinion ruled that the rate statute, as construed by the Minnesota Supreme Court, deprived the railroad of property without due process of law.[23] Chief Justice Melville W. Fuller assigned the task of preparing the Court's opinion to Justice Samuel Blatchford. One historian has suggested that this assignment was prompted by Fuller's belief that Blatchford, a compromiser, could fashion an opinion that would hold together a precarious majority for a significant constitutional innovation.[24]

The Court first rejected the railroad's contract clause argument. Justice Blatchford held that the general language in the company's charter conferring the power to collect tolls did not constitute a contract freeing the company from any legislative control. This finding simply affirmed the settled doctrine that corporate charters were strictly construed.

The justices, however, found a procedural infirmity in the Minnesota rate law. Although the precise nature of the defect was unclear from the opinion, the Court was obviously disturbed about the conclusive nature of the administrative process that determined rates. Justice Blatchford pointed out that the statute did not provide for notice or a hearing before the commission or for judicial review of rates.[25] This was a somewhat curious point because, in fact, the company received both notice and a hearing. Justice Blatchford was seemingly concerned that the commission might find rates to be unreasonable sua sponte without any hearing.

The Court then moved beyond this procedural objection and asserted the authority to review the fairness of rates imposed by state law. "The question of the reasonableness of a rate of charge for transportation by a railroad company, . . . " Justice Blatchford observed, "is eminently a question for judicial investigation, requiring due process of law for its determination." He added:

> If the company is deprived of the power of charging reasonable rates for the use of its property, and such deprivation takes place in the absence of an investigation by judicial machinery, it is deprived of the lawful use of its property, and thus, in substance and effect, of the property itself, without due process of law and in violation of the Constitution of the United States.[26]

Blatchford's opinion was somewhat nebulous with respect to the scope of judicial review and did not expressly direct a judicial investigation of rates. But the ruling has generally been understood as establishing that the reasonableness of rates was subject to independent court review. Thus, the *Chicago, Milwaukee* decision contradicted a fundamental principle of *Munn* that rate setting was solely a legislative function. Moreover, it signaled the Court's acceptance of the due process clause as a substantive restriction on state legislative authority.

Concurring "with some hesitation," Justice Samuel F. Miller provided a more compelling explanation of the constitutional need for judicial review of rates. He recognized that the states could exercise their authority to regulate transportation charges either by direct legislation or through a commission. But states could not apply either procedure to set a rate "which is so unreasonable as to practically destroy the value of property of persons engaged in the carrying business." It followed that there was "an ultimate remedy" for aggrieved parties in the federal courts, which had a duty to inquire into the reasonableness of rates.[27]

Speaking for the three dissenters, Justice Joseph D. Bradley complained that the decision effectively overruled *Munn* and made the courts "the final arbiter" in rate regulations. He maintained that the determination of reasonable charges was a legislative question, involving considerations of policy as well as remuneration. In his view, judicial relief was only available for fraudulent or arbitrary deprivation of property. He insisted that in this case there was no infringement of property rights "but merely a regulation as to the enjoyment of property."[28]

RESPONSE

Whatever the ambiguities of Justice Blatchford's opinion, contemporary observers were quick to perceive a sea change in the Supreme Court's attitude toward rate regulations. "It is everywhere regarded as a most important decision," the *New York Times* reported. Railroad officials were elated. An assistant general manager of the Chicago, Milwaukee & St. Paul Railway commented that "the decision is a ray of hope to railroads oppressed by confiscatory legislation." One railroad agent declared that the carriers "could now feel secure of their property." Another railroad manager added, "I think the action of the highest court in the country will call a halt on this [Granger] class of legislation." The *Winona Daily Republican* quipped: "Whenever you see a railroad man smile nowadays you may look to the Supreme Court decision for its inspiration."[29]

Reaction in Minnesota was generally hostile. As might be expected, the Populists were particularly bitter. The Executive Committee of the State Farmers' Alliance unanimously adopted a series of resolutions prepared by Ignatius Donnelly severely censuring the Supreme Court. The resolutions declared that the *Chicago, Milwaukee* decision signified "the subjection of the people and the states to the unlimited control of the railroad corporations of this country." Attacking the concept of judicial review, the resolutions appealed "from this second Dred Scott decision to the people of the nation; and we ask them to consider whether any other race would submit to have their liberties thus wheedled away from them, on technicalities, by a squad of lawyers, sitting as a supreme authority high above Congress, president and people." Lastly, the Executive Committee charged that in "our anxiety to protect the rights of property we have created a machinery which threatens to destroy the rights of man."[30]

Newspaper comment, while more restrained, was also largely negative. The *Minneapolis Tribune* maintained that "the Western Legislatures and commissions have in general been sufficiently lenient and reasonable in their demands for reduction of rates." Although agreeing that the railroads should have a right to be heard, the *Tribune* worried that the decision might allow the carriers "through tediously and cunningly delayed litigation to break down" the power of regulation. Similarly, the *Red Wing Argus* observed that the *Chicago, Milwaukee* ruling caused people to wonder "whether the legislators or the courts made the laws of the land." The *Winona Daily Republican* charged that the Supreme Court "takes the purely technical view of the question involved, and . . . looks first of all and chiefly to the interests of the roads."[31]

In contrast, the *St. Paul Dispatch* hailed the *Chicago, Milwaukee* ruling and decried the 1887 act as "the product of an unreasoning warfare upon the railroads." The *Dispatch* called upon the legislature to adopt "the more moderate policy" of the eastern states in supervising railroad operations. Likewise the *St. Paul Pioneer Press* commended the Supreme Court for fixing "an insuperable barrier against the tide of destructive agrarian and confiscatory legislation and judicial decisions which have threatened the unlimited spoliation of all railroad properties."[32]

Leading legal journals tended to look with favor on the *Chicago, Milwaukee* decision. An article in the *Albany Law Journal* defended judicial review of rates "because if otherwise, it would be giving to the Legislature the authority of deciding the constitutionality of their own acts." One commentator in the *American Law Register* construed the decision as strengthening the rights of property owners against the imposition of rates that resulted in a deprivation of property. His interpretation implied that "all lovers of individual liberty, of law and justice can properly rejoice. It is a most momentous decision." Such enthusiasm was not universal. A note in the *American Law Review* sharply criticized the ruling and emphasized the interpretative problems posed by Justice Blatchford's ambiguous opinion. The author was uncertain whether the decision turned on a narrow procedural point or established broad judicial supervision of legislative rate determinations. If it implied the latter, the decision was "an overturning of the fundamental principles upon which all our American governments are founded."[33]

As the debate over *Chicago, Milwaukee* raged, Minnesota officials worked to salvage the regulatory scheme. The railroad commissioners recommended that the law be amended to include judicial review of rates. This approach was adopted by Governor William R. Merriam, a Republican, in his 1891 message to the legislature. Avoiding any criticism of the decision, he pointed out that when the regulatory statute was enacted it was generally understood that the legislature was the final arbiter as to what rates were reasonable. Governor Merriam explained that the Supreme Court

> has determined that action upon such matters is not final either in a commission or in the legislature itself. The power of the legislature to make reasonable rates for common carriers is not denied, but whether a given rate so made is reasonable is a judicial question, and must be settled as other matters of law and fact are determined, through the medium of the courts.[34]

Accordingly, he urged a statutory amendment to provide a method of judicial review.

Heeding the governor's request, lawmakers amended the 1887 rate statute. Much of the earlier measure was unchanged, but the amendment stipulated that rates set by the commission should be treated only as prima facie evidence of reasonableness. The amendment also provided for notice and a full administrative hearing before the commission. Finally, the amended statute expressly established the right of a railroad to appeal commission orders to the state district courts, which had jurisdiction to examine "the whole matter in controversy."[35] These changes brought the Minnesota rate law into conformity with the constitutional requirements of *Chicago, Milwaukee*.

ASSESSMENT

Although a major victory for the railroads, the outcome in *Chicago, Milwaukee* did not inaugurate an era of laissez-faire in the transportation industry. The fears of the Populists to the contrary, the Supreme Court continued to recognize the power of state legislatures to regulate railroad and storage rates. The federal judiciary only protected carriers against unreasonable charges, and the railroads had to demonstrate their unreasonableness.[36] Still, the *Chicago, Milwaukee* ruling materially restricted state regulatory authority, and lawsuits seeking to invalidate state-imposed rates multiplied rapidly in the next decade.

Despite the Supreme Court's retreat from the *Munn* doctrine, the decision was not an abrupt departure from existing constitutional norms. Starting in 1886 the Court had cautioned in several cases that states could not, consistent with due process, impose confiscatory rates on regulated industries.[37] The justices came to realize that unlimited power of regulation might be used to destroy the value of railroad property. Once the Supreme Court distinguished between rate regulation and confiscation, judicial supervision of rates followed logically. Judicial oversight simply provided a vehicle by which the justices could vindicate property rights against confiscatory legislation. If the states had unlimited power to fix charges, then constitutional protection against confiscation was illusory and regulated industries had only those rights to use property that lawmakers chose to recognize.

Why did the Supreme Court move away from the *Munn* doctrine of unfettered legislative power to control rates? Scholars have sometimes depicted *Chicago, Milwaukee* as part of a pervasive pro-business bias on the part of the justices.[38] This rationale is problematic. After all, during the Gilded Age the Supreme Court upheld many state-imposed regulations on business activity. A more compelling explanation, offered by Mary Cornelia Porter, is that the Court "was less interested in rate regulation per se than in assuring that regulated utilities would continue to attract the investment capital necessary for expanding and improving services to the public."[39] The importance of investment security was clear to contemporary observers. One railroad official revealingly stressed that the *Chicago, Milwaukee* decision "will afford a very great safeguard to railroad investments." He explained that the ruling "comes at a very opportune time, for the reason that the frequent attacks in the West on railroad property by legislators and commissioners were beginning to sap the confidence of investors all over the world in the safety of investments in American railroad properties."[40] This was a crucial point because Europeans invested heavily in many western railroads, including the Chicago, Milwaukee & St. Paul Railway.[41]

Railroads long had feared that legislatively imposed rates would favor local interests and discourage long-term economic growth. An official of the Chicago, Milwaukee & St. Paul Railway explained that

> the railways have back of their adjustment of the rates the selfish interest of their own prosperity, which depends upon the prosperity of all the business on their lines, while a political commission if given this power would have nothing at stake but the political success of the influences which placed it in office.[42]

The growing intensity of rate regulation in the Gilded Age made the Court more aware of the deficiencies in the *Munn* doctrine and increasingly sympathetic to the position of the railroads. In short, experience served to undermine judicial confidence in legislative and administrative rate determinations. Gradually the justices saw *Munn* in a new light. While no doubt concerned about unwarranted intrusion on the property rights of the railroads, the Court also sought to fashion uniform national standards that guarded investment capital against impairment by inadequate compensation. Further, it became apparent that out-of-state investors had no meaningful opportunity to "resort to the polls" for protection, as suggested in *Munn*. Judicial redress was the only realistic remedy against unduly low rates.

Perhaps the most significant consequence of *Chicago, Milwaukee*, however, was its far-reaching impact on the constitutional protection of property rights generally. By mandating the judicial review of imposed rates, the Supreme Court implicitly recognized that protection of property went beyond title and possession. Ownership encompassed the right to use property for economic value. This step markedly enlarged the range of property interests secured by the Constitution.[43] In addition, the decision opened the door for the doctrine of economic due process. Once the Supreme Court accepted the notion that the due process clause mandated reasonableness in the context of rate controls, it was an easy step to apply this substantive restraint to economic regulations generally.[44] Soon the Court was assessing regulations against a reasonableness standard and striking down measures it deemed unduly restrictive of property rights.[45]

The *Chicago, Milwaukee* ruling also had implications for the reach of the takings clause of the Fifth Amendment. The Court's expressed worry that rate regulations might deprive the railroad of its property without due process portended extension of the takings clause to the states. In fact the dissenters had complained that the majority opinion proceeded on the assumption that the Constitution prohibited the states from taking private property without compensation. The dissenting justices pointed out that "there is no such clause" and that the states could make their own regulations governing the payment of just compensation.[46] Yet the majority opinion's tendency to assimilate due process protection of property with deprivation of lawful usage foreshadowed a prompt judicial move to enlarge the guarantees available to property owners under the Fifth Amendment. In *Chicago, Burlington and Quincy Railroad Company v. Chicago* (1897) the justices unanimously held that the just compensation requirement constituted an essential element of due process as guaranteed by the Fourteenth

Amendment.[47] Hence, the just compensation principle became in effect the first provision of the Bill of Rights to be applied against the states.

The *Chicago, Milwaukee* ruling had a particular impact on the states of the Great Plains. Responding to farmer dissatisfaction with the management of railroads, lawmakers in the prairie jurisdictions enacted a host of laws designed to restrict passenger and freight rates and the charges of grain elevators. Consequently, enlarged judicial review of railroad charges would be felt keenly in the Great Plains. Indeed much of the rate litigation after 1890 originated from the prairie states.[48]

An unresolved question raised by *Chicago, Milwaukee*, of course, was how to distinguish a valid rate regulation from a confiscatory rate. The Supreme Court wrestled with this complex issue in a number of cases during the 1890s. Eventually, in *Smyth v. Ames* (1898), the Court unanimously held that a utility was constitutionally entitled to a "fair return" upon the "fair value" of its property.[49] An attempt to protect regulated industries against confiscatory rates, the fair value rule proved difficult to administer. In the ensuing decades federal courts became heavily involved in supervising the rate-making process.[50] At the same time, Congress enacted a series of statutes that imposed more stringent federal controls over railroad charges.[51]

CONCLUSION

Chicago, Milwaukee was a landmark case in which the Supreme Court moved toward more vigorous protection of property rights. Historians, influenced by the Progressive school, have often criticized the decision for giving federal courts the power to review the substantive reasonableness of state-imposed rates. Charles Fairman, for example, championed the *Munn* doctrine and Justice Bradley's dissenting opinion in *Chicago, Milwaukee*. "Who can doubt," he asked, "that the Court would have done much better had it never quit the path Justice Bradley first pointed out?"[52]

One can, however, doubt. Farmers and shippers who called for railroad rate regulations often pursued an opportunistic course that benefitted their economic interests. In a sense, then, the movement for railroad regulation sought a redistribution of wealth from the carriers to consumers. State agencies frequently yielded to parochial pressures in setting rates, thereby threatening the long-term economic health of the railroads; yet only by generating a profit could the railroads attract capital investment and continue to provide services. It followed that state rate regulations had a direct impact on national transportation policy. Herbert Hovenkamp has pointed out that "the potential for abuse, particularly for free riding by the states, was substantial, and federal control by either legislation or judicial intervention was clearly necessary." The federal courts, he added, were "the only competent federal arm to control state free riding and protect the integrity of the national railroad system."[53]

Although criticized for granting the federal courts authority to review the substance of rates, the justices of the Supreme Court followed sound instincts. Judicial review placed some restraint on the marked tendency of legislators and regulators to set railroad rates at unrealistically low levels, often at the behest of special interest groups. Despite the rule of *Smyth v. Ames*, governmental regulation of railroad charges steadily increased in the early decades of the twentieth century. Indeed, several scholars have identified heavy-handed rate regulation and cumbersome rate-setting procedures as major factors in the decline of American railroads.[54] Arguably the Court should have reviewed rates more aggressively to protect the security of capital investment and thus encourage maintenance of an adequate rail service.

Lastly *Chicago, Milwaukee* has demonstrated impressive staying power. Following the constitutional revolution of 1937, the Supreme Court abandoned economic due process, retreated from meaningful review of rate fixing, and relegated property rights to a secondary position.[55] But the Supreme Court has never overruled *Chicago, Milwaukee* and continues to require judicial review of administrative decisions touching on constitutional rights. Recently the Supreme Court has even shown renewed interest in constitutional restraints on utility rate making. In *Duquesne Light Co. v. Barasch* (1989) Chief Justice William Rehnquist, speaking for the Court, reiterated the longstanding rule: "The guiding principle has been that the Constitution protects utilities from being limited to a charge for their property serving the public which is so 'unjust' as to be confiscatory."[56] Rehnquist stressed that a rate must afford adequate compensation. Thus after one hundred years *Chicago, Milwaukee* continues to influence constitutional law and provide at least symbolic protection to property rights.

NOTES

I wish to express my appreciation to Herman Belz, Jon A. Bruce, Barry Friedman, and Nicholas Zeppos for their helpful comments on earlier drafts of this article. I also wish to acknowledge the valuable research assistance of Susan E. Raines.

1. Harold U. Faulkner, *Politics, Reform, and Expansion: 1890–1900* (New York: Harper, 1959), p. 75.

2. Kermit L. Hall, *The Magic Mirror: Law in American History* (New York: Oxford University Press, 1989), pp. 197–98; Lawrence M. Friedman, *A History of American Law*, 2d ed. (New York: Simon & Schuster, 1985), pp. 446–47.

3. Hall, *The Magic Mirror*, p. 198; Solon J. Buck, *The Granger Movement: A Study of Agricultural Organizations and Its Political, Economic, and Social Manifestations, 1870–1880* (Lincoln: University of Nebraska Press, 1913), pp. 123–205. One authority has noted that the "real heart of the anti-railroad, or 'Granger movement' as it is usually known, came in the state regulatory laws of the Middle West." Robert Edgar Riegel, *The Story of the Western Railroads, from 1852 through the Reign of the Giants* (Lincoln: University of Nebraska Press, 1926), p. 143.

4. *Munn v. Illinois*, 94 US 113, 130, 140 (1877).

5. *Stone v. Farmers' Loan & Trust Co.*, 116 US 307, 331 (1886). See also *Dow v. Beidelman*, 125 US 680, 689 (1888) and *Chicago and North Western Railway v. Dey*, 35 Fd 866 (Cir. Ct., Iowa, 1888). As early as 1884 Chief Justice Waite observed in a rate challenge: "What may be done if the municipal authorities . . . fix upon a price which is manifestly unreasonable, need not now be considered." *Spring Valley Water Works v. Schottler*, 110 US 347, 354 (1884).

6. James W. Ely, Jr., *The Guardian of Every Other Right: Constitutional History of Property Rights* (New York: Oxford University Press, 1991), pp. 82–100.

7. *Wabash, St. Louis & Pacific Railway v. Illinois*, 118 US 557 (1886).

8. See Katha G. Hartley, "*Spring Valley Water Works v. San Francisco*: Defining Economic Rights in San Francisco," *Western Legal History* 3 (Summer/Fall, 1990): 287–308; *Spring Valley Water Works v. San Francisco*, 82 Cal 286, 307 (1890).

9. John E. Semonche, *Charting the Future: The Supreme Court Responds to a Changing Society, 1890–1920* (Westport, CT: Greenwood Press, 1978), pp. 16–20; David P. Currie, "The Constitution in the Supreme Court: The Protection of Economic Interests, 1889–1910," *University of Chicago Law Review* 52 (Spring, 1985): 324, 371–75. In a leading law casebook, *Cases and Material and Constitutional Law*, 11th ed. (Mineola, NY: Foundation Press, 1985), Gerald Gunther described *Chicago, Milwaukee* as "a significant turning point" but relegated consideration of the case to a footnote, p. 447, n. 8.

10. See Bernard H. Siegan, *Economic Liberties and the Constitution* (Chicago: University of Chicago Press, 1980); Richard A. Epstein, *Takings: Private Property and the Power of Eminent Domain* (Cambridge, MA: Harvard University Press, 1985); Note, "Resurrecting Economic Rights: The Doctrine of Economic Due Process Reconsidered," *Harvard Law Review* 103 (April, 1990): 1362–83.

11. The different names of the Chicago, Milwaukee & St. Paul Railway over time may give rise to some confusion. The carrier was commonly known as the St.

Paul Road in the late nineteenth century. Following a reorganization in 1928, the railroad was popularly called the Milwaukee Road. This article employs the title *Chicago, Milwaukee* to describe the Supreme Court case under investigation.

12. George H. Miller, *Railroads and the Granger Laws* (Madison: University of Wisconsin Press, 1971), pp. 117–39; Charles Fairman, "The So-called Granger Cases, Lord Hale, and Justice Bradley," *Stanford Law Review* 5 (July, 1953): 587, 600–606; Buck, *Granger Movement*, pp. 196–97. For agrarian distrust of the railroads in Minnesota, see William E. Lass, *Minnesota Bicentennial History* (New York: Norton, 1977), pp. 164–74.

13. Minn., "An Act to Regulate Common Carriers, and Creating the Railroad and Warehouse Commission of the State of Minnesota," ch. 10 (1887).

14. August Derleth, *The Milwaukee Road: Its First Hundred Years* (New York: Creative Age Press, 1948), p. 137 and Appendix A; John F. Stover, *The Life and Decline of the American Railroad* (New York: Oxford University Press, 1970), pp. 56–57; F. Stewart Mitchell, "The Chicago, Milwaukee & St. Paul Railway and James J. Hill in Dakota Territory, 1879–1885," *North Dakota History* 47 (Winter, 1980): 11. See also John W. Cary, *The Organization and History of the Chicago, Milwaukee & St. Paul Railway Company* (Milwaukee, WI: Press of Cramer, Aikens and Cramer, 1892, repr. 1981).

15. For the factual background and arguments of counsel, see "Third Biennial Report of the Railroad and Warehouse Commission as to Amendments and Revisions of the Railroad Laws of Minnesota, 1890," *Minnesota Executive Documents for Fiscal Year Ending July 31, 1890*, 3 (1891): 400–42.

16. *State ex. rel. Railroad and Warehouse Commission v. Chicago, Milwaukee & St. Paul Railway Company*, 38 Minn 281, 295, 37 NW at 784 (1888).

17. Ibid., pp. 296–97, 37 NW at 785–86.

18. *Peik v. Chicago and North-Western Railway Company*, 94 153 US 164 (1877); *Chicago, Milwaukee & St. Paul Railroad Company v. Ackley*, 94 US 179 (1877); *Stone v. Wisconsin*, 94 US 181 (1877).

19. Benjamin R. Twiss, *Lawyers and the Constitution: How Laissez Faire Came to the Supreme Court* (Westport, CT: Greenwood Press, 1942, repr. 1974), pp. 70–77, 161–62; John W. Cary, "Limitations of the Legislative Power in Respect to Personal Rights and Private Property," *American Bar Association Report* 15 (1892): 245–86.

20. Brief for Plaintiff in Error, John W. Cary, Counsel, pp. 14–17.

21. Ibid., pp. 18, 28, 23, 72.

22. Brief for Defendant in error, Moses E. Clapp and H. W. Childs, Attorneys, p. 14.

23. *Chicago, Milwaukee & St. Paul Railway Company v. Minnesota*, 134 US 418, 456–57 (1890). A companion case, decided the same day, arose out of a similar factual situation. The Minnesota Commission ordered a small local railroad to reduce its rate for handling and switching cars in Minneapolis. The company protested that the imposed rate was too low and provided an inadequate

compensation, thus depriving the company of its property. Reversing the rate decree, the Supreme Court held that the "views and considerations applicable to" *Chicago, Milwaukee* "apply with even greater force to the present case." *Minneapolis Eastern Railway Company v. Minnesota*, 134 US 467, 482 (1890).

24. Semonche, *Charting the Future*, p. 19.

25. *Chicago, Milwaukee & St. Paul Railway Company in Minnesota*, 134 US 418, 457 (1890).

26. Ibid., p. 458.

27. Ibid., pp. 459–60. For an analysis of Justice Miller's views, see Charles Fairman, *Mr. Justice Miller and the Supreme Court, 1862–1890* (Cambridge, MA: Harvard University Press, 1939), pp. 202–5.

28. *Chicago, Milwaukee & St. Paul Railway Company in Minnesota*, 134 US 418, 466 (1890).

29. New York *Times*, March 26, 1890; quoted in *Winona (MN) Daily Republican*, April 1, 1890; quoted in *St. Paul (MN) Dispatch*, March 25, 1890; quoted in *Daily Republican*, April 1, 1890.

30. Minnesota State Farmers' Alliance, Constitution and By-Laws, Declaration of Principles, Resolutions . . . (1890), p. 20.

31. Minneapolis *Tribune*, March 26, 1890; *Red Wing (MN) Argus*, April 3, 1890; *Winona (MN) Daily Republican*, March 26, 1890.

32. *St. Paul (MN) Dispatch*, March 25, 1890; *St. Paul (MN) Pioneer Press*, March 25, 1890.

33. Henry L. Harrington, "Legislative Interference With the Freedom of Railroad Corporation Contracts," *Albany Law Journal* 51 (April 20, 1895): 246, 249; William Draper Lewis, "Can Prices Be Regulated by Law?" *American Law Register* 41 (January, 1893): 9, 16; Note, "Regulation of Railway Fares: Rule that the Reasonableness of such Regulation is a Judicial Question: The so-called Minnesota Granger Case," *American Law Review* 24 (May-June, 1890): 516, 522.

34. Biennial Message of Governor William R. Merriam, 14 January 1891, *Minnesota Executive Documents for Fiscal Year Ending July 31, 1890*, 1 (1891): 37.

35. Minn., "An Act to Amend Chapter Ten [1887] Entitled 'An Act to Regulate Common Carriers, and Creating the Railroad and Warehouse Commission of the State of Minnesota'," ch. 106 (1891).

36. See Alton D. Adams, "Reasonable Rates," in William Z. Ripley, ed., *Railway Problems*, rev. ed. (Boston: Ginn and Company, 1913), pp. 604–9 (discussing *Chicago, Milwaukee* and judicial review of the reasonableness of rates). See also Cary, "Limitations on the Legislative Power," pp. 284–86, for an assessment of the *Chicago, Milwaukee* decision.

37. *Stone v. Farmers' Loan and Trust Co.*, 116 US 307 (1886); *Dow v. Beidelman*, 125 US 680 (1888); *Chicago and North Western Railway v. Dey*, 35 Fd 866 (Cir. Ct., Iowa, 1888).

38. Arnold M. Paul, *Conservative Crisis and the Rule of Law: Attitudes of the Bar and Bench, 1887–1895* (Ithaca, NY: Cornell University Press, 1960), pp. 39–45. Melvin I. Urofsky has sharply criticized the role of the federal courts in scrutinizing rates and contended that judicial review "gave railroads one more weapon to fight regulation." Melvin I. Urofsky, *A March of Liberty: A Constitutional History of the United States* (New York:, Knopf, 1988), p. 526.

39. Mary Cornelia Porter, "That Commerce Shall Be Free: A New Look at the Old Laissez-Faire Court," *The Supreme Court Review* (1976): 135, 143.

40. Quoted in *St. Paul Dispatch*, March 25, 1890.

41. Albro Martin, *Enterprise Denied: Origins of the Decline of American Railroads, 1897–1917* (New York: Columbia University Press, 1971), pp. 133–34; Dorothy R. Adler, *British Investment in American Railways, 1834–1890* (Charlottesville: University Press of Virginia, 1970), pp. 185, 191n, 199, 210. Riegel, *The Story of the Western Railroads*, p. 139.

42. Burton Hanson, *Unfair Railway Agitation* (Chicago: n.p., 1905), p. 51. Another railroad executive urged competition rather than regulation to hold down rates and pointed out that "the great majority of the railways in the United States are the creation of private enterprise and capital, and that the people in their collective capacity have not been taxed in order to construct them." Sidney Dillon, "The West and the Railroads," *North American Review* 152 (April, 1891): 451.

43. Stephen A. Siegel, "Understanding the *Lochner* Era: Lessons From the Controversy Over Railroad and Utility Rate Regulation," *Virginia Law Review* 70 (March, 1984): 187, 210–15.

44. Alfred H. Kelly, Winfred A. Harbison, and Herman Belz, *The American Constitution: Its Origins and Development* 6th ed. (New York: Norton, 1983), pp. 406–408; Urofsky, *March of Liberty*, p. 500.

45. See Paul Kens, *Judicial Power and Reform Politics: The Anatomy of Lochner v. New York* (Lawrence: University Press of Kansas, 1990).

46. *Chicago, Milwaukee & St. Paul Railway Company v. Minnesota*, 134 US 418, 465 (1890).

47. *Chicago, Burlington and Quincy Railroad Company v. Chicago*, 166 US 226 (1897).

48. E.g., *Brass v. North Dakota*, 153 US 391 (1894); *Smyth v. Ames*, 169 US 466 (1898).

49. *Smyth v. Ames*, 169 US 466 (1898).

50. Siegel, "Understanding the *Lochner* Era," pp. 215–59.

51. Stover, *Life and Decline*, pp. 113–16.

52. Fairman, "So-called Granger Cases," p. 670.

53. Herbert Hovenkamp, *Enterprise and American Law, 1836–1937* (Cambridge, MA: Harvard University Press, 1991), p. 160.

54. Stover, *Life and Decline*, p. 247; Martin, *Enterprise Denied*, pp. 354–60. Similarly, Forrest McDonald has maintained that railroads "became the first industry to be destroyed, in the long run, by an excess of regulation." Forrest

McDonald, *A Constitutional History of the United States* (Melbourne, FL: Krieger, 1982), p. 184.

55. Ely, *Guardian of Every Other Right*, pp. 119–34.

56. *Duquesne Light Co. v. Barasch*, 488 US 299, 307 (1989). See Richard J. Pierce, Jr., "Public Utility Regulatory Takings: Should the Judiciary Attempt to Police the Political Institutions?" *Georgetown Law Journal* 77 (August, 1989): 2031–2077.

Part III

Legalists of the Great Plains

The philosophy of law and the practice of law by legalists related to the Great Plains have been significant. There is clearly a jurisprudential aspect of Great Plains law that interests the rest of the nation, and an attorney-at-law practicing in the Great Plains can expect any number of unique legal consequences, whether it be in water law, Indian law, or conflicts of law.

The Great Plains has provided the setting for several of the greatest twentieth-century philosophers of law. One is Roscoe Pound, who, born in a small central Nebraska town, attended the University of Nebraska. Pound pursued a multitude of scholarly interests, including botany, philosophy, and law, and he is perhaps best known for his theories of sociological jurisprudence and his interest in the social impact of law.[1] A second major legal philosopher associated with the Great Plains and the subject of the first essay in this section is Karl Llewellyn. With E. Adamson Hoebel, a cultural anthropologist from the University of Minnesota,[2] Llewellyn was the co-author of *The Cheyenne Way*. Llewellyn also helped found the school of legal realism. In 1930 Llewellyn, then a law professor at Columbia University, together with Jerome Frank, a attorney in New York City, published a series of essays that distinguished between legal concepts and phrases and their application to the real world. Legal rules were, according to Llewellyn, rigid abstractions, and there was a fundamental distance between rules of a case and its practical settlement. To Llewellyn, behavior was the most basic legal constant that required empirical study. The decision, thus, was the law. In some ways Llewellyn was extending the ideas of Pound, but Pound eventually rejected Llewellyn as an extremist.[3]

The debate over sociological jurisprudence versus legal realism is in some ways akin to trying to understand the tremendous environmental diversity and climatic extremism of the Great Plains. Survival required adjustments, and reality called for innovation, not the adherence to older rules of survival. That justice must be tempered to society was true for the Cheyennes Llewellyn studied.

Practicing law just prior to Karl Llewellyn's writings on legal realism was William Jennings Bryan. Bryan moved to Lincoln, Nebraska, shortly after he completed law school in Chicago and spent a brief period practicing in Jacksonville, Illinois. He immediately formed a partnership with a law school friend, Adolphus Talbot. Their practice was typical of partnerships of the late nineteenth century in that it was composed primarily of civil debt cases with a smattering of criminal clients. It ranged from justice of the peace and county court appearances to arguing before the state supreme court. Although Bryan's time practicing law, 1887 to 1891, was brief, he became an important attorney in Nebraska, and it no doubt enhanced his future political career.[4]

Llewellyn and Bryan—it has the sound of a very important law firm that, of course, never was to be. In the essays that follow each legalist is discussed in terms of his relationship to law and the Great Plains. First, Scott Landers takes apart Karl Llewellyn's theories from his own words as found in his important work on the legal history of the Cheyenne. Landers discovers that Llewellyn sometimes did not practice what he preached and that Llewellyn ignores the obvious behavioral evidence in his collection and analysis of Cheyenne case law. Culture, to Llewellyn, was not a crucial factor in the settlement of disputes, and for Landers this seems hard to rationalize with the tenets of legal realism.

The practice of law on the Great Plains is examined in the second essay. C. Robert Haywood's *Cowtown Lawyers: Dodge City and Its Attorneys, 1876–1886*[5] constitutes the sum total of analysis of law as practiced by lawyers on the Great Plains. William Jennings Bryan is not thought to have been a successful lawyer primarily because his biographers have not examined the legal records of his law practice and because the Scopes trial at the very end of his career left a legacy of questioned competence even though he won a favorable verdict. Andrew Koszewski explains how Bryan was a successful appellate attorney who made a name before the Nebraska Supreme Court.

These two essays mark the beginning of research on the historical contributions of the legalists of the Great Plains. There remains much more to be uncovered and analyzed in order to understand the full history of the lawyers and legal thinkers of the region.

NOTES

1. See Roscoe Pound, "Mechanical Jurisprudence," *Columbia Law Review* 8 (July, 1908): 605–23; Edward A. Purcell, "American Jurisprudence between the Wars: Legal Realism and the Crisis of Democratic Theory," *American Historical Review* 75 (April, 1969): 424–46.

2. Karl Llewellyn and E. Adamson Hoebel, *The Cheyenne Way: Conflict and Case Law in Primitive Jurisprudence* (Norman: University of Oklahoma Press, 1941).

3. Karl Llewellyn, "A Realistic Jurisprudence—The Next Step," *Columbia Law Review* 30 (April, 1930): 431–65; Purcell, "American Jurisprudence."

4. Andrew B. Koszewski, "William Jennings Bryan's Law Practice in Nebraska, 1887–1891," M.A. Thesis, University of Nebraska-Lincoln, 1991.

5. C. Robert Haywood, *Cowtown Lawyers: Dodge City and Its Attorneys, 1876–1886* (Norman: University of Oklahoma Press, 1988).

6

Practicing What You Preach Against? Karl Llewellyn, Legal Realism, and *The Cheyenne Way*

Scott Landers

In *The Cheyenne Way*, Karl Llewellyn and Edward Hoebel asserted that they applied a legal realist methodology in their study of nineteenth-century Cheyenne legal culture.[1] Their methodology involves a behavioral approach to studying law, focusing on "cases of trouble and how they were handled."[2] This methodology is contrasted with what they call an "ideological" approach that emphasizes " 'rules' which are felt as proper for channeling and controlling behavior."[3] Although Llewellyn may not have denounced so much as urged supplementing an ideological or doctrinal approach,[4] he significantly underestimated its importance and the extent to which such an approach underpins his own methods.

In this chapter I assess the extent to which Karl Llewellyn and Edward Hoebel failed to adopt a genuinely non-ideological approach in investigating nineteenth-century Cheyenne dispute-settlement processes and offer a partial analysis of why any similar attempt would be likely to fail. If this assessment and analysis are correct, they support the following conclusions:

1. It is misleading for Llewellyn to characterize his method as an *alternative* to an ideological approach;
2. The sort of empirical study of law advocated by Llewellyn has value for jurisprudence only to the extent that it can fit within the general theoretical framework of rule-centered jurisprudence; and

3. Llewellyn failed to recognize the truth of these last two claims largely because he operated with a misconception of what a rule is.

Because critiques of rule-centered jurisprudence originally developed by legal realists continue to receive elaboration and support, a fuller understanding of Llewellyn's work is of continuing significance.[5]

THE COMPLEXITIES OF LEGAL REALISM

In his 1930 paper, "A Realistic Jurisprudence—the Next Step," Karl Llewellyn argued that "traditional precept-thinking," thinking that rules and principles form the core of law, should be displaced by a more empirical, scientific, behaviorist approach. Llewellyn thought of precepts as "merely verbal formulae" and suggested that Roscoe Pound, despite being "gifted with insight," was a "man partially caught in the traditional precept-thinking of an age that is passing."[6] Llewellyn's main conclusion was that "the clearer visualization of the problems involved [in thinking about law] moves toward ever decreasing emphasis on words, and ever increasing emphasis on observable behavior."[7]

Llewellyn joined other realists in the assault on conceptual jurisprudence originally directed against Christopher Columbus Langdell and Joseph Beale.[8] A focus on concepts was said to be doubly misguided. The first mistake was in thinking that common law evolution could be understood and predicted as the rational or "deductive" unfolding, at a social level, of fundamental concepts and related doctrines.[9] The second mistake consisted in thinking that at the level of individual cases judges should make decisions primarily by carefully analyzing relevant legal concepts and rules. The lines of attack merge when the case in question turns out to be a landmark decision.

An empirical approach, in contrast to a doctrinal one, was supposed to enable law to become less fiction-ridden and more effective as a flexible scientific instrument for directing social change. According to one observer, what united the realists "was their 'negation,' as Llewellyn put it, of the traditional focus on rules, principles, and doctrines."[10] The prescription that judges should not arrive at decisions in the manner dictated by traditional theory (i.e., by subsuming facts under concepts and rules) was usually grounded in various realist arguments that doing so was quite impossible.

The distrust of legal concepts and rules first took root in the practical realm, as a distrust of overly optimistic and uncritical *judicial* reliance on traditional legal categories and specific rules. Such distrust soon forced its way into the theoretical realm, as a distrust of categories and rules *per se*. What began as realism of a homey kind was pushed to what the realists regarded as its unavoidable conclusions, resulting in a highly *theoretical* form of realism. Because the realists were not complete anti-foundationalists, their theoretical pronouncements seemed to demand a philosophical basis at higher levels of abstraction, a basis many found in philosophical pragmatism.[11]

Given its philosophical roots in pragmatism, it is appropriate to judge realism by its practical consequences in two areas: judicial decision making by judges who subscribed to realism, and the application of realism's theories and approved methodologies to the sociological investigation of legal processes. Llewellyn's collaboration with anthropologist E. Adamson Hoebel on *The Cheyenne Way* thus presents a fair opportunity to judge the fruits of realism outside the arena of Anglo-American judicial decision making.

THE CHEYENNE WAY: AN EMPIRICAL APPROACH

In *The Cheyenne Way*, Karl Llewellyn and E. Adamson Hoebel took as their principal methodological dictum the requirement of focusing on "the trouble case." Their "theory of investigation" is "a case method procedure of going in the first instance after cases of trouble and how they were handled."[12] This method along with a focus on observable behavior while taking no interest in motivations for that behavior, in contrast to an ideological approach that focuses on beliefs, motivations, and doctrinal materials, is claimed as a hallmark of realistic jurisprudence.[13]

While *The Cheyenne Way* does bear the stamp of realistic jurisprudence, insofar as it focuses on dispute-settlement techniques and relies on data about how specific disputes were settled (rather than on data about nineteenth-century Cheyenne doctrine concerning how disputes, of general types, were supposed to be settled), *The Cheyenne Way* is hardly the paradigm of empirical scientific study one might legitimately expect from Karl Llewellyn. In "A Realistic Jurisprudence—the Next Step," Llewellyn suggested that the method of realistic jurisprudence is

> of a piece with the work of the modern ethnographer. He substitutes painstaking objective description of practice for local *report* of what the practice is, or for (what

is worse) a report either of local practice or of local ideology pleasantly distorted by the observer's own home-grown conventions. . . . What has been done in the last decades that has some touch of novelty is for theorizers to go beyond theorizing, to move . . . into the gathering and interpretation of facts about legal behavior.[14]

The "data" for *The Cheyenne Way* study, however, consist precisely of "local report of what the practice is," or rather, memories of what the practice had been when Cheyenne law formed an autonomously functioning system. Llewellyn and Hoebel were thus in no position to provide any "painstaking objective description of practice."

The dispute settlements Llewellyn's informants describe occurred between 1820 and 1880, while data were gathered in 1935 and 1936.[15] A total of fifty-three case histories are presented in *The Cheyenne Way*, ranging in length from a few sentences to five pages, though Llewellyn and Hoebel indicate that additional case histories were also used (cases too brief for significant discussion or cases borrowed from the works of George Bird Grinnell), and they add that "the reader should also realize the large background body of data and paralleling cases which are not included in the text . . . for obvious reasons of economy of space and reader's patience."[16] This last comment is surprising coming from someone suspicious of the possibility of defending a case interpretation on *a priori* grounds and without sufficient discussion of parallel cases.

Llewellyn worked with what little he had. Given the limited materials available, failure to conduct a more rigorous empirical study was unavoidable and, perhaps even on realist grounds, is therefore pardonable. It is nonetheless fairly astonishing to find little acknowledgement by Llewellyn of just how little, by realist standards, he did have to use.[17] Even putting aside these qualms, however, it is far from clear whether his case-law methodology differs more than superficially from a "doctrinal approach."

THE CHEYENNE WAY: RULES

Some difficulties in Llewellyn's approach stem from his view that *how* a trouble case is settled is more significant than either the nature of the trouble itself or how trouble cases evolve prior to being brought for settlement. The rules many theorists focus on, "primary rules" in H.L.A. Hart's terminology,[18] are to be recognized as "real" rather than empty verbal formulae—mere "paper rules," Llewellyn called them, where written down—only to the extent that they are "confirmed" by the facts of dispute settlement.

Llewellyn often seemed hostile to conceiving of law in terms of rules. What he frequently maintained in theory seems to place him within the camp of rule skeptics; yet Llewellyn waffled sufficiently to question whether that label applies. In *The Cheyenne Way* Llewellyn implicitly relied on the view that primary rules are extremely important for understanding law. Occasionally he explicitly recognized their significance for understanding an individual case.[19] Thus, he was not a rule skeptic of the sort who denies that rules play any significant role in law. Nonetheless, Llewellyn held that for an empirical legal science the only *significant* kind of "rules" is non-normative regularities disclosed by observing "practices." Llewellyn suggested that such behavioral regularities should not be thought of as rules at all:

> Real "rules" and rights [must be distinguished] from paper rules and rights. The former are conceived in terms of behavior; they are but other names . . . for the remedies, the actions of the courts. They are descriptive, not prescriptive. . . . "Real rules," then, if I had my way with words, would *by legal scientists* be called the practices of the courts, and not "rules" at all.[20]

The "rules" that are "real" rather than "paper" concern the behavior of dispute settlers rather than disputants. "Real rules," which legal scientists should not even call "rules," are general descriptions of court practices, according to Llewellyn. He apparently did not realize that court practices can scarcely be understood in abstraction from the practices of disputants. "Real rules" are to be distinguished from "paper rules" such as statutes (which Llewellyn sometimes denigrated as mere empty words).

Llewellyn most often thought of real rules as statements that describe rather than govern judicial practice. Sometimes a rule is said to be the practice rather than the generalization about it. Paper rules are of no intrinsic interest to the legal scientist; they are of interest only if their existence clearly influences judicial practice. How such influence might be demonstrated is not obvious, since according to Llewellyn a judge's merely *claiming* to apply a certain rule is not by itself very significant.[21]

Llewellyn seems interested in how courts behave but not in why they behave a particular way. The above conception of what a real rule is, then, as applied to the nineteenth-century Cheyenne, requires focusing on dispute-settlement techniques while seeking regularities in the behavior of dispute settlers. The overt behavior of the disputants themselves, and especially their motivations, is officially (in Llewellyn's view) irrelevant to what real rules the Cheyenne may have had.[22]

Llewellyn asserted that he found few rules in his Cheyenne data. He was convinced that despite the relative scarcity of rules, the Cheyenne were remarkably adept at settling disputes.[23] He concluded that perhaps the regularities found in Anglo-American judicial practice, like those found in Cheyenne dispute-settlement practice, can be attributed to forces at work other than those stressed by traditional jurisprudence.[24] This conclusion is the most significant claim, from the standpoint of social theory and general jurisprudence, made in *The Cheyenne Way*. Before such a conclusion can be embraced, however, the contention that the regularities in Cheyenne dispute-settlement practice cannot be largely attributed to the function of rules must be assessed.

Paradoxically, if Cheyenne dispute-settlement data exhibit regularities, then by Llewellyn's rough definition the Cheyenne *did* have what Llewellyn called "real rules." Llewellyn was correct that such "rules" do not in fact account for whatever regularities emerge from the data, but this is not an empirically verifiable contention because "real rules" merely *describe* the very regularities for which an account is sought. If real rules are merely descriptions of regularities in practices, then the existence of such rules cannot *explain* why those regularities exist.

Given how Llewellyn usually seems to have thought of rules, then, the claim that Cheyenne dispute-settlement data exhibit regularities but reveal few real rules is implicitly self-contradictory. It thus seems clear that Llewellyn must have another sort of rule in mind, other than real rules or paper rules, when he asserts that rules do not to a large extent account for regularities.

Llewellyn does not take much of an interest in whether the Cheyenne had this other sort of rule or how such rules might relate to Cheyenne dispute-settlement regularities because as a legal scientist he in effect barred himself from investigating prescriptive rules addressed to disputants. Nevertheless, Cheyenne disputes can be analyzed for regularities produced by precisely such rules.

THE CHEYENNE WAY: DISPUTES

If the role of prescriptive rules regulating disputant behavior is ignored, it becomes quite difficult to even understand the behavior of Cheyenne dispute settlers, let alone to join Llewellyn in seeing such behavior as exemplary of a "beautiful juristic technique." If Llewellyn's informants' accounts are stripped of all normative discourse, all that remains are accounts of disputes consisting of conflicting wills, rather than competing normative claims, and it is difficult to see what could count as *juristic* resolutions.[25]

Llewellyn does not, however, seem at all puzzled by the behavior of the Cheyenne dispute settlers. This is because in *The Cheyenne Way* he implicitly relied on assumptions about the existence and importance of genuinely prescriptive rules, in particular, of primary rules constituting basic social obligations and prohibitions. In coming to see his Cheyenne data as exhibiting juristic technique exquisitely adapted to nineteenth-century Cheyenne social conditions, Llewellyn either presupposed answers to questions about nineteenth-century Cheyenne legal concepts and primary norms, or instead relied on understandings of Anglo-American legal concepts and norms and then imposed these on his Cheyenne data. Llewellyn's reader is likely to follow suit, but such questions and answers are best assessed with care if they truly are significant to understanding dispute-settlement behavior.

It was inevitable that Llewellyn would implicitly rely on assumptions about nineteenth-century Cheyenne primary rules in order to understand Cheyenne disputes; it is this inevitability that undermines Llewellyn's moderate brand of rule skepticism.[26] In case analysis, the reported settlement of a dispute implicitly functions to confirm or disconfirm hypotheses about primary norms involved in generating the dispute itself. That we cannot always accept at face value the norms appealed to by disputants and dispute settlers as conclusive indications of a group's norms is a point well taken. Yet in theorizing, Llewellyn sometimes went beyond this humble point. At times he regarded methodology as determining theory. What the actual settlement of a dispute provides, however, is additional data for *evaluating* hypotheses and theories.

For Llewellyn and Hoebel, trouble cases themselves, disputes as they might be understood even prior to being brought for settlement provided hypotheses about what norms the nineteenth-century Cheyenne had; actual settlements provide only confirmation or disconfirmation of these hypotheses. It is thus only relative to disputes that settlements provide any indication of nineteenth-century Cheyenne law. In short, the investigation of settlements is methodologically necessary to knowing what the law is, but such an investigation cannot provide the conceptual framework within which to understand the nature of disputes.

Focusing on how trouble cases are handled is required to discover what norms, if any, and what processes come into play in settling disputes. A typical trouble case cannot be understood, however, without reference to primary normative rules because trouble cases are typically, even if not necessarily, normatively structured social interactions prior to being brought for settlement. A trouble case usually is normatively structured precisely because trouble typically arises as a result of the transgression of a primary norm. Thus, the settlement of a trouble case, to be conceived as having social significance, must be understood in relation to any primary norms that may structure the settled dispute. Naturally, settlement must also be understood in relation to *secondary* norms, if any exist, that regulate dispute settlement itself. Llewellyn's data show only that this latter type of norm was rare among the Cheyenne; his method precluded significant investigation of primary norms.

Ignoring the role that primary norms play during the generation of disputes requires that Cheyenne disputes be conceived, mistakenly, on a "hydraulic" or mechanistic model. According to such a model, disputes erupt merely from conflicting desires and opposing brute forces. Yet Cheyenne disputes, even as described by Llewellyn, did involve more than merely conflicting wills. Disputants conceived of their conflicts in terms of Cheyenne forms of property, marriage, government, and so on, institutions that may only be conceived of in terms of primary norms. Cheyenne disputes were about who owns a horse, or over wife stealing, or whether to compel a member of the Council of Forty-Four to attend a ceremony, or what to do about a murder. Trouble cases, then, were not thought of by Cheyenne disputants as involving merely conflicting desires, nor is there any reason to suppose they were so conceived or treated by Cheyenne dispute settlers.

A "hydraulic" conception of disputes, moreover, precludes distinguishing in theory, or understanding the distinction commonly made in practice, between legal and other disputes, or between justiciable and nonjusticiable ones. If not even a rough distinction of this sort can be made, then all disputes are legal ones, even though not all are legally settled. This is a consequence Llewellyn would not be comfortable with, for he argued that there are indeed "jobs" and techniques that are distinctively legal.[27] Llewellyn's attempt to identify "the legal" by identifying what is characteristic of legal settlements needs to be supplemented with an attempt to identify what is characteristic of legal disputes. Legal disputes typically involve not merely conflicting wills, but also some type of normative structure.

THE CHEYENNE WAY: SETTLEMENTS

Admittedly, dispute settlement of some sort can occur without anything like a judicial decision-making process that requires judging the relative merits of pleadings. In the Cheyenne cases Llewellyn discussed, however, there is evidence of something very much like pre-settlement rule-based "decision making." Those primary rules that do emerge in *The Cheyenne Way* seem to have been well entrenched, widely accepted, relatively few, simple, and easily applied to relatively uncomplicated fact situations. Thus, there was rarely actual doubt about what to count as wrongful conduct. Typically, the only problem that needed an explicit decision was what to do about wrongful conduct. This hardly implies that rule-based judgments were not being made by participants in Cheyenne dispute settlements. What Llewellyn's data reveal is the infrequency only of second-order disputes, disputes about what the primary norms were; the Cheyenne thus had a dearth not of rules generally, but of secondary rules for resolving second-order disputes. If Llewellyn's picture of the nineteenth-century Cheyenne is accurate, it seems to depict precisely the sort of legal culture H.L.A. Hart describes as a "regime of primary rules."[28] Far from showing the insignificance of rules in Cheyenne dispute settlements, then, Llewellyn's data may reasonably be attributed to the efficacy of primary rules among the Cheyenne. This is best seen by recognizing that both dispute evolution and dispute settlement can occur in stages.

At one stage there may simply be conflicting desires (which if acted upon may result in open aggression). These desires may, at a next stage, be articulated as claims, even if these claims merely report the desires—"I want those horses"; "So do I."[29] This move represents a significant advance over the first stage, for it indicates the preliminary stage of an attempt to avoid physical aggression between the parties.

At a third stage the conflict may transcend to a level at which the claims become normative rather than psychological. Even the simple "those horses are *mine*" differs significantly from "I want those horses." This stage shades into a stage at which explicit justification of claims may take place —"I got to those horses first," "I saw their tracks first, and the tracks come before the horses." Note that "the tracks come before the horses" cannot adequately be thought of merely as a descriptive claim, surface grammar notwithstanding. Its function and significance in the evolution of dispute and settlement are clear: it has the force of an appeal to a putative rule entitling the track finder to the horses. The track-finder rule need not explicitly be formulated or referred to as such, for where rules are widely accepted they may shape dispute evolution and settlement even while going unmentioned. What makes "I saw the tracks first" relevant and worth pointing out by one of the disputants is the existence of the rule as a social fact.[30]

The normative structure of a dispute is the product of processes that transform a conflict of wills into a dispute ripe for settlement. As Martin

Golding puts it in describing "jural-like dispute settling," the dispute that reaches the dispute settler is a "persuasive conflict" that is "an offshoot of an antecedent conflict."[31] Elsewhere, in discussing adjudication in particular, Golding comments: "The dispute that is settled by the third party is not the original conflict, with all its overtones and complexities, but rather the controversy that is presented by the parties for resolution. In order to achieve finality in the adjudicatory situation, the original conflict is superseded by the second-level dispute that is presented to the third party."[32] Golding further points out that in adjudication, settlement of the persuasive conflict may leave the original conflict largely intact or, in some contexts, may even exacerbate it.

Part of the juristic beauty Llewellyn found among Cheyenne dispute settlements seems to lie precisely in the Cheyenne ability to settle disputes without the need for legalistic transformation of conflicts beyond recognition by the original parties. The Cheyenne thereby seem to have achieved legal settlements that avoided merely placating disputants temporarily while risking future social disruption.

ANALYZING CHEYENNE HOMICIDE

The epistemological importance for law of understanding a culture's primary norms and the values reflected in them can be illustrated by considering the nineteenth-century Cheyenne law of homicide that Llewellyn depicted. On the positive side, Llewellyn showed that knowing formulations of primary norms, without knowing what remedies were available for their transgression, is not enough to fully understand the role of those norms within Cheyenne culture. Knowing that a Cheyenne's killing of a Cheyenne was prohibited is important, but understanding specifically how the Cheyenne responded to such behavior increases understanding not only of secondary (reactive) behavior but also of the primary behavior itself. On the critical side, Llewellyn ignored the extent to which investigation must be directed toward primary norms and their associated legal categories, and away from dispute settlements, to understand the nineteenth-century Cheyenne law of homicide.

Llewellyn explained that homicide was responded to by banishing the offender for a period of years and "renewing the sacred arrows," which was a purification ritual designed to ward off supernatural sanctions against the tribe.[33] The offender was expected to be reformed by banishment before readmission to the tribe. To many this will seem an extremely humane, generous, and enlightened way to deal with murder. For Llewellyn's reader it is yet another instance of the beauty, clarity, and fitness of Cheyenne juristic technique.[34] Before such a judgment can be rendered, however, it is important to consider differences among characterizing the offense first as a killing, then as a homicide, and last as a murder.

These are not discriminations to be found among the nineteenth-century Cheyenne as portrayed by Llewellyn. They are important to some ways of thinking about the value of human life and the norms some cultures have concerning the taking of human life. It is surprising to find such distinctions absent from the thinking of Llewellyn's Cheyenne, but it is far from clear what conclusions, if any, may be drawn from that absence. Obviously, the Cheyenne distinguished killing in general from homicide in particular, as indicated by differential treatments of killing a buffalo and a person. In informants' reports, sometimes the words "murder" and "murderer" are used, sometimes "kill" and "killer," but it is unclear whether this is a product of language translation problems and whether the Cheyenne distinguished murder from other forms of homicide. To regard all homicides as murder merely because tribal responses were similar, as Llewellyn does, seems risky. By doing so he may be conflating offenses distinguished in other ways by the Cheyenne but which called for similar sanctions. Llewellyn regarded cruelty to a daughter who then commits suicide as constituting murder among the Cheyenne, for example, but his evidence seems tenuous and could equally support alternative views of the sole case that is truly on point.[35]

Before concluding that the nineteenth-century Cheyenne were far advanced in treating and rehabilitating offenders, then, it is necessary to appreciate nineteenth-century Cheyenne attitudes concerning the inviolability of human life. It is important to understand the nature of the offense before the nature of the sanction can be understood. In addition to investigating "cases of trouble and how they were handled," therefore, an investigation of nineteenth-century Cheyenne fundamental legal categories and associated primary norms is needed. This latter line of inquiry is just the sort Llewellyn frequently criticized.

LLEWELLYN AND PRIMARY RULES

This essay has focused on the extent to which Llewellyn relied on understandings (and perhaps misunderstandings) of Cheyenne primary rules that he failed to mention. Admittedly, Llewellyn did not entirely avoid mentioning specific primary legal rules in *The Cheyenne Way*. His treatment of explicitly mentioned primary rules, however, presents one last stumbling block for Llewellyn's reader for here Llewellyn's failure to practice what he preached is most evident. What he preached is that any contention that a rule exists must be subject to empirical confirmation. The nature of such confirmation on Llewellyn's view is, however, far from clear.

Most often his model of confirmation seems akin to empirical confirmation and disconfirmation of hypotheses in natural science. Putting aside the fact that even within natural science the nature of confirmation and disconfirmation is far from unproblematic, such a model is nothing but problematic when applied to prescriptive rules rather than empirical regularities.[36] The judicial disposition of a single case, viewed in isolation, cannot be legitimately regarded as capable of falsifying the contention that there is a rule requiring a contrary result. Realists often treated prescriptive rules as if they are significantly similar to empirical universal generalizations corresponding to natural regularities, however, and it is because of this that they failed to formulate a theory of judicial mistake.[37]

Unlike empirical universal regularities, rules will fail to have their characteristic results if they are ignored or misapplied. They are not, however, thereby disconfirmed. Perhaps it was because prescriptive rules cannot be forced into the mold of laws of nature that many realists rejected a rule-centered view of law, but such a rejection seems to beg questions. If rules do not fit a particular empiricist model, it remains an open question whether it is rule-centered jurisprudence *or that model* that should be rejected.

Because *The Cheyenne Way* does not involve comparing behavioral data to any already given set of rule formulations, Llewellyn avoided the mistake of thinking that a putative rule's existence can be disconfirmed by appeal to a single case. In *The Cheyenne Way* Llewellyn was guilty, however, of the vice of taking the single case, or small numbers of cases, as confirming the existence of a rule. In discussing the only case of a Cheyenne abortion Llewellyn found, he concluded that the fetus was regarded as having recognizable "legal personality" and that the case was thus subsumable under the nineteenth-century Cheyenne law on homicide. This view is held despite the fact that his informant hardly conceptualized the case in such terms.[38] This and other cases reveal Llewellyn's infidelity to his own demand that rule-existence claims be confirmed by appealing to behavioral consequences.

This last case, among others, also forces us to question what significance legal concepts have for Llewellyn. Given Llewellyn's realist hostility to relying on traditional legal concepts in their native habitat, it is curious how often he relied on Anglo-American law to characterize nineteenth-century

Cheyenne law. His remark made in discussing a case near the end of *The Cheyenne Way*, that he and Hoebel "are not urging that the participants thought in the terms we use, or in remotely equivalent Cheyenne concepts,"[39] merely provokes inquiry into the formation, evaluation, and use of concepts for cross-cultural investigations.

Though harsh, it is fair to say that Llewellyn's distrust of "ideology"—of relying on concepts, doctrines, and rules, whether native or foreign to the culture being studied—apparently extended only to his own legal culture. Indeed, at times his treatment of Cheyenne law appears to be quite a bit more naive than realistic. As evidence of Cheyenne law he often accepts, apparently at face value, what must be regarded as mythologized and ideologically infused accounts of dispute settlements.

Legal myth and ideology, where widely accepted and transmitted across generations, are nonetheless more important aspects of a legal culture than is often supposed. What law's mere subjects believe is quite as important as what law's officials believe for lawyers no less than judges must wait for cases to be brought to them, and judges no less than juries are influenced by ideology.

CONCLUSION

A close analysis of *The Cheyenne Way* supports the conclusion that even a jurisprudence that focuses on dispute-settlement behavior inevitably must also investigate fundamental legal categories and primary norms. This latter line of inquiry cannot be postponed while drawing conclusions from data gained by an empirical study of dispute-settlement processes.

While Llewellyn did at times acknowledge the importance of primary norms in shaping Cheyenne socio-legal relations, he did not attempt to see their significance in a general way. Lewellyn frequently placed the word "rule" within quotation marks in the theoretical sections of *The Cheyenne Way*, typically dropping the quotation marks when constrained to mention a rule in the case study sections. This suggests that at the time *The Cheyenne Way* was written Llewellyn still held that legal practices, understood in factual rather than normative terms, constituted the proper subject matter of legal science,[40] a science intended to displace "the traditional precept-thinking of an age that is passing."

Nonetheless, *The Cheyenne Way* shows just how difficult the escape from traditional precept-thinking is when attempting to understand legal practices. As a whole perhaps Llewellyn's work, and legal realism generally, is best thought of as suggesting techniques for testing the fit between traditional legal theory and actual legal practice. Legal realism cannot supply a competing legal theoretic framework, however, nor undermine the general framework of rule-centered jurisprudence.

Nothing in the above discussion counts against an empirical study of law, so long as such an approach involves an empirical study of norms. Despite their many insights and the attempt by some to rely on a pragmatic epistemology, the legal realists were misled, in much of their critique of rule-centered jurisprudence, by an inadequate epistemology for understanding social phenomena. By recapturing the hermeneutic theme of H.L.A. Hart's work, and further developing Hart's discussions of primary rules while overcoming his occasional reliance on an objectionable formalism, it should be possible to take into account the insights found in *The Cheyenne Way* and other legal realist literature—while *fortifying* rather than displacing rule-centered jurisprudence.

NOTES

1. Karl N. Llewellyn and Edward Adamson Hoebel, *The Cheyenne Way: Conflict and Case Law in Primitive Jurisprudence* (Norman: University of Oklahoma Press, 1941).

2. Ibid., p. viii.

3. Ibid., p. 20.

4. Karl Llewellyn, "On Reading and Using the Newer Jurisprudence," *Columbia Law Review* 40 (April, 1940): 581–614; reprinted in Karl Llewellyn, *Jurisprudence: Realism in Theory and Practice* (Chicago: University of Chicago Press, 1962), p. 152. See also William Twining, *Karl Llewellyn and the Realist Movement* (London: Weidenfeld and Nicolson, 1973).

5. The contemporary Critical Legal Studies (CLS) movement is partly rooted in the American legal realist movement. See Scott Landers, "Wittgenstein, Realism, and CLS: Undermining Rule Scepticism," *Law and Philosophy* 9 (1990): 177–203 and see the relevant works cited therein.

6. Karl Llewellyn, "A Realistic Jurisprudence—the Next Step," *Columbia Law Review* 30 (April, 1930): 431–65, reprinted in Llewellyn, *Jurisprudence*, p. 7. Roscoe Pound responded with an attempt to characterize legal realism in his largely unsympathetic "The Call for a Realist Jurisprudence," *Harvard Law Review* 44 (March, 1931): 697–711. Llewellyn's response to Pound, "Some Realism about Realism—Responding to Dean Pound," *Harvard Law Review* 44 (June, 1931): 1222–64, effectively destroyed Pound's characterization.

7. Llewellyn, "A Realistic Jurisprudence," *Jurisprudence*, pp. 39–40.

8. Karl Llewellyn, "On the Good, the True, the Beautiful, in Law," *University of Chicago Law Review* 9 (February, 1942): 224–65; Llewellyn, *Jurisprudence*, pp. 167–213.

9. Compare Oliver Wendell Holmes, *The Common Law*, Mark DeWolfe Howe, ed. (Boston: Little, Brown and Co., 1963; first published in 1881), p. 5.

10. Martin Golding, "Jurisprudence and Legal Philosophy in Twentieth-Century America—Major Themes and Developments," *Journal of Legal Education* 36 (December, 1986): 441–80, especially 452.

11. Llewellyn applauded the work of John Dewey, in Karl Llewellyn, Review of *Jurisprudence*, by Roscoe Pound, *University of Chicago Law Review* 28 (Autumn, 1960): 174–82. Reference to the early pragmatists (to Charles S. Peirce, William James, and John Dewey) can be found scattered throughout the realist literature.

12. Llewellyn and Hoebel, *Cheyenne Way*, p. viii.

13. Compare Chapter 2 of *Cheyenne Way* to "A Realistic Jurisprudence." For the official lack of interest in motivations, see Llewellyn and Hoebel, *Cheyenne Way*, pp. 34–35. See also Twining, *Karl Llewellyn*, pp. 158–66, regarding the contrast between a realist approach and what he calls a focus on "perspectives, i.e., on what people think" (p. 159).

14. Llewellyn, "A Realistic Jurisprudence," *Jurisprudence*, pp. 28–29.

15. Llewellyn and Hoebel, *Cheyenne Way*, pp. viii and 29. For an account of the history of the *Cheyenne Way* study itself, see Twining, *Karl Llewellyn*, pp. 153–56.

16. Llewellyn and Hoebel, *Cheyenne Way*, p. 341.

17. See ibid., especially pp. 29–40, for Llewellyn's recognition of the possible limitations of his data.

18. See H.L.A. Hart, *The Concept of Law* (Oxford: Oxford University Press, 1961), pp. 77–96.

19. Llewellyn and Hoebel, *Cheyenne Way*. See, for example, Case 7 and Llewellyn's comments: "A tribal chief could not be deposed, no matter what his conduct," which Llewellyn first called a "principle" and then a "generalization" (p. 79) and later maintained that "an impeachment would be unconstitutional" (p. 81). Regarding Case 11, Llewellyn commented: "The duty of all the members of a [soldier] society to participate in the administration of punishment and the liability of all members to discipline in case of neglect were stated by all informants as generalized rules and are borne out in several cases" (p. 113). Both Llewellyn and his informants spoke variously of a no-hunting "rule" and of no-hunting "decrees." On page 114: "One tribal rule was for the soldiers of the society of the Sun Dance pledger to march afoot before the tribe when they were making the ceremonial move preparatory to giving the Sun Dance." The text continues with a discussion of the sanction for violating that rule. In Case 17 the informant reported a chief saying, "Now we shall make a new rule. There shall be no more borrowing of horses without asking" (p. 128). Llewellyn described this as "important, . . . the crystallization of a new social policy, the formulation of a law making it a crime to borrow another's horse without his expressed permission" (p. 128) and as "legis-

lation" (p. 129); elsewhere he described the new rule as an "ordinance" (p. 343). Many additional examples can be given.

20. Llewellyn, "A Realistic Jurisprudence," *Jurisprudence*, p. 21.

21. Ibid., p. 17.

22. In a defensive posture Llewellyn reminded the reader that "the accounts move in terms of *behavior*, rarely in terms of reasons therefore." Llewellyn and Hoebel, *Cheyenne Way*, p. 35.

23. Ibid., pp. 312–13.

24. Ibid., p. 334.

25. For example, see Llewellyn and Hoebel, *Cheyenne Way*, Case 1, pp. 3–6. Case 1 contains the following normative or institutional terms and underlying concepts: gift, property, soldier, prohibition, spokesperson, agreement, promise, acceptance, rescinding a gift, pledge, crier (a position of importance among the Cheyenne), scouts, our people, release from a vow, adoption of a son, tribal chief, taking temporary charge of a tribe, permission. In his comments on page 162, Llewellyn added the following phrases of his own: "sole claimants," "self-appointed executors or trustees," "propriety," "socially justifying," "the entire tribe's changing its normal constitutional status," "war-party constitution," and "authority." These do not seem reducible to descriptive behavioral terminology. Stripped of such discourse, however, the case would scarcely be intelligible. The reader might try reading one of the cases with normative discourse removed to see how difficult a task understanding then becomes.

26. For arguments aimed at undermining more extreme forms of rule skepticism, especially when it is pitched at higher levels of abstraction, see Landers, note 5 above.

27. On Llewellyn's "law-jobs" theory, see Llewellyn and Hoebel, *Cheyenne Way*, Chapters X and XI; Karl Llewellyn, "The Normative, the Legal and the Law Jobs: The Problem of Juristic Method," *Yale Law Journal* 49 (June, 1940): 1355–1400 and "Law and the Social Sciences—Especially Sociology" (1949) in *Jurisprudence*, pp. 352–71; and Twining, *Karl Llewellyn*, pp. 174–84.

28. Hart, *The Concept of Law*, pp. 89–91.

29. For the Cheyenne dispute over horses referred to here and in the following paragraph, see Llewellyn and Hoebel, *Cheyenne Way*, Case 49, pp. 224–25.

30. On the idea of a "social fact" generally, see Maurice Mandelbaum, "Societal Facts," *British Journal of Sociology* 6 (1955): 305–17.

31. Martin Golding, *Philosophy of Law* (Englewood Cliffs, NJ: Prentice Hall, 1975), p. 110.

32. Martin Golding, "On the Adversary System and Justice," in Richard Bronaugh, ed., *Philosophical Law: Authority, Equality, Adjudication, Privacy* (Westport, CT: Greenwood Press, 1978), p. 103.

33. Llewellyn and Hoebel, *Cheyenne Way*, Chapter VI.

34. Compare also Karl Llewellyn, "The Anthropology of Criminal Guilt" (1950), reprinted in *Jurisprudence*, pp. 439–50, especially pp. 447–49.

35. Llewellyn and Hoebel, *Cheyenne Way*, pp. 160–61. Llewellyn treated the preceding case as though the informant's account places the two cases on an exact par, but it is noteworthy that the informant does not claim that the mother of the suicide victim, in the preceding case, was banished via a decree of exile pronounced by a conference of the tribal chiefs, as was standard procedure for cases regarded as murder.

36. On the problematic nature of confirmation in natural science, see Clark Glymour, *Theory and Evidence* (Princeton: Princeton University Press, 1980); Carl Hempel, *Aspects of Scientific Explanation and Other Essays in the Philosophy of Science* (New York: The Free Press, 1965); and Israel Scheffler, *The Anatomy of Inquiry: Philosophical Studies in the Theory of Science* (Indianapolis: Hackett Publishing, 1981).

37. Felix Cohen "assumed that only ethical criticism is appropriate for judicial decisions, that there is no such thing as legal criticism of decisions, and that decisions cannot be criticized as correct or incorrect [i.e., there is no such thing as a judicial *mistake*], but only, in a utilitarian sense, as good or bad." Martin Golding, "Realism and Functionalism in the Legal Thought of Felix S. Cohen," *Cornell Law Review* 66 (June, 1981): 1032–57, quotation from page 1041.

38. Llewellyn and Hoebel, *Cheyenne Way*, pp. 118–19, 166.

39. Ibid., p. 322; see also pp. 318–19.

40. Compare also Llewellyn, "Law and the Social Sciences—Especially Sociology," *Jurisprudence*, pp. 354–57.

7

William Jennings Bryan, Attorney Before the Nebraska Supreme Court

Andrew B. Koszewski

Historians and biographers of William Jennings Bryan tend to examine his life only in terms of his political ambitions or his place in late nineteenth-century social movements while neglecting his legal career. What biographers have focused on about Bryan's early years in Nebraska was his relationship with J. Sterling Morton and his wing of the state Democratic party, as well as Bryan's rise as a public speaker and a political force. Very little research has been done on Bryan's career in the Nebraska bar from 1887 to 1891. Biographers, such as Paolo Coletta, have commented that Bryan viewed law as a means to political success and not as an end in itself.[1] Other biographers, such as Paxton Hibben, described Bryan's Nebraska practice as "hit and miss," and Louis Koenig commented that Bryan achieved only moderate success as a lawyer.[2]

Bryan was a young attorney in Jacksonville, Illinois, when he decided to move to frontier Nebraska in 1887. He was more fortunate than other lawyers new to the area in that he was acquainted with a Lincoln attorney, Adolphus Talbot. Talbot and Bryan met while both attended Union College of Law in Chicago and began a friendship that influenced Bryan to relocate to Lincoln. By the time Bryan arrived, Talbot had already dissolved a partnership, which allowed Bryan to enter into a partnership with his friend and avoided the difficult task of beginning a solo practice or forming a partnership with someone he did not know.

Talbot and Bryan's law firm was typical of this era. Firms usually consisted of no more than two or three partners. The work arrangement of Talbot and Bryan was also typical for such partnerships. Bryan and Talbot prepared cases jointly, with one constructing the arguments they thought pertinent to the case, and the other attempting to construct the adversary's counter arguments. At the end of the month they added the receipts together and divided the amount between them. A unique element of Bryan and Talbot's partnership was that Bryan excluded from the firm the money Talbot received for serving as counsel to the Missouri Pacific Railroad. At the beginning of their relationship, Bryan wanted nothing to do with railroads.[3]

THE BRYAN LEGAL MYTHOLOGY

Historians have clearly established that Bryan was politically ambitious. Upon his move to Lincoln on October 1, 1887, he brought with him two letters of introduction, one from Illinois Congressman William M. Springer to J. Sterling Morton, and one from Jacksonville judge Carl Epler to Jefferson H. Brady, a Lincoln attorney. Following these introductions Bryan plunged into Nebraska party politics. At the Lancaster County Democratic Convention in April, 1888, Bryan argued in favor of a motion to elect T. Sterling Morton delegate-at-large to the national convention. Morton won.[4]

At this convention Bryan delivered a tariff speech that moved him into a position of importance within the state party. This culminated in his election as a United States Representative in 1890, when Bryan defeated Republican incumbent William Connell by 32,376 votes to 25,663.[5] Bryan was devoted to the Democratic party, and he worked tirelessly to strengthen it. Yet his law practice was his sole source of income, and this explains why Bryan made references to his law firm in political speeches.[6] Bryan was furthering two goals in his early Nebraska years: helping the Democratic party *and* building his law practice.

Historical assessments of Bryan's legal career strangely have their origins in his presidential bid in 1896. It was in the 1896 presidential campaign that opponents leveled vehement attacks against Bryan's competency as a lawyer. Naturally, Bryan defended his legal practice from such criticism. The most noted rebuttal came from Bryan's wife, Mary. She wrote, "Those who complain should consider that he entered the profession at twenty-three and left it at thirty, and during that period began twice, and twice became more than self-supporting."[7]

This debate has continued into the various works on Bryan's life. Paxton Hibben and other biographers have maintained that Bryan, though diligent, lacked an insightful, intelligent mind.[8] Usually to illustrate such a description, they point to Bryan's performance during the Scopes trial. Furthermore, even those biographies sympathetic to Bryan have qualified his abilities as a lawyer. These historians have discussed Bryan's abilities as a jury lawyer only in terms of his oratory skill.[9] Recent biographer Robert Cherny stressed Bryan's speaking ability to juries rather than his intellectual legal skills.[10]

This conclusion regarding William Jennings Bryan's abilities as a lawyer, that had he remained in the profession and not moved on to an influential political career, he would have made a good jury lawyer, has been most persistent. This comment is attributed to fellow Lincoln lawyer and friend of Bryan, Charles G. Dawes.[11] Dawes, a Republican, also went on to a successful political career, becoming vice-president under Calvin Coolidge, and though Dawes opposed Bryan politically, he commented that Bryan would have made a successful jury lawyer. This characterization was meant to emphasize Bryan's oratory powers, but it has been interpreted over time to have certain negative connotations.

PRACTICING BEFORE A STATE SUPREME COURT

Sympathetic biographies of Bryan, describing him as a jury lawyer, have slighted the work Bryan did in front of the Nebraska Supreme Court. The cases that Talbot and Bryan or Bryan argued before the court indicate that Bryan was a successful appellate lawyer and that Talbot and Bryan was an important emerging Lincoln law firm by 1891.

Lawyers formed partnerships to increase the number of clients and also to allow individual lawyers to specialize within a given field. The task facing any lawyer or law firm was to build up enough legal work from which one could make a living. For the firm of Talbot and Bryan this meant amassing a sizable amount of legal work, being retained for appellate actions while trying to avoid the unpleasant and less remunerative task of debt collection. One of the ways to examine how successful Bryan was at building his legal practice is by assessing Bryan's participation before the Nebraska Supreme Court. How often Bryan had cases before the Nebraska Supreme Court and what these numbers mean give an indication of Bryan's legal acumen.[12]

Previous biographers have numbered Bryan's supreme court cases at nine. However, the Nebraska Supreme Court dockets contain eleven instances where the names Talbot and Bryan or William Jennings Bryan appear. Bryan had one case before the court during the July 1889 term, and he argued three cases, two of them independent of the firm, during the January 1890 term. The last case occurred during September 1890. By the September term Bryan already had been nominated as the Democratic congressional candidate, and he was beginning to turn from his law practice to concentrate on his campaign.

According to Table 7.1 which indicates the number of lawyers appearing before the Nebraska Supreme Court in a given term, the vast majority of lawyers never argued more than one or two cases before the Nebraska Supreme Court. Talbot and Bryan were part of this majority in the July 1888 term and the January 1889 term. By the September 1889 term and the January 1890 term, however, Bryan achieved a higher level of demand. In the September 1889 term, Bryan's practice did better than nearly 691 of the lawyers or law firms that appeared before the court. This percentage increased to 69.4 percent in the next term, January 1890. These figures suggest that Bryan had the foundation of a strong legal practice not only as a jury lawyer but also as an appellate attorney before the Nebraska Supreme Court.

Bryan's eleven Supreme Court cases can be divided by subject into three different categories. The first category deals with those cases concerning the recovery of some financial debt. The next category involves cases that required court interpretation of particular state statutes, and the final category concerns those cases of a political nature where an election was contested.

BRYAN AND DEBT ACTIONS

Table 7.2 provides the basic information about each case in the context of debt action appeals. The first Supreme Court case involving the recovery of a debt that the firm Talbot & Bryan participated in was *Wood v. O'Hanlon*.[13] Talbot & Bryan served as counsel for Edward Wood in his suit to recover $530.80 from Peter O'Hanlon. O'Hanlon incurred the debt when he purchased an Iowa hotel from Wood. O'Hanlon placed a down payment on the property, leaving $1,500 outstanding. In the course of events, the hotel caught fire and burned to the ground. O'Hanlon had insured the hotel for $2,000, but only realized $1,400 from the insurance. He paid Wood $1,000 plus interest but used the remaining money to pay off other debts.

Table 7.1
Frequency That Lawyers/Law Firms Appeared Before the Nebraska Supreme Court, January Term, 1888 through September 1890 and the Percentage Each Represents from Total in That Term

no. of times appearing before court	number of lawyers or law firms					
	Jan. 88	*July 88*	*Jan. 89*	*Sept. 89*	*Jan. 90*	*Sept. 90*
1	177	186	171	255	322	295
	58.2%	53.6%	57.6%	52%	54.4%	52.3%
2	55	61	53	81	89	98
	18.1%	17.6%	17.8%	16.5%	15%	17.4%
3	26	33	40	43	63	58
	8.6%	9.5%	13.5%	8.8%	10.6%	10.3%
4	20	24	9	28	32	33
	6.6%	6.9%	3%	5.7%	5.4%	5.9%
5	11	16	12	22	26	20
	3.6%	4.6%	4%	4.5%	4.4%	3.5%
6	9	10	5	21	17	16
	3%	2.9%	1.7%	4.3%	2.9%	2.8%
7	4	9	1	7	16	11
	1.3%	2.7%	.3%	1.4%	2.7%	2%
8	1	3	4	6	7	13
	.3%	.8%	1.3	1.2%	1.2%	2.3%
9	0	3	0	4	8	6
	0%	.8%	0%	.8%	1.4%	1.1%
10 or more	1	2	2	23	12	14
	.3%	.6%	.6%	4.7%	2%	2.4%

Source: Bar Docket of the Nebraska Supreme Court (1888–1890), Nebraska State Capitol Library, Lincoln, NE.

O'Hanlon also owned some other property in Iowa which he sold for $700. He then gave his wife $500 that he claimed was rightfully hers based upon her assets prior to their marriage. This left O'Hanlon insolvent and released him from the remaining amount he owed Wood.

With his wife's $500 Peter O'Hanlon traveled to Chadron, Nebraska, for the purpose of purchasing a certain piece of property. On the day of the sale, O'Hanlon was unable to attend, so his brother Patrick went in his place and bought this property in Peter O'Hanlon's name. This was an alleged mistake on Patrick's part and to mend the mistake Peter conveyed the title of

Table 7.2
Debt Cases Talbot & Bryan/W.J. Bryan Had Before the Nebraska Supreme Court, 1887–1891

Debt Cases	Date Opinion Filed	Attorney(s) for Plaintiff	Attorney(s) for Defendant	Decision
Wood v. O'Hanlon	May 1889	Sprague, Fisher & McCann Talbot & Bryan	Alfred Bartow	For O'Hanlon
Cornish & Tibbets v. Russell	July 1891	Cornish & Tibbets	S. P. Davidson D. F. Osgood Talbot & Bryan	For Russell
Watte v. Wickersham	Oct. 1889	Talbot & Bryan	Lam, Ricketts & Wilson	For Wickersham
Reynolds v. Dietz	March 1892	J. B. Cessna	M. A. Hartigan Talbot & Bryan	For Reynolds

property to Patrick who then conveyed it to Peter's wife, Margaret. Edward Wood alleged that this was all a scheme created to defraud him of the remaining money Peter O'Hanlon owed him, but the court ruled in favor of the O'Hanlons, claiming that the attorneys for Wood failed to disprove any of the O'Hanlons' testimony.

Talbot and Bryan had only a minor role in this case.[14] The other firm serving Edward Wood, Sprague, Fisher and McCann, argued the case. The brief filed on Wood's behalf only bears their firm's name, and the transcript of the case mentions only their names as attorneys for Edward Wood. Talbot and Bryan performed some service as the docket does mention their name. This is supported by a letter found in the case file.[15] Alfred Bartow, attorney for the O'Hanlons, allowed Talbot and Bryan to examine the records of the case for two days, so they probably performed some research services for Sprague, Fisher and McCann.

Talbot and Bryan had a similar role in *Cornish and Tibbets v. Russell*.[16] In this case James Russell sought to garnish funds in the possession of Cornish and Tibbets, a Lincoln law firm. Russell alleged that this law firm held money won by Mary Bidwell in her successful $1,100 lawsuit against the Johnson County Bank of Sterling, Nebraska. Cornish and Tibbets denied they had any money belonging to Mary Bidwell because it was assigned to the Riverside Land Company of Wichita, Kansas. Russell claimed that this was undertaken for the purpose of avoiding her debt. Since Russell won his case in district court, Cornish and Tibbets appealed the case to the Nebraska

Supreme Court, hoping the court would overturn the lower court's decision. The supreme court heard the case but rejected the arguments made by Cornish and Tibbets and affirmed the lower court's judgment.

This case was unusual because there was no mention of Talbot and Bryan in the supreme court's opinion, and yet, on August 8, 1889, the docket stated, "service accepted Talbot and Bryan attorneys for plaintiff."[17] The case transcript gives no indication that the firm participated substantially in the supreme court proceedings. The brief submitted in Russell's behalf bears only the firm name of D. F. Osgood and S. P. Davidson.[18] However, upon examination of the case file, Talbot and Bryan were listed counsel for James Russell at the district court, so they probably consulted with Davidson and Osgood.

Watte et al. v. Wickersham et al. was a case in which Talbot and Bryan solely represented Joseph Watte, Frank Axtell, and Finley Forbes in their suit against Charles Wickersham and Henry Ware.[19] Watte, Axtell, and Forbes were partners in the firm of Elmendoff, Watte, and Company, a corporation that placed orders for clients on the Chicago Board of Trade. They claimed that Wickersham and Ware bought and sold grain using Elmendoff, Watte, and Company as their agent. In October 1886, Wickersham and Ware received a statement indicating the amount they owed for Elmendoff, Watte, and Company's services. Wickersham and Ware refused to pay, maintaining that they would only be liable for losses incurred from the buying and selling of grain contracts. The attorneys for Wickersham claimed that the transactions constituted illegal gambling contracts and, therefore, were void. They attempted to show that the contracts made for Wickersham were never intended for use to buy or sell grain but rather only to engage in grain speculation. This reduced the contracts to wagers, which were illegal. Talbot and Bryan argued that contracts to buy or sell commodities for future delivery were valid and legal contracts, but the district court ruled in favor of Wickersham, and Talbot and Bryan appealed and lost.

The supreme court based its decision on its earlier ruling in *Sprague v. Warren*.[20] The *Watte* decision, written by Justice Amasa Cobb, ruled that the facts in this case were no different from those of *Sprague*. Justice Cobb quoted *Sprague*, stating that contracts are valid only if the parties deal with actual property. Here there was no intent to deliver real goods between the two parties. The court opposed enforcing contracts that represented wagers on the rise and fall of commodity prices.

The remaining debt case that Talbot and Bryan worked on was *Reynolds v. Dietz*.[21] This case involved the attempt by Lewis Reynolds to collect an $8,625 mortgage on a piece of property in Adams County. There were fifteen defendants in this case and Talbot and Bryan represented four of them, Joseph Boehmer, Alexis Halter, B. J. Brotherton, and Thomas Hyde. Reynolds obtained the property's mortgage from Gould and Lenora Dietz, and Edward and Carrie Stickney, but the Dietzs and Stickneys sold the land to Harrison Bostwick, who acted as an agent for the other defendants in the case. Reynolds claimed that by selling the land to Bostwick and the other defendants, they were now responsible for the money owed to Reynolds. The case tried before the district court held only that the Dietzs, Stickneys, and Bostwick were liable for the money owed Reynolds.

This case was appealed to the Nebraska Supreme Court by Lewis Reynolds, and in the process of appealing the case the attorneys for Reynolds served Harrison Bostwick with a bill of exception. A bill of exception is a written statement that contains the objections made by a party to a lower court's decision. Done for the benefit of the appellate court, this bill must be given to the adverse party. Talbot and Bryan's brief argued for a motion to void Reynolds' bill of exception.[22] They alleged that a bill of exception had to be delivered to the adverse party, and Harrison Bostwick did not constitute an adverse party because he had a vested interest in seeing the liability spread to all the parties in the suit. The court dismissed the motion, stating that since Bostwick was a trustee for all the defendants in the purchase of property, it was sufficient that the bill was served to him, and it also overturned the district court's finding and ruled that since the defendants purchased the property they had to pay.

The obvious generalization about the debt cases handled by Talbot and Bryan is that the firm was only mildly successful. However, Talbot and Bryan had only a minor role in *Wood v. O'Hanlon* and though they only had a silent role in *Cornish and Tibbets v. Russell*, they successfully argued the case in the district court. The last two cases where the firm of Talbot and Bryan directly represented clients resulted in lost decisions. In the *Watte* case, the firm had the difficult task of trying to differentiate their facts from those of the *Sprague* case. Perhaps more disappointing to the firm, and particularly to Bryan since he actually argued the firm's position, was the *Reynolds* case. Bryan failed to persuade the court to dismiss the case on the grounds that the actual parties in the case had not been served notice as to the case's appeal.

BRYAN AND STATUTORY CONSTRUCTION

Bryan's next set of cases dealt with arguments about how certain state statutes should be interpreted (see Table 7.3). This function of the state

Table 7.3
Talbot & Bryan Cases Involving Statutory Interpretation, 1887–1891

Cases	Date Opinion Filed	Attorney(s) for Plaintiff	Attorney(s) for Defendant	Decision
Stewart Chute Lumber Co. v. Missouri Pacific Railroad	Sept. 1889	Mason & Whedon	A. R. Talbot Talbot & Bryan	For Stewart first, for MoPac Railroad on retrial
Beach v. Emmons	Sept. 1889	J. L. Caldwell	Cassidy & Wolfe Talbot & Bryan	For Emmons
Bell v. Templin	Jan. 1889	Darnell & Kendall	Henry Nunn Talbot & Bryan	For Templin
Getchell v. Benton	Sept. 1890	B. B. Wiley Talbot & Bryan	H. C. Brome N. D. Jackson William Leese	For Getchell

supreme court, to decide the precise meaning of words in a particular statute, was and still remains one of its most important functions.

Bryan's first supreme court case concerning statutory interpretation, *Stewart Chute Lumber Company v. Missouri Pacific Railroad*, involved the meaning of a statute granting liens for "material furnished" or labor performed for the construction of a railroad.[23] Marcus Kavanaugh was a subcontractor who graded certain sections of land for a track that would extend into Lincoln. He was hired by Casement, Carlile & Company, a contracting firm retained to grade the line for the Missouri Pacific Railroad. Kavanaugh purchased wood from the Stewart Chute Lumber Company, which was used to build shantytowns and barns. These buildings were to house his men and work animals. When Kavanaugh tried to pass the bill for the lumber onto the railroad company, the company refused to pay it, and the lumber company filed a lien against Missouri Pacific Railroad and the contractor.

The railroad argued that the word "furnished" in the statute applied only to those materials physically used in the construction of the railroad. This argument was rejected by Justices Cobb and Manoah B. Reese. In overturning the lower court's decision they ruled in favor of the lumber company. Justice Samuel Maxwell dissented from the majority opinion.

Maxwell argued that such an interpretation would extend liability too far. Railroads could be liable for the food or clothes workmen used while building a track. Maxwell had the opportunity to make his opinion known a second time when the case was again appealed to the Nebraska Supreme

Court on technical grounds. By the time of the second appeal, T. L. Norval had replaced Justice Reese on the court, and he agreed with Maxwell. The court then reversed its earlier decision and ruled in favor of the railroad.[24]

Adolphus Talbot argued the case on behalf of the railroad. Bryan's anti-railroad sentiments prevented him from accepting money for Talbot's cases for the railroad or from having his name mentioned as an attorney for a railroad. What makes this case interesting is that the firm of Talbot and Bryan appeared also as counsel for Casement, Carlile and Company.[25] There was even a brief filed on behalf of the contracting company that bears the firm's name.[26] The transcripts of the case indicate that Talbot appeared on behalf of both the railroad and the contractor.[27] It is difficult to evaluate Bryan's individual contribution to the case. Because Bryan and Talbot prepared cases jointly, one might assume that Bryan played some role, but in this particular case, Bryan may have deferred to his partner.

Bryan's role in *Beach v. Emmons*, however, is much more visible and easier to evaluate. In this case, involving whether or not a constable could demand payment before summoning a jury, Talbot and Bryan served as co-counsel with the firm of Cassidy and Wolfe.[28] Not only did Talbot and Bryan file a joint brief with Cassidy and Wolfe, but this was one case where evidence exists showing that William Jennings Bryan personally argued in front of the court on behalf of James A. Emmons.[29]

Emmons filed a complaint against Alva Pound, Joseph Mitchell, and Frank McClelland, charging the three with assault and battery. These individuals were arrested and upon a hearing demanded a jury trial. After selecting a jury, the district court judge directed constable A. B. Beach to summon the jurors. He refused to do so, stipulating that his fees had to be paid in advance. Bryan, acting as counsel for Emmons, argued for a writ of mandamus, which would force Beach to summon the jurors.

The argument contained in the brief written by Talbot and Bryan with Cassidy and Wolfe asserted that although a justice of the peace may demand certain securities before issuing a warrant, nowhere is there a statute that allows a constable to demand advance payment of his fees.[30] The Nebraska Supreme Court agreed with Bryan and granted Emmons his writ. The opinion written by Justice Maxwell mirrored the arguments put forth by Talbot and Bryan.

In *Bell v. Templin* the issue before the court was whether it had original jurisdiction in cases that contested the election results for the position of county attorney. The action arose out of an election held in Howard County on November 6, 1889. According to the election results, T. T. Bell, the

Republican candidate, lost to his Democratic challenger, J. W. Templin, and Bell challenged these results.[31]

Bell's attorney argued that the court had original jurisdiction in this case because the court could decide election disputes involving judges to the supreme court, judges to the district courts, "district attorneys," and regents of the University of Nebraska. Moreover, the legislature passed an act in 1885 that established the election and duties of the office of "county attorney" and stipulated that wherever the term "district attorney" appeared in the state laws, it should be replaced by "county attorney."[32] Bell's lawyers concluded that this gave the supreme court jurisdiction in this case.

Talbot and Bryan argued that the jurisdiction for county attorney rested within the county court, and Justice Maxwell held that since a county attorney was a county officer, the county court had original jurisdiction. The state supreme court had original jurisdiction in certain cases but not this one, so it dismissed the case.

One final case handled by Bryan and Talbot, *Getchell v. Benton*,[33] concerned whether or not certain bonds issued by the city of Neligh could be used to aid in the construction of a sugar beet processing factory. On May 20, 1890, Neligh held an election concerning whether or not to issue bonds of $14,800 for the purpose of building a sugar beet processing factory. The bond issue passed overwhelmingly. However, John Getchell believed that the bonds were aiding a private corporation and therefore were illegally issued. Bryan argued this case for Getchell personally in front of the Nebraska Supreme Court.

Generally, historians have discussed late nineteenth-century legal developments in terms of laissez-faire economic policies. Kermit Hall argues that such a description contains inherent problems because state legislatures were not debating whether or not government should interfere in the economy, but how it should promote or regulate economic production.[34] States used local aid bills to allow municipalities to underwrite and subsidize railroad developers, but after the Panic of 1873, state governments increasingly withdrew from economic promotion. Bryan's case is significant because it is illustrative of this trend away from state and local government economic promotion.

The Nebraska Legislature passed an act in 1869 that established the procedure for issuing bonds for works of internal improvement. Talbot and Bryan argued that the court's decision in *Traver v. Merrick County* defined what kind of mill could be a work of internal improvement.[35] According to Chief Justice Cobb's opinion in *Traver*, mills were allowed to be constructed with funds if public milling rates were determined by county commissioners. Talbot and Bryan argued that bonds issued to develop a mill whose rates were not determined by a city, county, or state official did not constitute a work of internal improvement within the meaning of the act.

The court agreed with Bryan's arguments and concluded that the planned Neligh sugar beet factory constituted private property and not a public project. The *Neligh Advocate* immediately published the results of the case and five weeks later ran a story regretting that the financial backers of the sugar beet factory had backed out. "The mechanics and laboring men of Neligh must have work to do or they will be compelled to go elsewhere."[36] To those who favored the public development of sugar beet factories, Bryan was an enemy, and this group vehemently opposed Bryan in his future Nebraska political campaigns.[37]

Talbot and Bryan were much more successful in this group of cases than any others. These cases also demonstrated Bryan's success at arguing before the court. Of the two cases that Bryan personally argued, both were won for Bryan's clients.

BRYAN AND POLITICAL ISSUES

The final three cases concern elections that were contested for reasons of fraud (see Table 7.4). *Bell v. Templin* is not included in this category because the issue in that case was only whether the supreme court had jurisdiction and did not directly involve charges of election fraud.

What distinguishes these cases is that they depended upon the meaning of election regulatory laws. Charges of election fraud were frequently heard

Table 7.4
Talbot & Bryan/W.J. Bryan Cases Involving Election Fraud, 1887–1891

Fraud Cases	Date Opinion Filed	Attorney(s) for Plaintiff	Attorney(s) for Defendant	Decision
Hanna v. Kavanagh	July 1888	Marquett Deweese & Hall	Talbot & Bryan T. J. Doyle, H. G Bell, W. R. Kelly	For Kavanagh
State, ex. rel. Easterday v. Howe	Jan. 1890	N. Z. Snell W. J. Bryan A. S. Tibbets	Charles Hall Adams, Lansing & Scott	For Easterday
State, ex. rel. Stearns v. Foxworthy	Jan. 1890	N. Z. Snell W. J. Bryan A. S. Tibbets	Charles Hall Adams, Lansing & Scott	For Foxworthy

throughout the United States during the 1880s,[38] and eventually this uproar led to the adoption of the Australian or secret ballot in the early twentieth century.

According to Nebraska statutes, the election of any person to any public office may be contested for specific grounds: fraud or corruption on the part of election judges; when the incumbent was convicted of a felony and had lost his or her civil rights; or when illegal votes were counted or legal votes rejected.[39] A joint session of the Nebraska House of Representatives and Senate heard and determined the contested elections of executive department officers. The Nebraska Supreme Court heard and decided contested elections dealing with judges of the supreme court, judges of the district courts, district attorneys, or regents of the university. District courts decided contested elections of county judges, and county courts decided contests of all other county and city officers. However, a party could appeal a decision from the county or district court to the next higher court, either the district court or the supreme court.

Hanna v. Kavanagh was the first case that the firm of Talbot and Bryan ever argued in front of the supreme court.[40] The case concerned a special election held in Greeley County to decide whether or not to move the county seat from Scotia to Greeley Center. The case, as Bryan described it, was really a power struggle between the Union Pacific and Burlington railroads.[41] The election on January 17, 1888, was both close and controversial. The *Greeley Center Independent* ran this article about the election returns:

> Never before has man thought that in this fair land where right, truth and freedom were watch words of liberty, that red handed fraud could steal the privileges of ballot and set at naught the will of the people. In this hellish act suspicion must rest on Scotia whom a "blind man though a fool" could but say would profit by it.[42]

The article specifically mentioned votes being thrown out in the Spring Creek precinct. Talbot and Bryan represented John Kavanagh, the head of the canvassing board that rejected the ballots from the Spring Creek precinct and who was on record as being sympathetic to Greeley Center.[43]

The discrepancy arose when the sealed envelope delivered to the county clerk showed visible signs of having been opened. The returns contained 117 votes in favor of the relocation and 4 votes against it. After investigating the situation, the canvassing board discovered that 61 names had been added to the list. The original ballots cast were 47 for relocation and 13 against. The canvassing board ordered the election board of Spring Creek to file correct returns. After its failure to refile the ballots, the canvassing board refused to count any of the ballots from Spring Creek. J. R. Hanna, M. B. Gearon, and J. R. Swain undertook a suit on behalf of Greeley Center to force the canvassing board to count the ballots. The attorneys for Hanna contended that Kavanagh lacked any authority to reject the ballots and should simply count the votes.

Bryan argued that it was the duty of Kavanagh to count only proper ballots, and because these ballots were not proper, Kavanagh acted correctly. The opinion of the court, written by Chief Justice Reese, stated that the canvassing board could not be compelled to canvass returns that were not genuine and refused to issue a writ to force Kavanagh to count the Spring Creek ballots. One ironic twist of the case was that Bryan ultimately was successful against the interests of his client. Kavanagh wished to lose the case because the votes were so predominantly in favor of relocation.

Bryan's last two cases were instances when his political life and his law practice merged. This aspect, ignored by historians, seems only fitting given Bryan's commitment to the Democratic party. If a need arose where Bryan could assist the party with his legal skill, he would do so. Both cases, *State, ex rel. Easterday v. Howe* and *State, ex rel. Stearns v. Foxworthy*, concerned the election of a justice of the peace in Lincoln on November 5, 1889.[44] These two cases were remarkable because Bryan worked on them apart from the firm, the only two instances when this occurred. Working with Bryan was Nova Snell, from the law firm of Sawyer and Snell, and Addison Tibbets, from the firm of Cornish and Tibbets, as they defended the Democratic and Prohibition party candidate Martin Easterday.

Easterday ran for justice of the peace in the Third District. The original returns indicated that the Republicans had swept not only the state, but the local elections.[45] Shortly afterward there was confusion over how to canvass the votes for justice of the peace. *The Daily Nebraska State Journal* attempted to clarify the situation by explaining that the Republican candidates ran on a double-headed ticket.[46] Their tickets were labelled for individual districts in the city and for the city as a whole, but Democratic candidates ran in the districts only. The Democratic paper, the *Omaha Bee*, ran a short article about Easterday in which he vowed to fight the election results.[47]

The problem involved in the case first centered on how justices of the peace were elected in cities such as Lincoln. Lincoln was divided into wards numbered one through six. The wards that constituted the Third District were the fourth and sixth wards. According to the statutes covering the election of a justice of the peace for the Third District, a plurality of votes was necessary in the fourth and sixth wards. The controversy centered on the wording of the ballot for that election. Under the ballot heading "Justice of the Peace for the Third District," Easterday canvassed 144 votes and Charles Foxworthy 200 votes. Under the ballot heading "Justice of the Peace," Easterday canvassed 465 votes and Foxworthy 405 votes. Finally, under the ballot heading "Justice of the Peace for the First District," Easterday canvassed three votes and Foxworthy none.

The total results indicated that Easterday had 612 votes to Foxworthy's 605. County clerk O. C. Bell refused to add together the votes for Easterday, claiming that the exact wording of the ballot prevented them from being counted together. He only counted the ballots with the heading "Justice of the Peace for the Third District" and declared Foxworthy the winner. Martin Howe was elected county clerk after Bell, but he too refused to recount the votes, arguing that since Foxworthy was already in office, switching could cause serious damage to the administration of justice. Moreover, he argued that the statutes covering the election of justices of the peace were unclear. He was unsure whether to honor the statute that provided for the election of justices of the peace from the city at large or the other statute that provided for the election of justices of the peace by district only.[48]

The court ruled that in cases of conflicting statutes the more recent statute is controlling, and, therefore, the statute that called for the election of justices of the peace by district was the prevailing law. Justice Norval accepted the argument made by Bryan, Snell, and Tibbets, that the wording of ballots should not prevent the adding together of the ballots cast for Easterday,[49] and he issued a writ compelling Martin Howe, the new county clerk, to recount the votes.

The next step taken by Bryan, Snell, and Tibbets was to attempt to remove Charles Foxworthy from his position as justice of the peace in *State, ex rel. Stearns v. Foxworthy*. Royal Stearns was the Lancaster County attorney working with Bryan, Snell, and Tibbets. In this case the attorneys for Charles Foxworthy argued that in the disputed election Martin Easterday received 575 Democratic votes and 37 Prohibitionist votes. The Prohibitionist ballots (see Table 7.5) violated Section Forty of Chapter Twenty-six in *Nebraska Compiled Statutes* because ballots having a greater number of names than needed for that office were fraudulent ballots and could not be counted in this instance for Easterday.[50]

Bryan, Snell, and Tibbets once again argued that the people of the Third District understood that Martin Easterday was the candidate for justice of the peace and the votes sufficiently indicate the voters' intentions, but the court ruled against Easterday. The justices concluded that since the Prohibitionist ticket did not specifically indicate who the candidates were for

Table 7.5
Republican and Prohibition Party Tickets in State, ex rel. Stearns v. Foxworthy (1890)

Republican City Ticket	*4th Ward Prohibition Ticket*
For Justice of the Peace of the First District of the City of Lincoln, and for the City of Lincoln,	For Justice of the Peace,
J.H. Brown.	S.J. Kent, S. S. Roice M. L. Easterday.
For Justice of the Peace of the Second District of the City of Lincoln, and for the City of Lincoln,	For Assessor, W. M. Fullerton.
S. T. Cochran.	For Constables, J.R. Cochran, G. C. Small.
For Justice of the Peace of the Third District of the City of Lincoln, and for the City of Lincoln,	
Chas. H. Foxworthy.	

Source: *State, ex. rel. Stearns v. Foxworthy* (1890) case file (Nebraska State Historical Society, Lincoln, Nebraska).

what district, the ballots were illegal and not countable. Foxworthy retained his position as justice of the peace.

The cases of *Easterday v. Howe* and *Stearns v. Foxworthy* are clear examples of Bryan's law practice used in the service of the Democratic party. They also place Bryan's relationship with elements within the Democratic party in a new light. Nova Snell, who ran for county attorney in 1890, was a law partner with Andrew J. Sawyer. Sawyer, a close friend of J. Sterling Morton, was a local political force within the Democratic party, having been elected mayor of Lincoln in 1887 and having served as chairman of the Committee on Resolutions for the state Democratic party. Sawyer was one of the conservative Democrats who opposed Bryan's nomination as the Democratic congressional candidate in 1890.[51] This was mentioned by state Democratic managers as they discussed with Bryan his candidacy for Congress. This conversation took place months prior to the Nebraska State Democratic Convention, which was held on August 14, 1890. The opinion reached in the *Foxworthy* case was issued in April 1890, four months prior to the state convention. Though one cannot conclude that Bryan spoke to Sawyer through Snell, it does suggest that because of his involvement in the *Easterday* cases, Bryan himself bridged a political chasm.

CONCLUSION

From this description of the cases that had the names Talbot and Bryan or Bryan on the Nebraska Supreme Court docket, only eight cases can be described as having Bryan act as a direct participant. Of the six cases that Talbot and Bryan argued together, the firm won four and lost two. Of the cases that Bryan argued before the court, either with the firm or alone, Bryan won four and lost two. Though Bryan lost both cases involving the recovery of debts owed, his cases cover a wide array of legal problems. The more successful of Bryan's cases were those that challenged the meaning of state statutes.

Bryan was a knowledgeable lawyer who could successfully argue cases in front of the state supreme court, but he did not operate in a vacuum. Talbot undoubtedly contributed in all the cases handled under their firm's name, and the extent to which one was more knowledgeable than the other is not possible to determine. One can conclude, however, that Bryan and Talbot were able to build a successful practice. This was a considerable accomplishment given that Bryan's practice in Nebraska lasted less than four years and that Talbot, prior to Bryan's move to Nebraska, worked almost exclusively for the Missouri Pacific Railroad. Though Bryan left the legal profession for politics, he did so after having achieved a certain position of significance with Nebraska's highest court and within Nebraska's legal community.

NOTES

1. Paolo E. Coletta, "William Jennings Bryan's First Nebraska Years," *Nebraska History* 33 (June, 1952): 75.

2. Paxton Hibben, *The Peerless Leader: William Jennings Bryan* (New York: Russell G. Russell, 1929), p. 122; Louis W. Koenig, *A Political Biography of William Jennings Bryan*, (New York: G. P. Putnam & Sons, 1971), p. 56.

3. William J. Bryan and Mary B. Bryan, *The Memoirs of William Jennings Bryan* (Chicago: United Publishers of America, 1925), pp. 69–70, 76, 82.

4. Coletta, "Bryan's First Nebraska Years," pp. 76, 79.

5. James F. Pederson and Kenneth D. Wald, *Shall the People Rule? A History of the Democratic Party in Nebraska Politics, 1811–1972* (Lincoln, NE: Jacob North, 1972), p. 75; Paolo E. Coletta, "The Morning Star of the Reformation: William Jennings Bryan's First Congressional Campaign," *Nebraska History* 37 (June, 1956): 109; Charles Morrow Wilson, *The Commoner: William Jennings Bryan* (Garden City, NY: Doubleday, 1970), p. 155.

6. Robert W. Cherny, *A Righteous Cause: The Life of William Jennings Bryan* (Boston: Little, Brown, 1985), p. 24.

7. William J. Bryan, *The First Battle* (Chicago: W. B. Cunkey, 1896), p. 48.

8. Hibben, *Peerless Leader*, p. 121. Besides the biographers already mentioned, see David D. Anderson, *William Jennings Bryan* (Boston: Twayne Publishers, 1981), pp. 33–34; Albert L. Gale and George W. Kite, *Bryan the Man: The Commoner at Close Range* (St. Louis: Thompson Publishers, 1908), p. 24; J. C. Long, *Bryan the Great Commoner* (New York: D. Appleton, 1928), pp. 42–49; M. R. Werner, *Bryan* (New York: Harcourt, Brace, 1929), p. 22. None of these biographies go into much detail about Bryan's law practice. Completely ignoring his practice is Kendrick A. Clements, *William Jennings Bryan: Missionary Isolationist* (Knoxville: University of Tennessee Press, 1982) which discusses Bryan as a Christian statesman in every respect of his life but his legal career. Also, Paul W. Glad, *The Trumpet Soundeth: William Jennings Bryan and His Democracy, 1896–1912* (Lincoln: University of Nebraska Press, 1960) does not discuss Bryan's law practice. The Scopes trial also contributed to damaging Bryan's image as a lawyer. For sources on that trial, see John T. Scopes, "Denouement at Dayton," in Paul W. Glad, ed., *William Jennings Bryan, a Profile* (New York: Hall and Wang, 1968), pp. 229–35; Leslie H. Allen, ed., *Bryan and Darrow at Dayton* (New York: Arthur Lee, 1925), pp. 133–57; and Ray Ginger, *Six Days or Forever? Tennessee v. John Thomas Scopes* (Boston: Beacon Press, 1958).

9. Coletta, "Bryan's First Nebraska Years," p. 74; Koenig, *Political Biography of Bryan*, p. 55.

10. Cherny, *Righteous Cause*, p. 24.

11. See ibid.; Coletta, "Bryan's First Nebraska Years," p. 74; Koenig, *Political Biography of Bryan*, p. 55. All these biographies mention that Bryan would have made a good jury lawyer. Only Coletta's article mentions the Dawes quote directly, but this sentiment is found in the other two biographies.

12. The Nebraska Supreme Court during Bryan's legal career consisted of three popularly elected justices. The composition of the court changed only once during the period in which Bryan practiced law in Lincoln. The justices who served from 1887 to 1891 were Amasa Cobb, Manoah B. Reese, Samuel Maxwell, and T. L. Norval, who replaced Chief Justice Reese after the Republican party refused to renominate Reese in 1889.

13. *Wood v. O'Hanlon* 26 Neb 527 (1889).

14. *Wood v. O'Hanlon*, Nebraska Briefs, Nebraska State Capitol Library, Lincoln, NE, 51: 576–586.

15. *Wood v. O'Hanlon*, Nebraska Supreme Court Docket, Clerk's Office of Supreme Court, State Capitol Building, Lincoln, NE, no. 3292; *Wood v. O'Hanlon* case file, Nebraska State Historical Society, Lincoln, NE.

16. *Cornish and Tibbets v. Russell* 32 Neb 397 (1891).

17. *Cornish and Tibbets v. Russell*, Nebraska Supreme Court Docket, no. 3784.

18. *Cornish and Tibbets v. Russell*, Nebraska Briefs, 63: 8–12.

19. *Watte, et al. v. Wickersham et al.* 27 Neb 457 (1889).

20. Ibid. at 473.

21. *Reynolds v. Dietz* 34 Neb 265 (1892).

22. *Reynolds v. Dietz*, Nebraska Briefs, 66: 630–644.

23. *Stewart Chute Lumber Company v. Missouri Pacific Railroad* 28 Neb 39 (1889); Nebraska, Consolidated Statutes of Nebraska 2170, 470 (1891).

24. *Stewart Chute Lumber Company v. Missouri Pacific Railroad* 33 Neb 30–32 (1890).

25. *Stewart Chute Lumber Company v. Missouri Pacific Railroad*, Nebraska Supreme Court Docket, no. 3261.

26. *Stewart Chute Lumber Company v. Missouri Pacific Railroad*, Nebraska Briefs, 55: 23.

27. *Stewart Chute Lumber Company v. Missouri Pacific Railroad* case file, Nebraska State Historical Society, Lincoln, NE.

28. *Beach v. Emmons* 27 Neb 398 (1889).

29. W. Bryan and M. Bryan, *Memoirs*, pp. 78–79.

30. *Beach v. Emmons*, Nebraska Briefs, 50: 580–83.

31. *Bell v. Templin* 26 Neb 249 (1889).

32. Nebraska, *Consolidated Statutes of Nebraska*, 3105, 712 (1891).

33. *Getchell v. Benton* 30 Neb 870 (1890).

34. Kermit L. Hall, *The Magic Mirror: Law in American History* (New York: Oxford University Press, 1989), p. 190.

35. *Getchell v. Benton* 30 Neb 873 (1890).

36. *Neligh (NE) Advocate*, December 25, 1889, and January 29, 1891.

37. Coletta, "Bryan's Second Congressional Campaign," p. 275.

38. "Richard Jensen, *The Winning of the Midwest: Social and Political Conflict, 1888–1896* (Chicago: University of Chicago Press, 1971), pp. 34, 40.

39. Nebraska, *Consolidated Statutes of Nebraska*, 1646, 369 (1891).

40. *Hanna v. Kavanagh* 24 Neb 506 (1888).

41. Bryan and M. Bryan, *Memoirs*, p. 80.

42. *Greeley Center (NE) Independent*, January 20, 1888.

43. W. Bryan and M. Bryan, *Memoirs*, pp. 81–82.

44. *State, ex rel. Easterday v. Howe* 28 Neb 619 (1890); *State, ex rel. Stearns v. Foxworthy* 29 Neb 341 (1890).

45. *Nebraska State Journal* (Lincoln, NE), November 6, 1889.

46. Ibid., November 7. 1889.

47. *Omaha (NE) Bee*, November 9, 1889.

48. See Nebraska, *Compiled Statutes of Nebraska*, section 7, chapter 26, 387 (1887) for the old statute concerning how justices of the peace were elected. The new statute was approved in 1889 and can be found in *Laws of Nebraska*, 360 (1889).

49. *State, ex rel. Easterday v. Howe* 28 Neb 619 (1890).

50. *State, ex rel. Stearns v. Foxworthy* 29 Neb 314 (1890).

51. Paolo E. Coletta, "Morning Star," p. 106.

Part IV

Judiciaries of the Great Plains

Judging in the Great Plains has not been the subject of systematic investigation. Other regions' judiciaries have been chronicled, such as the justices of the peace in the Pacific Northwest[1] or state supreme courts in the Rockies[2] or county courts in the South,[3] but not those of the Great Plains.

Plains courts are complicated. The range of judicial experiences is diverse. All of the Plains states contain Native American courts. These include the nineteenth-century Courts of Indian Offenses, the twentieth-century tribal courts set up as a result of the Indian New Deal, and the twelfth-century or earlier traditional courts of the Pueblos. New Mexico contains courts from the Spanish, Mexican, and territorial periods. Texas, similarly, boasts Spanish and Mexican courts plus its own nine-year Republic judiciaries. Aside from Texas, all of the Plains states went through various territorial periods. All were unique. Courts from Louisiana Territory, Indian Territory, Dakota Territory, the Missouri District, and Washington Territory all extended to the Great Plains. Extra-legal court proceedings punctuated the range cattle industry throughout the Plains and mining in the Black Hills.

Indian courts and territorial courts of the Great Plains have not been systematically studied. Similarly, the ten state court systems have been ignored. Federal courts on the Great Plains have also not enjoyed scholars' attentions. Much remains to be done to this virgin territory of American legal history.

The two essays that follow are but a beginning. They include studies of the federal judiciary of the Western District of Missouri and modern tribal courts with specific reference to those functioning in South Dakota on Sioux reservations.

Lawrence H. Larsen, in his overview of the hundred-year history of federal judging in Missouri, explains the contributions federal district judges made to national jurisprudence. The Western Missouri District Court originally covered the entire northern Plains region but eventually was geographically restricted to the Plains periphery, headquartered out of Kansas City. This court's contributions range from direct participation in *Dred Scott v. Sandford*[4] and reconstruction legalisms to monitoring prohibition, prosecution of urban political corruption, and modern antitrust struggles. For Larsen, the federal judges at this particular court were careful, serious, competent judges. They were not bought-off political hacks who cared little about justice. The Western Missouri District Court even spawned a U.S. Supreme Court justice, Charles Whittaker.

Frank Pommersheim, himself a tribal court judge, offers a broad sweep of the problems confronting modern Indian courts in terms of their abilities to make a jurisprudential impact. Judge Pommersheim explains how significant it is for tribal courts to develop their judicial record with tribal customs in mind. He tells how the Rosebud Sioux Tribe severed its relationship with the federal government in the conduct of its tribal courts and how it is traveling the road of constitutionalism. He shows how the Chief Justice Marshalls—John Marshall of the U.S. Supreme Court and Sherman Marshall of the Rosebud Sioux Tribal Court—have tried to place Native American judges within a framework that includes the conflicting residues of sovereignty and colonialism.

NOTES

1. John R. Wunder, *Inferior Courts, Superior Justice: A History of Justices of the Peace on the Northwest Frontier, 1853–1889* (Westport, CT: Greenwood Press, 1979).

2. John D. W. Guice, *Rocky Mountain Bench* (New Haven, CT: Yale University Press, 1972).

3. Robert M. Ireland, *The County Courts in Antebellum Kentucky* (Lexington: University Press of Kentucky, 1972) and *Little Kingdoms: The Counties of Kentucky, 1850–1891* (Lexington: University Press of Kentucky, 1977).

4. *Dred Scott v. Sandford*, 19 US 303 (1857).

8

Observations on One Hundred Years of Federal Judging in Western Missouri District Court

Lawrence H. Larsen

It can be said that the judges of the United States District Court for the Western District of Missouri from 1857 to 1960[1] were not facile, compliant judges. They were not political hacks of little personality and few ideas who were intent on doing the bidding and carrying out the policies of the presidents who appointed them to the federal district bench. Rather, with perhaps one or two exceptions, they were, in the true sense of the word, leaders who displayed a great deal of judicial independence.

What is now known as the Western District of Missouri was originally the District of Missouri. At its creation in 1822, it covered roughly the northern half of the Louisiana Purchase that was unsettled. Federal judicial business for the central and northern Plains was carried to the Missouri region. After the Kansas-Nebraska Act of 1854, the district shrank significantly to encompass just the state of Missouri. Three years later Missouri was divided into two federal districts, the Eastern and Western Districts. Since 1857 the Western District of Missouri has been geographically stable.

The center for the Western District court eventually revolved around Kansas City. On the periphery of the Great Plains, Kansas City was evolving into a major metropolitan area. During the last quarter of the nineteenth century and the first quarter of the twentieth century it established itself as an economic and cultural magnet for the central Plains region.

JUDGE ROBERT WELLS

Originally, Missouri was one Federal District and President James Monroe appointed James H. Peck as the first judge in 1822. He served until his death in 1836 in a rather uneventful capacity.[2] Robert Wells succeeded Peck, functioning as a federal trial judge from 1836 until 1864. During Wells' tenure he witnessed the modern evolution of the Western District. He presided on circuit courts over the vast expanse of the central and northern Plains until 1854, over all of Missouri until 1857, and over the consolidated Western District until his death seven years later.

In 1857, because of the rapid growth of St. Louis and a sharp increase in steamboat cases, Congress divided Missouri into Eastern and Western Districts. Judge Wells was designated the Western District judge and Samuel Treat, a St. Louis politician and civic leader, became the first Eastern District judge. Judge Treat served for thirty years in the Eastern District, sitting in St. Louis. After he retired, he arranged and edited his papers prior to presenting them to the Missouri Historical Society, but he culled out any correspondence with the Western District judges, not considering it important enough to save for posterity.[3]

Judge Wells died in 1864 and his successor, Arnold Krekel, presided in the Western District from the spring of 1865 until he retired in 1888. On the surface, Judge Wells and Judge Krekel were very different men. Wells was a native-born American and Krekel a foreign-born German. Wells was a slave holder and Krekel an abolitionist. Wells felt that a federal judge should keep a hand in state affairs—Krekel felt the opposite. Wells was a Jacksonian Democrat, Krekel a Lincoln Republican.

Yet, despite the surface differences, the two eminent jurists shared many similarities. Both were of humble origin. Both went to a new state where they quickly rose to positions of trust and honor. Both served in the Missouri General Assembly. Both were prosecuting attorneys of St. Charles County, Missouri. Both wanted to establish colleges in Jefferson City—Wells failed, Krekel helped to found Lincoln University. Both were presidents of Missouri constitutional conventions. Both worked as surveyors. Although Wells owned slaves, both had a strong attachment to the Union and opposed the secession of Missouri. Krekel joined the Union forces and rose to the rank of colonel. While Wells was too old for service, one of his sons-in-law was an officer in the Union army.[4]

Wells remained very active in politics even after he became a judge. Although he resigned as attorney general of Missouri when he assumed the bench, he was a member of the state's Democratic committee, lobbying the

Missouri legislature to establish a state lunatic asylum and running successfully as a delegate to a state convention to write a new constitution for Missouri. Wells continued to operate a farm and when asked about the profitability of his agricultural operation, he replied, "Very good, but what bothers me is that Lawyer Wells has to pay too many of Farmer Wells' bills."[5]

Wells' most famous case was *Dred Scott v. Sandford.* Under the federal judiciary structure at that time, Wells was a circuit judge in Missouri and he presided over the *Dred Scott* case alone because the other circuit judge, James M. Wayne, was busy with the Missouri Supreme Court. Wells instructed the jury that Scott was still a slave, relying on a previous Missouri Supreme Court decision. *Dred Scott* was appealed to the United States Supreme Court, and Chief Justice Roger Taney ruled in his famous decision that Scott could not sue in federal court because he was not a citizen, that Congress had no power to restrict slavery in the territories, and that the Missouri Compromise was null and void. Wells indicated to friends that his feelings were in favor of Scott, and he wished the law was in his favor.[6]

JUDGE ARNOLD KREKEL

Arnold Krekel, who succeeded Judge Wells in 1865, was one of Lincoln's last appointments. Because of Judge Krekel's strong pro-Union attitudes, a large number of Missourians disliked him, considering him little more than an occupation judge. Krekel certainly had strong views. He required grand jury members to swear to an ironclad oath that they had not assisted or attempted to assist any person connected with the Confederate cause. A prospective juror, B. Gentry, a Columbia dry goods merchant who described himself as an "uncompromising Union man," volunteered that over his protests his brother had joined the Confederate forces of General Sterling Price. Gentry told the judge:

> At the battle of Wilson's Creek (near Springfield, Missouri), my brother was wounded in the knee, and later the surgeons amputated on his leg three times. He was about to die, and wanted to be brought to Columbia; and my mother, who lived in Columbia, wanted him brought home. I hired a teamster with a hack and obtained a permit from the Federal authorities to go through the lines to Springfield and return. He reached Springfield two hours before my brother's death, and he buried my brother in that city. I paid the teamster out of money belonging to my brother's estate, of which I was later the administrator. That, sir, is the only time I ever attempted to assist anyone connected with the cause of the South.

Judge Krekel replied, "Well, Mr. Gentry, if you did that, you are not qualified to serve on the United States grand jury. Stand aside."[7]

Judge Krekel had a practical sense of justice and of his role on the bench. A young German immigrant convicted of a crime threw himself on the mercy of the court, explaining that he had trouble supporting himself because he could not read or write English. The judge engaged in innovative sentencing. He sentenced the young man to jail with the stipulation that he be released upon acquiring English language skills. Under the compulsion of Judge Krekel's sentence, he passed a satisfactory language examination after a very brief confinement.[8] Over the years, Judge Krekel developed a serious hearing problem that impaired his performance, but he showed no sign of leaving the bench even though he was entitled to retire. After much thought, a group of distinguished members of the bar went to see him and asked him to consider retirement. The judge replied, "Vat, me retire? I should say not. When I go down the street now people say, 'Der comes Judge Krekel.' But if I should retire, they would say, 'Der comes that old Dutch son-of-a-bitch.' "[9]

JUDGE JOHN PHILIPS

Judge Krekel finally resigned in June 1888, a month before he died of Bright's disease. John Finis Philips, a member of the Kansas City Court of Appeals, succeeded him. Philips, a powerful figure in Missouri Democratic politics, was a Union colonel in the Civil War and a former U.S. Congressman.[10] Philips campaigned to become U.S. district judge even before Judge Krekel finally resigned.[11] Philips had a reputation as a very able lawyer, and the only question about him as a judge concerned his judicial temperament. It was said that he occasionally showed flashes of charm and humor, but that he was usually harsh, domineering, and sarcastic.

Philips was a resolute person who did not always follow convention. In 1883, while serving as a commissioner of the Missouri Supreme Court, an appellate position, he successfully defended Frank James, the brother of Jesse, in one of the most famous criminal proceedings in the history of the Show-Me-State, held in Gallatin. Philips, in closing arguments, destroyed Dick Liddel, the state's surprise star witness, recently released from an Alabama penitentiary, who placed Frank James at the crime scene. Philips, describing Liddel, said,

> He has been smuggled, hid and concealed from all other eyes than those of his master and trainer in Kansas City. Like some animal brought from an eastern jungle

for exhibition, he has been kept concealed from the public until the circus opened. He has been fed and housed at the courthouse in Kansas City under the guardianship of supple officers of that county, exercised, I presume, only between suns.[12]

In a bootlegging case tried by Judge Philips, an American Indian witness professed ignorance of the English language. After several attempts failed to elicit replies, Philips turned to the federal marshal and said, "Take this Indian out in the back yard and shoot him." Before that could be done, the Indian broke in that he understood.[13] In another case tried in the Ozarks of Missouri, a local lawyer by the name of Jim Moore kept addressing the witnesses by their first names, saying, "Now, Sam," "Now, George," "Now, Bill." Judge Philips admonished Moore by stressing, "You are accustomed to practicing in a justice of the peace court. This is a federal court. Discontinue addressing these witnesses by their given names." Moore apologized, but the next witness was an archetypical hillbilly. Lawyer Moore, forgetting himself, said, "Now, Rube, wasn't it this?" Judge Philips interrupted, "Well, as far as this witness is concerned, we shall waive the rule. You may call him Rube."[14]

Judge Phillips' most controversial actions came when he imprisoned many elected Missouri officials for failing to raise money to pay off railroad bond issues. These bonds had been issued years before by the counties to help build the railroads, and when the counties defaulted on the bonds, the bondholders sued in federal court. When officials in the Western District refused to raise taxes to pay off the bonds, Philips responded by finding them in contempt and either threatening or putting them in jail for varying lengths of time. One set of county administrative judges remained behind bars from October 1893, to May 1894.[15]

On June 25, 1910, Judge Philips, at the age of seventy-six, officially retired from the federal judiciary. The U.S. attorney in the Western District, Arba S. Van Valkenburgh, replaced Philips. A University of Michigan graduate, Van Valkenburgh had practiced law and had been a leader of the Republican party in Kansas City. As a U.S. attorney, Van Valkenburgh displayed inherent qualities of common sense in solving problems. In rebate cases, he stopped the illegal practices but declined to prosecute several obviously guilty prominent Kansas City businessmen who included close social friends in order to save the cost of a trial. The object was to find solutions and move along, even if it meant stretching the letter of the law. He displayed the same qualities on the bench, although during World War I he became caught up in wartime hysteria, handing down a very harsh ten-year sentence to a wealthy woman radical in an Espionage Act case. Van Valkenburgh was a federal judge until 1925, when he went to the Eighth Circuit Court of Appeals. He retired in 1933, remaining active until his death in 1944. Memorial resolutions emphasized his fine judicial temperament.[16]

THE REEVES AND OTIS REPUBLICAN TEAM

On January 24, 1923, President Warren G. Harding appointed Albert L. Reeves as an additional district judge in the Western District of Missouri. From the standpoint of Harding's corrupt administration, this proved to be an excellent appointment. Reeves, a rather grim-looking man with wire glasses, had seemingly perfect conservative Republican credentials. A respectable, but unspectacular individual, he appeared to be ordinary in every respect, a perfect Babbitt or Mr. Bridge. He belonged to the soundly correct Blue Hills Golf Club and the Kansas City Club. Although he had once run and lost a bid for Congress on the Republican ticket, his two Kansas City law partners were both Democrats. One, Fred Boxley, handled Harry S Truman's legal affairs. Reeves was appointed as a commissioner of the Missouri Supreme Court in 1921 and remained one until he became a federal judge. Judge Reeves had hardly settled in as a federal judge when he became the senior judge in the Western District.[17]

In 1925, when Judge Van Valkenburgh advanced to the Eighth Circuit Court of Appeals, his replacement was Merrill E. Otis. Judge Otis had received a bachelor's degree from the University of Missouri in 1906, a master's in 1907, and a law degree in 1910. He never belonged to a social fraternity because, according to him, "One had to have at least two sets of clothes to be eligible, and I was never able to qualify."[18]

A number of the cases handled by Reeves and Otis involved bootlegging. The standard sentence was a year and a day in jail. Under discretionary guidelines, unless the violator was a repeat offender, the amount of time behind bars was less, usually three or four months. Judge Reeves made sentencing for many Prohibition felons the most pleasant part of the trial experience, suggesting they were about to receive a vacation at federal expense. Judge Otis was just the opposite. He specialized in stern lectures on the evils of wrongdoing and made transgressors feel small and worthy of their punishment. His methods backfired, however, when he sentenced the mayor of Westphalia for bootlegging. Westphalia, a community near Jefferson City, had a heavily German populace who considered it their God-given right to ignore all federal laws that pertained to the demon drink.

A stranger seeking a place to buy illegal whiskey once asked the town marshal in Westphalia for directions. The marshal pointed to the highest point in town, which was the steeple of the Roman Catholic Church, and said, "Any place but there." The local populace did not take kindly to Judge Otis sentencing their mayor to a jail term. On the day he reported for sentencing in Jefferson City before Judge Otis, the town band accompanied him. When he left for jail, the band serenaded him. During his time behind bars, the mayor won a triumphant reelection. Upon completion of his sentence, the band played, the citizens cheered, and he returned home a conquering hero.[19]

The most famous case that Judges Reeves and Otis handled was the 1939 Thomas J. Pendergast income tax evasion case. Pendergast, the powerful political boss of Kansas City, ran the city as if it was his own personal business. Judge Reeves handled the federal grand jury that charged Pendergast with tax evasion and Judge Otis handled the case for trial. Pendergast changed his plea from not guilty to guilty and threw himself on the mercy of the court. Judge Otis imposed a sentence of fifteen months in the penitentiary and a $10,000 fine and five years of probation.[20] Pendergast became very sick while in jail and suffered a series of heart attacks. Although Judge Otis received a storm of criticism in newspaper editorials and from people all over the state who felt the sentence was grossly inadequate,[21] then-senator Truman approached President Franklin D. Roosevelt about a pardon for Pendergast. FDR refused in strong language to act favorably on the request.[22]

Truman bitterly denounced Reeves and Otis as the villains out to get Pendergast. He charged, "The federal court in Kansas City is presided over by two as violently partisan judges as ever sat on the federal bench." Truman called attention to Reeves' appointment by "that great advocate of clean, non-partisan government, Warren G. Harding," and to Otis' appointment by "that other great progressive non-partisan, Calvin Coolidge." Truman claimed that a Jackson County Democrat, the home county of both himself and Pendergast, had as much chance of a fair trial in the Western District "as a Jew would have in a Hitler court or a Trotsky follower before Stalin."[23] Judge Reeves, who had recently presided over vote fraud trials in Kansas City that resulted in many convictions of Pendergast henchmen and the striking from the roles of over 60,000 "ghost voters," passed Truman's remarks off as "a speech of a man nominated by ghost votes, elected by ghost votes, and whose speeches probably are written by ghost writers."[24]

NEW JUDGES IN MID-CENTURY

In 1937, the Western District gained another judge, John Caskie Collet, a member of the Missouri Supreme Court at the time of his appointment. Apparently, his selection resulted from a broker meeting at Pendergast's headquarters, 1908 Main Street in Kansas City, attended by Missouri's two Democratic Senators, Bennett C. Clark, Jr., and Truman.[25] Technically, although he sat in Kansas City, Judge Collet was a "roving judge," serving both Missouri federal judicial districts. At the end of World War II, while still a federal district court judge, Collet served President Truman in a cabinet level position. Judge Collet became an Eighth Circuit appellate judge in 1947.[26]

In 1943, the Western District gained another "roving judge," Richard N. Duncan. Judge Duncan had practiced law in St. Joseph, Missouri, where he was city counselor from 1927 to 1930. In 1932, he gained the backing of Tom Pendergast and won a seat in Congress from the Third District of Missouri in an at-large election. He won successive terms until he was defeated in 1942. In Congress, his chief claim to fame was a slavish support of Roosevelt and the New Deal.[27] Judge Duncan, realizing that he was probably going to be defeated in his bid for reelection, started working on trying to be designated as a federal judge. His plan of attack was to get Judge Otis, fresh from sending Pendergast to jail, elevated to the Eighth Circuit Court of Appeals. In pursuance of that strategy, he talked with Attorney General Robert Jackson. Jackson had never attended college or a college-affiliated law school. He was, however, a member of the American Bar Association and had heard Otis make a speech to the organization in which he stated that only college-trained individuals should be admitted to the bar.[28] After hearing Duncan extol Otis' qualifications, Jackson exerted all his power as attorney general of the United States against the nomination of Otis, stating, in effect, "Tell him [Otis] I heard that American Bar speech and that I will never help nominate him to be an appeals judge."[29] That was a message that Congressman Duncan understood, so he pursued other routes in his quest for a federal judgeship.

Judge Duncan was a close friend of Senator Truman. In early 1943, Truman proposed Duncan for a federal judgeship, a new post in the Western District. Attorney General Francis Biddle believed the folksy Duncan to be an incompetent. Federal Bureau of Investigation reports showed that all the lawyers interviewed in St. Joseph considered Duncan to be an inexperienced and mediocre attorney. The local bar association voted 23 to 1 against endorsing him, the only "yes" vote coming from his former law partner.

Attorney General Biddle noted that Duncan had never gone to law school. Biddle attempted to persuade Truman to select someone else. Truman would not back off. Biddle then tried to get President Roosevelt to deny the nomination, but FDR wrote to Biddle,

> I have done a great deal of checking and in spite of what you say about his legal ability I have a hunch that he has as much legal ability as at least half the people we put on the District Bench. What you need on a District Bench is old-fashioned, homespun common sense. This is more important than being able to teach at Harvard Law School.[30]

Duncan's name was sent up and he was confirmed.

Probably the most important case that Judge Duncan handled was the *Kansas City Star* antitrust case. The jury found that the *Kansas City Star* conspired to run its weak competitor, the *Kansas City Journal Post*, out of business. Judge Duncan handed down a harsh sentence. He fined the *Star* a million dollars, ordering it to stop its monopolistic business practices and to divest itself of a radio and television station. Losing the suit was a humiliating and costly episode for the proud and powerful Republican newspaper and civic institution in Kansas City. Judge Duncan had two framed excerpts from the *Star* side by side in his family room. One contained a black-bordered editorial denouncing his appointment to the federal bench; the other headlined that he had fined the paper one million dollars.[31]

Albert Ridge replaced Judge Otis, who died of cancer on December 23, 1944, at the age of sixty-two. Ridge, who had served in World War I in the 129th Field Artillery, Battery D, 35th Division, commanded by Captain Harry S Truman, saw action in France and received a citation for bravery. Ridge was a private first class at the time of his 1919 discharge. In 1921, he enrolled in the Kansas City School of Law. He did a great deal of his studying on the balcony of a downtown haberdashery shop run by Truman and another Battery D veteran, Eddie Jacobson. Ridge passed the Missouri bar in 1923 and graduated from law school in 1925. Truman nominated Ridge in January 1945, shortly before becoming vice president. President Roosevelt signed Ridge's commission on April 7, 1945, only five days before his death. During his sixteen years as a trial judge, Ridge distinguished himself by working to reform rules of procedure.

A FUTURE SUPREME COURT JUSTICE

In 1954, Judge Reeves retired and he was replaced by Charles E. Whittaker.[32] Whittaker had passed the Missouri Bar in 1923 and graduated the following year from the Kansas City School of Law. For many years, he was a lawyer in the important Kansas City law firm of Watson, Gage and Ess. Whittaker represented the *Kansas City Star* and its powerful editor, Roy Roberts. Whittaker was considered a skilled trial lawyer. Roberts was instrumental in persuading Dwight D. Eisenhower to run for president of the United States and helped him to be elected. When an opening developed on the bench of the Western District, Roberts suggested Whittaker and he was quickly nominated and confirmed. Judge Whittaker, while on the district bench, tried a sensational case involving Ross Brown, who in broad daylight kidnapped the wife of a Kansas City automobile dealer. Brown, at the point of a gun, forced his victim to drive into Johnson County, Kansas, where he raped and brutally murdered her and buried her in a shallow grave. Convicted and sentenced to death, Brown died in the Missouri gas chamber.[33]

In 1956, President Eisenhower appointed Judge Whittaker to the Eighth Circuit Court of Appeals, where he sat for nine months before his elevation to the Supreme Court of the United States to replace Justice Stanley F. Reed. Although Whittaker was easily confirmed, he had an unhappy time on the Supreme Court. He was a conservative and a believer in moderation and judicial restraint. He was on a very activist court. Justice William O. Douglas indicated that Whittaker could not make up his mind and kept switching his vote.[34] Apparently, the torment of the cases caused him to suffer from health problems that further hurt his performance. Justice Whittaker resigned from the Supreme Court in 1962 and returned to Kansas City. He maintained chambers in the Federal Court Building until his death in 1972. He had wanted to try cases, but Chief Justice Earl Warren refused to grant permission. He supposedly told an intermediary, "Tell him that I never could get him to make up his mind, and I'll be damned if I will let him do that to me again trying cases. So the answer is no."[35]

Justice Whittaker's replacement in the Western District, R. Jasper Smith, a former Republican Missouri legislator from Springfield, also believed in judicial restraint.[36] He came on the court at a time when his views of justice increasingly were out of fashion. He tried no major cases and died in 1962, replaced by another independent-minded judge, John W. Oliver, a Democrat and a legal activist. Traditions of independent judging set much earlier in the Western District continued to prevail.

CONCLUSION

Over one hundred years of judging in the Western District of Missouri federal courts have been characterized by strong judicial leadership. Thirteen judges have contributed markedly to the federal establishment of the rule of law in America's heartland.

The record includes a number of important decisions. Slavery issues, such as *Dred Scott v. Sandford*, and reconstruction concerns, such as the administration of the ironclad oath, were grappled with by Western District judges. Prohibition, local political corruption, the Pendergast Machine, and the *Kansas City Star* antitrust case all figure prominently in the federal court's work. Moreover, the Western District proved to be the setting for the initial judicial experience of a future U.S. Supreme Court justice, Charles Whittaker. The history of the federal judiciary of the district court of Missouri and the Great Plains offers a rich legacy.

NOTES

As the designated historian of the United States District Court for the Western District of Missouri, I wish to thank the help and support of the Historical Society of the United States District Court for the Western District of Missouri, especially that of U.S. Senior Judges Scott O. Wright, Howard F. Sachs, and the late William H. Becker, and of Society President F. Russell Millin.

1. A "Table of Succession" for the District Courts of Missouri can be found in Table 10, Theodore J. Fetter, *A History of the United States Court of Appeals for the Eighth Circuit*, Judicial Conference of the United States Bicentennial Committee (n.p., 1977). See generally Lawrence H. Larsen, *Federal Justice in Western Missouri: The Judges, the Cases, the Times* (Columbia: University of Missouri Press, 1994).

2. Charles B. Davis, "James Hawkins Peck," *Missouri Historical Review* 27 (October, 1932–July, 1933): 3–20; "James Hawkins Peck, Missouri's First Federal Judge—1788–1936," *Missouri Bar Journal* 3 (June, 1932): 92–93.

3. Samuel Treat Papers, Missouri State Historical Society, St. Louis, MO.

4. Roy T. King, "Robert William Wells, Jurist, Public Servant, and Designer of the Missouri State Seal," *Missouri Historical Review* 30 (January, 1936): 107–31; "Arnold Krekel: Second Judge of the United States District Court for the Western District of Missouri," Archives of the United States District Court for the Western District of Missouri, Kansas City, MO [hereafter referred to as Western District Archives].

5. Quoted in King, "Robert William Wells," pp. 107–31.

6. *Dred Scott v. Sandford*, 19 US 303 (1857). See also Harold Schwartz, "The Controversial Dred Scott Decision," *Missouri Historical Review* 54 (April, 1960):

262–72; Vincent C. Hopkins, *Dred Scott's Case* (New York: Antheneum, 1967); Don E. Fehrenbacher, *The Dred Scott Case: Its Significance in American Law and Politics* (New York: Oxford University Press, 1978).

7. North Todd Gentry, "Some Missouri Judges I Have Known," *Missouri Historical Review* 34 (April, 1940): 342–56.

8. Merrill E. Otis, "My Predecessors," in Alexander M. Meyer, ed., *In the Day's Work of a Federal Judge: A Miscellany of Opinions, Addresses and Extracts from Opinions and Addresses* (Kansas City, MO: Brown-White Co., 1937), p. 259.

9. Quoted in ibid., pp. 259–60. See Howard F. Sachs, "Missouri's Gilded Age, as Viewed by Judge Arnold Krekel," *Kansas City Bar Journal* 30 (June, 1955): 4–5, 13.

10. Howard F. Sachs, "Without 'Mawkish Deference': Notes on the Judicial Career of John Finis Philips, United States District Judge for the Western District of Missouri" (Draft, September, 1986), Western District Archives. See Floyd C. Shoemaker, "In Memorial: Judge John F. Philips," *Missouri Historical Review* 13 (October, 1918–July, 1919): 282–87.

11. "Appointment Files on John Philips," Department of Justice, Record Group 60, National Archives, Washington, DC.

12. Quoted in John T. Barker, "The Trial of Frank James," *Journal of the Missouri Bar* 13 (January, 1957): 3–6.

13. Merrill E. Otis, "Addresses to and About Lawyers," in Meyer, *Day's Work*, p. 229.

14. Quoted in ibid., p. 228.

15. Edwin L. Lopata, *Local Aid to Railroads in Missouri* (New York: Parnassus Press, 1937; repr. 1981). See "Imprisonment of State Officials by the Federal Courts: Message of Governor Stone of Missouri to the Legislators," *American Law Review* 27 (May-June, 1893): 393–402.

16. "Memorial Services for Arba S. Van Valkenburgh," Non-Record, National Archives—Central Plains, Kansas City, Missouri; *United States v. Rose Pastor Stokes*, Case No. 3536, Criminal Cases, 1879–1964, Kansas City Division, United States District Court for the Western District of Missouri, Records of United States District Courts, Record Group 21, National Archives—Central Plains [hereafter referred to as National Archives—Central Plains].

17. Floyd Calvin Shoemaker, *Missouri and Missourians: Land of Contrasts and People of Achievements*, 5 vols. (Chicago: Lewis Publishing Co., 1943), 5: 106–7; Albert L. Reeves, Jr., to Howard F. Sachs, December 17, 1986, January 8, 1987, Western District Archives.

18. Quoted in "Our Jurist President," *Kansas City Law Review* 1 (April, 1933): 1–2. See Shoemaker, *Missouri and Missourians*, 4: 55–57.

19. Quoted in meeting with William H. Becker, January 10, 1987, Western District Archives.

20. *Kansas City Star*, May 22, 1939. See Lyle W. Dorsett, *The Pendergast Machine* (Lincoln: University of Nebraska Press, 1980); Maurice M. Milligan, *Missouri Waltz: The Inside Story of the Pendergast Machine by the Man Who Smashed It* (New York: Scribner's Sons, 1948); William M. Reddig, *Tom's Town: Kansas City and the Pendergast Legend* (Philadelphia: J. B. Lippincott Co., 1947).

21. For example, see *Kansas City Times*, May 23, 1939; *St. Louis Globe Democrat*, May 23, 1939; *St. Louis Star-Times*, May 23, 1939; *Columbia [MO] Daily Tribune*, May 23, 1939; *St. Joseph [MO] Gazette*, May 23, 1939.

22. Quoted in John K. Hulston, *An Ozarks Lawyer's Story: 1946–1976* (Republic, MO: n.p., 1976), p. 90.

23. Quoted in Reddig, *Tom's Town*, p. 292.

24. Quoted in ibid.

25. *Kansas City Star*, December 24, 1936; *Kansas City Times*, January 1, March 10, 1937.

26. "In Memoriam: John Caskie Collet," Non-Record, National Archives—Central Plains.

27. "Missouri's New Federal Judges," *Missouri Bar Journal* 14 (June, 1943): 135–41.

28. Otis, "Intelligence at Bar, in Box, on Bench," in *Day's Work*, 213–20.

29. Quoted in Meeting with William H. Becker, March 26, 1988, Western District Archives.

30. Quoted in Francis Biddle, *In Brief Authority* (Garden City, NY: Doubleday, 1962), 202–4.

31. Hulston, *Ozark Lawyer's Story*, 90. See *United States v. Kansas City Star*, Case No. 7989, Criminal, Kansas City, Western District, National Archives—Central Plains.

32. "The Honorable Charles E. Whittaker Installed as United States District Judge," *Kansas City Bar Journal* 29 (September, 1954): 8–9; "Charles Evans Whittaker," *University of Kansas City Law Review* 42 (Fall, 1973): iii; "Charles E. Whittaker, 1901–73," *Journal of Missouri Bar* 30 (January-February, 1974): 61–62.

33. *United States v. Arthur Ross Brown*, Case No. 19376, Criminal, Kansas City, Western District, National Archives—Central Plains.

34. William O. Douglas, *Court Years: The Autobiography of William O. Douglas, 1939–1975* (New York: Random House, 1980), pp. 173–250. See Daniel M. Berman, "Mr. Justice Whittaker: A Preliminary Appraisal," *Missouri Law Review* 24 (January, 1959): 1–15; David N. Atkinson, "Retirement and Death on the United States Supreme Court: From Van Devanter to Douglas," *University of Missouri-Kansas City Law Review* 45 (Fall, 1976): 1–27.

35. Quoted in Meeting with William H. Becker, April 6, 1988, Western District Archives.

36. "Testimony of R. Jasper Smith, Nominee, June 26, 1956," File No. Sen 84B-A3; Nominations, Special Subcommittee of the Committee on the Judiciary, 84th Cong., Records of the U.S. Senate, Record Group 46, National Archives, Washington, DC.

9

Tribal Courts: Constitutional Decision Making and an Opportunity for Transformation

Frank Pommersheim

American Indian tribal courts are increasingly recognized as being important forums for the resolution of disputes that arise on reservations.[1] The growth in the stature and responsibility of tribal courts raises questions not only regarding how and what law will be applied in these forums,[2] but also raises questions of a different and more important order. This is especially true at the appellate and constitutional level and includes such questions as what narrative, what interpretive framework, and what aspirations, if any, will permeate these decisions.

Constitutional decision making in tribal courts provides a unique opportunity for the tribes, in the framework of actual cases, to develop a body of indigenous constitutional law. More specifically, this process promises, in part, to illuminate the role sovereignty will play in how tribal societies transform the present by integrating the best of the past with a liberating view of the possibilities of the future.[3] Within this larger context, there are also a number of textual and analytical questions concerning the nature and process of tribal constitutional adjudication. It is issues such as the nature of tribal foundational documents, theories of tribal constitutional adjudication, and the relationship of tribal constitutional decision making to federal and state constitutional processes that are the focus of this essay. Needless to say, all of this must be examined in a context that often provides for the perilous overview and review authority of Congress and the federal courts.[4] In addition, these issues will be examined in relation to tribal culture and institution building.

TRIBAL CONSTITUTIONS AS FOUNDATIONAL DOCUMENTS AND SOURCES OF MEANING

Tribal court constitutional decision making, like similar judicial decision making in state or federal courts, is *not* the simple utilization of the formula that calls for the application of the appropriate law to the facts, which, in turn, yields a credible decision. A more significant question is the principled direction that such decision making seeks to advance. Without awareness of the policy-making attributes of constitutional decision making, tribal courts are in danger of mimicking the sterile analytical rigor so often recommended to them, but that is often unhinged from the cultural context and vision of tribal communities. With this in mind, it is instructive to review the history and meaning of tribal constitutions and other tribal foundational documents.

It is important to note that in American political and legal culture the United States Constitution is authoritative—indeed supremely authoritative.[5] The authority vested in the Constitution requires controversies to be decided according to it. In addition, the Constitution is viewed as a *text* that is meaningful in the sense of being meaning-ful, full of meaning.[6] These observations serve to highlight some important threshold questions in the area of tribal court constitutional and appellate adjudication.

When examining tribal constitutions, it is not to be presumed that these documents are either supremely authoritative or a text full of meaning. The reason for this is rooted in the origins of most tribal constitutions, as well as the existence of other organic sources of authority, namely treaties, that may have an equal or even more ascendant claim as supremely authoritative and full of meaning. Many tribal constitutions were adopted pursuant to the enabling provisions set forth in the Indian Reorganization Act of 1934[7] (hereinafter IRA). Originally, section 17 of the IRA provided:

> Any Indian tribe, or tribes, residing on the same reservation, shall have the right to organize for its common welfare, and may adopt an appropriate constitution and bylaws, which shall become effective when ratified by a majority vote of the adult members of the tribe, or of the adult Indians residing on such reservation, as the case may be, at a special election authorized and called by the Secretary of Interior under such rules and regulations as he may prescribe. Such constitution and bylaws, when ratified as aforesaid, and approved by the Secretary of Interior. . . . Amend-

ments to the constitution and bylaws may be ratified and approved by the Secretary in the same manner as the original constitution and bylaws.[8]

This almost unlimited approval authority of the Secretary of the Interior has only recently been somewhat narrowed. The Secretary must now exercise his or her authority within forty-five days of the tribal election or the inaction will be considered as approval.[9] More importantly, it must approve any tribal constitution or amendment unless there is a finding "that the proposed Constitution and bylaws or any amendments are contrary to applicable laws."[10]

In light of this overarching secretarial authority, a salient question emerges concerning the quality and authenticity of the tribal constitutions adopted pursuant to the IRA authorizing legislation. These constitutions did *not* come into being as the result of tribal constitutional conventions that might have distilled the wisdom and insights of tribal people and their traditions, but rather from the handiwork of the top-down Bureau of Indian Affairs. Throughout the 1930s when most tribes organized under the IRA, the Department of the Interior prepared model constitutions for tribes.[11] A leading survey of tribal courts noted that, "the boilerplate provisions of this model were adopted by virtually all tribes which voted to organize under that Act. . . . Thus, although the IRA was designed to restore residual powers to tribal sovereignty, the extent and exercise of those powers were determined largely by the Interior Department."[12]

Many of these constitutions provided for an ongoing review authority by the Secretary of the Interior to approve amendments to tribal constitutions, as well as tribal ordinances adopted pursuant to these constitutions. The paternalistic and colonizing agenda of the Bureau of Indian Affairs knew few, if any, bounds. As noted by the Supreme Court, "The BIA had a policy of including provisions for secretarial approval, but that policy was not mandated by Congress."[13]

Indeed, these "model" constitutions omitted at least two hallmark provisions from the "model" United States Constitution, namely the protections of the Bill of Rights and the doctrine of separation of powers. Not coincidentally perhaps, these very omissions are the ones that tribes are most criticized for, when in fact the blame lies elsewhere.[14] Of course, the IRA did not mandate the absence of these protections.

As a result, many tribes were effectively cut off from incorporating important tribal values into their constitutions, as well as shackled with "model" constitutions that blatantly ignored the distinctive and crucial elements that made the United States Constitution the emulative model in the first instance. It is, therefore, not difficult to understand that tribal constitutions do not, as a rule, occupy within their own communities the same high moral and legal ground as the United States Constitution holds in American legal and political culture.

LAKOTA CONSTITUTIONAL CONCERNS FOR TRIBAL COURTS

In spite of this problematic history, tribes are increasingly adept and conscious of the necessity to seize and to bend their constitutions in order to make them more responsive to a tribally defined understanding of present and future needs and aspirations. For example, a number of tribes, including the Rosebud Sioux Tribe,[15] adopted Bill of Rights amendments to their constitutions before enactment of the Indian Civil Rights Act of 1968[16] mandated such guarantees throughout Indian country.

More recently, the Rosebud Sioux Tribe adopted a constitutional amendment which, on one hand, removed the review authority of the Secretary of the Interior from tribal council legislative decisions.[17] This tribal constitutional provision effectively abolished the Secretary's authority to "interfere" in the duly elected tribal council's exercise of its legislative functions. On the other hand, and even more transformative, the tribe adopted an amendment that explicitly allows for the calling of a tribal constitutional convention. The requirements are:

> Upon receipt of a petition that contains the signatures of at least thirty (30) per cent of the voters in the last tribal election, the Tribal Secretary shall refer the petition to the next Tribal Council meeting which shall call a Tribal Constitution convention to commence within thirty (30) days and to appoint a seven member Tribal Council, to conduct this Convention for the purpose of hearing proposed amendments, and to approve those of which shall be referred to the Secretary of Interior, and upon receipt of them, it shall be the duty of the Secretary of Interior to set an election as described in Section 1 above.[18]

Such actions reflect a deliberate and concerted effort to breathe new life into documents of hierarchy and control.

The Rosebud Sioux Tribe has not yet utilized this provision to call a constitutional convention. However, I have witnessed and participated in numerous conversations with tribal members about the possibility. These conversations are marked by excitement, challenge, and a deep sense of historical and cultural responsibility. The constitutional amendment process "is an important instrument with which the political community can exercise its stewardship over the living tradition. If constitutional adjudication is one occasion for moral discourse and growth, the amendment process is another such occasion."[19]

Such efforts may be complemented by tribal efforts to identify other vital sources of law with which to shape the contours of tribal aspiration. A most likely source here, of course, is treaties. Treaties are significant on a number of different levels. Treaties, at least for many tribes, represent a high point of tribal sovereignty when tribes dealt with the federal government on a true government-to-government basis. Treaties represent the political and legal adjustments between the western march of an expansionary American society and the staunch resistance of established tribal societies.[20]

Treaties not only represent a high point of tribal sovereignty, but are also instrumental in establishing a permanent and constitutional link between the tribes and the federal government:

> The treaties that established reservations did much more. They helped create the enduring and special legal and moral relationship that exists between the federal government and Indian tribes. Treaties also reflect a set of sovereign promises and expectations that continue to be at the heart of defining the modern contours of this relationship.[21]

It is also important to note that many tribes, including the Sioux Tribes of South Dakota, did not view the treaty as mere expedience and the power politics of the day, subject to future accommodation of other emerging national interests. Every treaty was settled with the smoking of the pipe. As noted by Father Peter John Powell, the well-known historian and anthropologist:

> [W]hites, rarely, if ever, have understood the sacredness of the context in which treaties were concluded by Lakota people. . . . "The pipe never fails," my people, the Cheyennes say. For the pipe is the great sacramental, the great sacred means that provides unity between the Creator and the people. Any treaty that was signed was a sacred agreement because it was sealed by the smoking of the pipe. It was not signed by the Chiefs and headmen before the pipe had been passed. Then the smoking of the pipe sealed the treaty, making the agreement holy and binding.
>
> Thus, for the Lakota, the obligations sealed with the smoking of the pipe were sacred obligations.[22]

Treaties are, of course, recognized as the "supreme law of the land" under the United States Constitution's Supremacy Clause[23] and serve as the legal and moral cornerstone for many tribes. Treaties are therefore sufficiently located in tribal law and history to be properly considered "supremely authoritative" and full of meaning. All of this, however, is subject to potentially debilitating federal review—both legislative and judicial[24]—but it does, nevertheless, identify a potential core of tribal foundations law with which to address contemporary goals and issues.

Treaties and tribal constitutions, when placed side by side, provide a valuable complement and reinforcement to each other as brackets of tribal authority and meaning. Treaties are, in many ways, most suited as the primary legal vector to orient tribal-federal government to government relations. In addition, treaties served to establish and to advance the appropriate legal and diplomatic protocols to maintain tribal territorial and governmental integrity. Tribal constitutions, in turn, are more central to the task of identifying day-to-day values and principles that are vital to developing tribal societies which are committed to the flourishing of individual and communal life within their borders. These parameters are not, of course, mutually exclusive, but rather represent zones of activity and concern with different centers and overlapping common areas.

There are, of course, other potential sources of tribal foundational law such as tradition and custom including, for example, principles that are part of the oral tradition. However, the significant point is the overriding importance of engaging in the on-going process of identifying authoritative legal sources of tribal aspiration in order that tribal court decision making be as meaningful as possible.

THEORIES OF TRIBAL CONSTITUTIONAL ADJUDICATION

Having identified the potentially "supremely authoritative" tribal foundational documents that are most meaningful, the next question is how tribal courts might approach their interpretive function when they encounter tribal foundational law. The two most likely theories of constitutional adjudication that might pertain to tribal constitutional adjudication are of originalism and non-originalism. These theories bracket the broad range of interpretive possibilities, which are also often spoken of somewhat imprecisely, as from conservative to liberal or from "strict" construction to "loose" construction. The important point to emphasize in this area is the issue of choice in adopting an appropriate interpretive strategy that is politically and culturally resonant from the tribal point of view.[25] These terms, in turn, suggest a broad range of interpretive possibilities.

The notion of originalism holds that: [T]o "interpret" the Constitution is to ascertain the original meaning—the beliefs the text was originally understood to symbolize—and then to answer the question of what significance, if any, those beliefs have for the conflict at hand, what those beliefs mean for the conflict at hand, what those beliefs if accepted, require the court to do, if anything, with respect to the conflict at hand.[26]

This describes the prototype of legal analysis: identify the applicable "rule" and apply it to the facts of the case. Admittedly, in the context of originalist constitutional adjudication, the search for the "rule" also includes a search to identify the original meaning or value assigned to the constitutional provision by the framers and ratifiers of the Constitution. This may not always be an easy task and is one which is fraught with its own hermeneutic problems. Yet it is not difficult to view the process as essentially frozen in time, independent of, and potentially cut off from, contemporary reality and political discourse. For many, in fact, this would constitute a good thing.[27]

Non-originalism, on the other hand, does not reject originalism, but simply goes beyond its singular approach. To the non-originalist, the constitutional text is meaningful in its original sense, but it is meaningful in an additional sense in that at least some constitutional provisions signify fundamental aspirations of the American political tradition.[28] A text is not constrained to a singular meaning, and in the case of the constitution, it may be argued that it has grown to include "certain basic, constitutive aspirations or principles or ideals of the American political community and tradition."[29] The best examples here include the free speech, press, and religion provisions of the First Amendment; the due process clause of the Fifth Amendment; and the due process and equal protection clauses of the Fourteenth Amendment.

The originalism approach applied to tribal constitutional adjudication is deeply problematic. Given the colonialist intrusion and presence of the Bureau of Indian Affairs in many tribal constitutions, it hardly makes sense to regard this handiwork as unduly authoritative. Undoubtedly, most provisions in tribal constitutional texts, as with the federal constitution, are reasonable and without substantial controversy.[30] Nevertheless, it is critical that indigenous people, if they are to pursue a true course of liberation and self-determination, identify a foundational text(s) and a theory of constitutional interpretation that enhances this potential development. Non-originalist constitutional theory holds promise in assisting this development. Therefore, one of the major tasks of tribal constitutional adjudication is to identify and to evaluate the fundamental aspirations and ideals of the tribal community.

In the context of tribal court constitutional adjudication, these models raise important questions. While the originalist approach is basically straightforward legal analysis, application of the non-originalist approach is not so easy to identify in the tribal court setting. The aspirational component of the political-legal community, and the tradition that it reflects, emerges over time. Tribal courts are very young. Most were established after the IRA of 1934 and most have become significantly active only within the last fifteen to twenty years. Therefore, this part of the tribal tradition is quite recent in its development. Treaties, however, are significantly older. Tribal culture and tradition, of course, are quite ancient.

This configuration presents some unique challenges. Tribal courts do not, as a general rule, have access to a body of established tribal constitutional precedent that helps to form and to provide guidance to the potential aspirational component of tribal constitutional adjudication. This problem, in turn, is exacerbated by the external Bureau of Indian Affair roots of most tribal constitutions. These items do not in any way constitute an insuperable bar. Rather, these facts suggest a cautionary note that the efforts of the tribal courts will need be both venturesome and circumspect; venturesome, in the sense of identifying the sources of the aspirational components. However, they must also be circumspect in the sense of properly grounding decisions within the matrix of reasonable analytical processes and legal reasoning.[31]

In this regard, the early decisions in Indian law authored by Chief Justice John Marshall are instructive. In the seminal cases of *Johnson v. McIntosh*,[32] *Cherokee Nation v. Georgia*,[33] and *Worcester v. Georgia*,[34] the Supreme Court was confronted with important questions about the rights and status of Indian tribes within a young republic. In these cases, with minimal guidance from the text of the Constitution,[35] Justice Marshall articulated a vision of tribes as possessing a unique position as "domestic dependent nations" and "distinct, independent political communities" within an emerging national federalism.[36] This position was grounded in a recognition of tribal sovereignty that was largely to be independent of state aggression and interference.[37] These nascent doctrines were not grounded in precedent because there was none. Rather, they were fashioned from some combination of political-legal expediency and a certain moral urgency. These views have been seriously vitiated and increasingly attenuated over the years, but they have not been overruled or completely abandoned.[38]

Paradoxically, these early cases also framed a despotic imperialism and racism to justify federal title to Indian land and attendant federal hegemony in Indian affairs. This is most apparent in *Johnson v. McIntosh*, which rested almost entirely on the spurious and self-serving "doctrine of discovery."[39]

This federal hegemony developed without constitutional safeguard or limits and, ultimately, spawned the astounding doctrine of congressional "plenary power" in Indian affairs.[40] This bifurcated, if not fully schizophrenic, approach to tribal sovereignty as either extensive and enduring, or marginal and fleeting, has further complicated the context in which tribal court constitutional adjudication takes place. This federal inconsistency has been exacerbated by the tendency of the federal courts and Congress to approach Indian tribes as little more than legislative objects rather than free-standing constitutional subjects.

In addition, elaboration of the concepts of community and tradition is required to interpret a foundational constitutional text. A functional definition of community describes the concept as a group of persons united principally by their identification of themselves as the present bearers of, and participants in, a tradition. Tradition, in turn, is perhaps best understood as the history or narrative in which the central theme is an aspiration to achieve a particular form of life and to certain projects, goals, and ideals. The central discourse within the tradition is an argument about how that form of life is to be cultivated and revised.[41] The purpose of constitutional and other foundational texts is to charter and mandate the form of life to which a particular community and tradition aspire. The foundational text, therefore, symbolizes the mandate.[42]

These definitions of a foundational text and its community and tradition will seem to many, perhaps, as more pertinent to interpretation in the "sacred" as opposed to any "constitutional" sense. But that is just the point—the analogy to "sacred texts" is very resonant to a "non-originalist" conception of constitutional adjudication.[43] Such texts, whether "sacred" or "constitutional," particularly given their "aspirational" and indeterminate nature, become irrepressible with an "excess of meaning."[44] For example, Justice Harlan in *Poe v. Ullman*[45] spoke of the importance of "approaching the text which is the only commission for our power not in a literalistic way, as if we had a tax statute before us, but as the basic charter of our society, setting out in spare but meaningful terms the principles of government."[46] Such an emphasis on community, tradition, and "sacredness" is also likely to be more resonant with Native American cultures and history.[47]

Yet there is not only this making or creating of meaning and tradition, but its complement of being creatures of that tradition. It is this double yoke of creating and creatureliness—the tension between the dynamic verb and the stately noun—that makes for the essence of the mediation of the past and the present that is at the heart of the acts of interpretation and stewardship.[48] This description is certainly well understood within Indian culture and tradition. For example, as noted by Vine Deloria, Jr., and his co-author Clifford Lytle:

> First, there must be a structural reform of tribal governing institutions that is fundamental but also permits a continuity between past and present. . . . Second, some kind of determined and lasting cultural renewal must take place to resolve the question of Indian identity in the modern world; here emotional continuity must be recognized and considered seriously.[49]

The response to these challenges will do much to determine the nature and quality of tribal and reservation life in the immediate future. Tribal court constitutional adjudication will be a significant strand in the braid of that response. Without such tribal constitutional underpinnings, there can be a tragic loss of identity and purpose to the pervasive intrusion of extrinsic legal demands and forces.

As suggested by the late Robert Cover,

> No set of legal institutions or prescriptions exists apart from the narratives that locate it and give it meaning. For every constitution there is an epic, for each decalogue a scripture. Once understood in the context of the narratives that give it meaning, law becomes not merely a system of rules to be observed, but a world in which we live.[50]

In part, this insight describes the legacy that tribal courts inherit and must necessarily confront and transform in the process of their development and decision making. The traditional law and narrative of many tribes, and most certainly, the Sioux Tribes of South Dakota, place emphasis on community, cooperation, and relatedness. However, the dominant legal narrative of majoritarian jurisprudence is often rooted in individualism, competition, and autonomy. Therefore, tribal court decision making inevitably confronts the necessity of developing a blend of these values, a transmutation that synthesizes the tension created by these pressures of dominant intrusion from "above" and of culture and tradition from "below."[51]

The dilemma of the Sioux Tribes is not unlike the situation that all tribal institutions face as they seek to navigate between the tradition and roots of their past and the often uncharted frontiers of the present and future. It is important to note the essential fragility of law and legal decisions that are not grounded in a supporting culture and social reality. The law helps to shape the community reality and ideal, as well as, in return, being shaped and informed by it. Tribal court decision making which is unhinged from this process will surely become irrelevant and even inimical to the achievement of a meaningful tribal future. It is this perspective of law as both tradition and aspiration defining the "world in which we live" that most eloquently illustrates the law's responsibility and meaning within tribal culture at large.

COMMUNITY AND INSTITUTION BUILDING

The law is also about power—the jurisdictional power to render justice and achieve other socially enhancing goals. However, the ability to realize worthy objectives requires more than jurisdiction and power; it requires expertise, resources, and community support. Practitioners and scholars of Indian law are often not cognizant enough of this political and social reality. Theory and practice in Indian law are too often unhinged from the political commitment to institution building which is necessary to make the possibilities of the law meaningful. Any tribal jurisdictional authority confirmed by Congress or the U.S. Supreme Court must, in turn, be complemented by tribal resources and institutions capable of implementing that authority in such a way that the ideals and principles of the law are realized in practice. Without this understanding, much Indian law scholarship is, or is in danger of, becoming a misleading abstraction cut off from the frontiers of significant tribal development. A supportive body of federal Indian law is a necessary, but not sufficient, condition for building a flourishing cultural and institutional future in Indian country. The field of Indian law needs to extend its range, to ground itself in tribal reality, and to avoid the temptation of becoming a thing unto itself—a useless reification.[52]

An important and related caution to heed is the fact that the law in general, and Indian law in particular, cannot be an end in itself. The law does not make things happen, but rather creates a normative space[53] in which to realize and effectuate individual and cultural values. The normative space created by tribal sovereignty validated by federal Indian law stands in need of creative and viable tribal institutions in order to achieve the social and cultural objectives embodied in the law. This latter effort is often a long, unheralded struggle, but it is, arguably, the most important foundation for the future. It is important not to lose sight of the fact that all significant public values are realized through institutions. Better institutions are essential to better lives.[54]

Unfortunately, many in the field of Indian law, including scholarly commentators, often pay insufficient attention to this issue.[55] The result is to create a grossly distorted picture of the relationship of law to sovereignty.

It further obscures the relationship of politics and institution building to law and the realization of significant tribal values. For example, the fact that tribal sovereignty and federal Indian law currently endorse the significance of tribal courts[56] cannot deflect concern from the concomitant necessity for tribal courts to continue to develop their resources, competence, and insights. For it is, after all, both theory and practice, both authority and its implementation, that determine the quality of justice rendered.

This foundational predicate includes the necessity of developing increasing political support and understanding of tribal courts. Institutional support needs to come from all quarters, but particularly from both the Indian and non-Indian communities subject to the authority of tribal courts, including those members of the legal profession who practice before them. For example, on the Rosebud Sioux Reservation, Chief Justice Sherman Marshall[57] holds an annual week-long Tribal Court Open House in which members of the tribal and general public are invited to visit the courthouse and listen to a series of presentations on the policies and procedures of the Tribal Court. The topics of these presentations range from the filling out of forms to the structure and function of the tribal court appellate system. Chief Justice Marshall also makes it a point to visit all the tribal communities to explain the nature and duties of the Tribal Court. This is particularly important, because as Chief Justice Marshall notes,[58] many tribal people do not understand, and have a negative view, of their tribal courts.

In addition, Chief Justice Marshall has organized a group of Indian and non-Indian attorneys, who appear regularly before the Rosebud Sioux Tribal Court, to serve as an advisory group concerning legal practice issues before the court. This group is clearly a precursor to a functioning tribal bar association.[59] Without this kind of understanding and action, tribal sovereignty and federal Indian law are in danger of becoming abstractions disconnected from the reality and challenge of community and institutional life on the reservation. Even worse, tribal sovereignty itself may be threatened by the very failure to establish an adequate base of financial resources and institutional development. For example, at recent hearings of the U.S. House of Representatives Committee on Interior and Insular Affairs in South Dakota, most of the testimony provided about tribal courts focused on how well they are working or not working in their day-to-day operation, rather than on their theoretical or jurisdictional underpinnings. This is the kind of "reality," rightly or wrongly, that is likely to affect Congress rather than any general analysis of federal Indian law.

Much of the problem concerning tribal sovereignty within the national, state, and even many tribal legal communities is the absence of any foundational web of beliefs about tribal sovereignty. Without this foundational agreement or understanding that tribal sovereignty exists and what its roots and baseline horizons are, the entire field flounders. Tribal sovereignty often seems to be extraordinarily precarious and at risk. For example, the overwhelming membership of the state and federal practicing bar and judiciary have no training in Indian law. Furthermore, since the Indian law presence is only nominal in other parts of the curriculum,[60] most members of the practicing bar and judiciary have no sense of what tribal sovereignty and the principles of self-determination mean. As a result, the legal and constitutional context of tribal sovereignty is not readily apparent. Therefore, almost every instance of discourse on Indian law requires substantial "education" in order to achieve any threshold understanding of the most important concepts within the field. This is an incredibly burdensome but necessary task, which reflects the pervasive ignorance and distortion that permeate the understanding of sovereignty and Indian law doctrine within the national and state legal communities.

This problem is exacerbated because the thrust of tribal sovereignty is often "counter" to the thrust of that of other minority groups within this country. The object of almost all litigation of other minorities in this society is increased access to rights and institutions within the dominant society. This goal is well understood, even if resisted, within the dominant legal and judicial community. However, the object of most, if not all, tribally initiated or defended Indian law litigation is to establish and vindicate a historical, non-assimilated right to an autonomy that seeks to preserve a "measured separatism."[61] This emphasis is not recognized within the national and state legal communities' web of beliefs. Therefore mutuality and dialogue in the context of federal awareness and understanding of tribal court decision making is critical to expand the foundational web of beliefs that federal and state legal communities bring to Indian law matters.

Belief in tribal sovereignty does not, at least to me, mean that tribes always "win." Rather, it means that their basic sovereignty is recognized as permanent, enduring, and located in, and vouchsafed by, the federal constitution. Only when this is accomplished will it be truly possible to determine the specifics of tribal sovereignty in the thick detail and practice of adjudicating individual cases, just as it occurs in the context of state and federal sovereignty.

The absence of any truly constitutionalized understanding of tribal sovereignty is problematic not only at the level of political and legal rhetoric, but more significantly, it is a serious destabilizing force in the day-to-day political, cultural, and institutional life of tribes. Any project, particularly one that is relative to law and jurisdiction, is subject to unilateral defeasance by Congress or the federal courts.[62] A sovereignty of sufferance, oxymoronic on its face, does not provide an environment conducive to meaningful self-determination or realization.

The process of tribal court constitutional adjudication promises to articulate an emerging vision of tribal sovereignty. It will also, in parallel fashion, advance the ongoing process which recognizes, from the tribal perspective, the authenticity of tribal courts as legitimate and significant tribal institutions. Tribal authenticity is, of course, not a given because tribal courts, like most other tribal institutions, do not have their structural roots in pre-contact, pre-colonial times.[63] This "inside/out" authenticity, in turn, must meet the potential strictures and constraints of judicial and congressional review that are necessary to achieve a complementary "top-down" authenticity. It is the synthesis that results from this delicate passage between these often competing sources of validation that holds the key to a meaningful and flourishing future.

COMPARATIVE HORIZONS

Constitutional decision making in tribal courts can also potentially perform other important functions, in addition to its central task of illuminating the distinctive markers of tribal sovereignty. These functions include delineating the relationship of tribal courts to federal courts, providing tribal interpretations of federal standards, and incorporating international legal norms into tribal jurisprudence. These are all relevant and promising avenues of development for tribal courts.

Congress has failed to address the relationship of tribal courts to federal courts.[64] The United States Constitution is silent on this matter. Therefore, to date, the task of attempting to describe these parameters has largely fallen to the federal courts, especially the U.S. Supreme Court. The Supreme Court has begun this task in the *National Farmers Union Insurance Company v. Crow Tribe of Indians*[65] and *Iowa Mutual Insurance Company v. LaPlante*[66] cases, by staking out some of the territory relevant to review of tribal court assertions of jurisdiction. Both of these decisions make it clear that the Supreme Court expects tribal courts to fully articulate their own view of the scope of tribal jurisdictional authority.[67] Federal review, when it follows, is a *de novo* consideration of the federal question presented by tribal assertions of jurisdiction.[68] Therefore, it is incumbent upon tribal courts, even when direct tribal constitutional questions are not involved, to persuasively develop convincing legal rationales to support assertions of tribal jurisdiction.

There are intriguing questions about the potential deference to, rather than review of, some tribal court jurisdictional decision making. While it is clear, for example, that federal courts may review tribal court jurisdictional decision making in light of alleged mistakes about the contours of federal law relevant to tribal jurisdiction, it is less clear what a federal court should do when the alleged tribal court mistake is not one of federal law, but rather of tribal law.[69] Here, tribal courts need to articulate the rationale that just as federal courts are bound by the construction of state law of the highest state court, they ought to be similarly bound by the interpretation of tribal law by the highest tribal court. In many instances, tribal constitutional adjudication will come into play only if the tribal court has jurisdiction in the first place. It is therefore necessary for tribal courts to deploy sufficient analytical rigor to maximize the likelihood of success at the jurisdictional level which, in turn, will often open the way to a proper consideration of tribal constitutional law.

Tribal constitutional adjudication may also be fruitfully compared to the growing trend and attention paid to state constitutional adjudication.[70] This growth can be traced to two important developments: state willingness to provide greater civil liberties protections for its citizens than those required by the United States Constitution,[71] and state interest in insulating its decisions from Supreme Court review.[72] These developments have sparked a small but noticeable shift in law school curricula toward developing courses and materials in this area.[73] Similar developments in Indian law would alleviate the tendency to confine Indian law to the margins of the law school curriculum.[74]

These developments suggest similar options for tribes and tribal courts to consider. Although tribes are bound by the Indian Civil Rights Act of 1968, as the states are by the federal Bill of Rights, they would have a free hand to develop their own view of civil rights protection as a matter of tribal constitutional law. This is already true of some tribal constitutions[75] and seems an obvious building block of tribal sovereignty. The question becomes: how do the tribes and tribal courts construe the parameters of basic civil rights guarantees completely apart from any federal mandate, such as the Indian Civil Rights Act of 1968? In addition, tribes need to pursue creative avenues to limit federal court review of tribal court decision making. This raises even broader questions about tribal constitutions and their relationship to state and federal constitutions. The federal constitution is a charter of enumerated powers, while state constitutions are general limitations on the otherwise wide-ranging sovereign power of the states. "Therefore, the great questions of federal constitutional interpretation involve implied *powers*, whereas the great questions of state constitutional interpretation concern implied *limitations*.[76]

This fundamental difference between state and federal constitutions would seem to be a matter of significant tribal constitutional importance. Little has been written in this area. Obviously, the "plenary power" doctrine suggests limited tribal authority, but that is not quite the question. The initial question is the meaning of a tribal constitutional text as interpreted by the highest tribal appellate court. For example, many tribal constitutions make reference to specific enumerated powers and broad unspecified reserved powers.[77] Is the tribal constitutional text a charter of only limited powers or one of extensive powers with only implied limitations? This issue thus raises the question of the parameters of tribal sovereignty and tribal constitutional authority within the national republic. Thoughtful tribal constitutional exegesis of these issues can play a vital role in resolving questions at the tribal level and inaugurating and contributing important dialogue at the national level.

Tribes and tribal courts are also poised to consider pathbreaking constitutional constructions. While the heart of traditional constitutional "faith" is its commitment to those individual rights vouchsafed in the Bill of Rights, that constellation of aspiration may be inadequate to capture the real essence of a complementary tribal goal to preserve and enhance a set of cultural rights. In this vein, the emerging set of international norms relevant to indigenous people provides a rich benchmark for tribal consideration. These norms include: (1) recognition of the distinctive nature of indigenous peoples' collective rights; (2) the centrality of territorial rights to indigenous survival; (3) the recognition of indigenous peoples' right to self-determining autonomy; and (4) international legal protection of indigenous rights.[78] This international core of indigenous peoples' rights could be constitutionalized directly through the amendment process and/or that process of constitutional interpretation of the relevant tribal constitutional text. All of these steps, taken individually or collectively, offer the potential to advance tribal constitutional foundations and aspirations, as well as enrich the national jurisprudence of pluralism and equality.

FEDERAL CONSTRAINTS AND OPPORTUNITIES

Any opportunity for transformation within tribal court appellate and constitutional decision making faces potential impediments and constraints from the pervasive federal authority over Indian affairs. These potential limiting factors come from two different sources within the federal government: first, the power of federal courts to review much of tribal court decision making[79] and second, the overarching "plenary power"[80] of Congress in Indian affairs.

The dialectic of these twin forces is, perhaps, best illustrated within the context of the Indian Civil Rights Act of 1968.[81] The act requires all tribal governments, as a matter of federal law, to provide a wide range of rights, drawn largely from the Bill of Rights, to all persons within a reservation. The only remedy specified in the act is the writ of habeas corpus.[82] In *Santa Clara Pueblo v. Martinez*,[83] the Supreme Court held that habeas relief was the exclusive remedy created by the act and it did *not* authorize any implied civil rights cause of action independent of habeas relief.[84] The Court also indicated that one of the effects of its decision was to change the law that tribal courts would have to apply.[85] Thus, under the *Santa Clara* holding, claims not amenable to habeas corpus relief are diverted to tribal court. Decisions of tribal courts in these matters do not appear to be reviewable in federal courts.

This result has provided some controversy. Amending legislation has been introduced in Congress to increase the purview of federal district court reviewing authority of tribal court decisions made under the Indian Civil Rights Act.[86] This pending legislation clearly falls within the wide-ranging plenary authority of Congress in Indian affairs. Yet it epitomizes the tension between pervasive federal review on one hand and respect for tribal sovereignty on the other. This debate further illustrates the deeper question of what the purpose of federal review is in the first place—to encourage law that emanates from another strand in the braid of American pluralism, with review reserved for situations that diverge only markedly from the federal canon? Or is it to insure a similarity of result and assimilation of difference? The answers to these questions are not obvious, but it is important, nevertheless, to consider them.

There is some helpful guidance in the form of lower federal court jurisprudence developed prior to the Supreme Court's *Martinez* decision in 1978. These decisions suggest that federal courts are prepared to envision tribal courts as not having to rotely adhere to the federal definitions of many of the key provisions of the Indian Civil Rights Act of 1968.[87] With the appearance of *Martinez*, this process came to an abrupt halt because most of the cases were no longer amenable to federal court review. Yet these cases provide one possible benchmark for considering that, even when there is federal review, it ought to be flexible with regard to both tribal court objectives and the resource constraints that affect many tribes. The federal courts need to be informed of tribal objectives and "story" in order that their decision making may be informed and dialogic rather than the product of "imperial" largesse.

The big swipe of Congress' plenary authority seems best left on the sidelines in order to allow this process of localized and narrow judicial review to develop further. Such an approach would encourage, rather than impede, the mutual craft of articulating a sovereignty that proceeds slowly but surely through the process of limited federal review.

This question of federal policy highlights the darker specter of federal courts' acting in a "jurispathic" capacity. This term, originally coined by Robert Cover, means the authority of courts to kill law created by communities.[88] Efforts of tribal courts may be struck down by federal courts as simply too divergent from the majoritarian canon to be tolerated within the federal system.[89] Tribal courts and culture are obviously different from state courts and culture. Therefore, there are real questions of how to understand and to judicially think about this potentially authentic divergence.[90] In many ways, this is the heart of the problem and it goes all the way back to the beginnings of the federal republic. The focal point is the inability to envision and determine how tribal sovereignty and culture are to be integrated within a dynamic federal system. No one knows the answer, but certainly there is a cautionary note that unilateral actions and pronouncements, whether judicial or congressional, do not offer much hope beyond that of assimilation and coercion. Empathy, dialogue, and respect for emerging tribal jurisprudence hold out the most meaningful promise for achieving a future that honors and respects differences rooted in the past, but transfigured in the present, in order to achieve a secure and flourishing future for all.

CONCLUSION

The opportunities and challenges that face tribal courts are manifold and include such things as how and what law will apply. Perhaps more significant are questions related to tribal court appellate and constitutional decision making. These questions include how decisions will be influenced by tribal constitutional texts and theory, as well as tribal aspiration. The processes of law and legal decision making are not "merely a system of rules to be observed, but a world in which we live."[91] The truth of this assertion carries special meaning for Indian tribes and their tribal courts. Indian tribes have struggled from the very beginning of contact with European intruders to preserve their cultures and vindicate their claim of sovereignty. The law has played a critical role, for better or worse, in this struggle.

This world of law in which we live therefore has a deep and abiding effect on the actions of indigenous, colonized, and developing tribal communities within this republic. This pervasive influence of law needs to be transformed within tribal courts as a means to develop and to communicate tribal constitutional and moral aspirations and to elucidate the legal narrative and foundational thrust of tribal culture and sovereignty.

Tribal constitutional decision making is also vital in that it potentially sheds abstraction in favor of context that is grounded in the flesh and blood of actions and concerns of tribal communities. Such tribal constitutional narrative challenges the dominant canon that there is "only one true version of a story and that there is only one right way to tell it."[92] It is, ultimately, this challenge and the response to it that will likely determine much of the future of Indian law, as well as the quality of tribal life and the integrity of the national commitment to the treaty-based promises of flourishing "measured separatism."

NOTES

1. See *National Farmers Union Insurance Cos. v. Crow Tribe of Indians*, 471 US 845 (1985); *Iowa Mutual Insurance Co. v. LaPlante*, 480 US 9 (1987).

2. See Michael Taylor, "Modern Practice in the Tribal Courts," *University of Puget Sound Law Review* 10 (Winter, 1987): 231–75; Frank Pommersheim, "The Contextual Legitimacy of Adjudication in Tribal Courts and the Role of the Tribal Bar as an Interpretive Community: An Essay," *New Mexico Law Review* 18 (Winter, 1988): 49–71; Frank Pommersheim, "The Crucible of Sovereignty: Analyzing Issues of Tribal Jurisdiction," *Arizona Law Review* 31 (Number 2, 1989): 329–63.

3. Frank Pommersheim, "Liberation, Dreams, and Hard Work: An Essay on Tribal Court Jurisprudence," *Wisconsin Law Review* 1992 (Number 1): 411.

4. Obviously, some tribal court decisions are reviewable by federal courts, while tribal authority as a whole is caught within the net of Congress' "plenary authority" in Indian affairs. See *National Farmers Union*, 471 US 845 (1985); *Iowa Mutual*, 480 US 9 (1987); and *Lone Wolf v. Hitchcock*, 187 US 553 (1903).

5. Michael J. Perry, *Morality, Politics, and Law: A Bicentennial Essay* (New York: Oxford University Press, 1988), p. 131. Of course, it is important to note that for African Americans (and other minorities including women) the U.S. Constitution (at least in its original form) may be seen as enshrining majoritarian dominance. See e.g. Thurgood Marshall, "Reflections on the Bicentennial of the United States Constitution," *Harvard Law Review* 101 (November, 1987): 1.

6. Ibid., p. 132.

7. U.S., *United States Code* [hereafter *U.S.C.*] 25 (1990): sec. 461–79. Strictly speaking, this Congressional enabling legislation was not required to "authorize" tribes to adopt tribal constitutions. Tribes clearly retained such authority as part of their sovereignty and reserved powers not explicitly extinguished by Congress. See David H. Getches and Charles F. Wilkinson, *Federal Indian Law: Cases and Materials*, 2d ed. (St. Paul, MN: West Publishing Co., 1986), p. xxv; Felix S. Cohen, *Handbook of Federal Indian Law* (Washington, D.C.: U.S. Department of Interior, 1942) and rev. ed., Rennard Strickland and Charles F. Wilkinson, eds. (Charlottesville, VA: Michie Bobbs-Merrill, 1982), pp. 231–42. As to the numbers themselves, note that

> [D]uring the two year period within which tribes could accept or reject the IRA, 258 elections were held. In these elections, 181 tribes (129,750 Indians) accepted the Act and 77 tribes (86,365 Indians, including 45,000 Navajos) rejected it. The IRA also applies to fourteen groups of Indians who did not hold elections to exclude themselves. Within twelve years, 161 constitutions and 131 corporate charters had been adopted pursuant to the IRA.

Comment, "Tribal Self-Government and the Indian Reorganization Act of 1934," *Michigan Law Review* 70 (April, 1970): 955, 972. Many other non-IRA tribes adopted written constitutions, which are often quite similar to IRA constitutions. Some tribes, such as the Navajo, do not have a written constitution. Ibid., pp. 972–73.

8. U.S., *U.S.C.* 25 (1988): sec. 476.

9. Ibid., 25 (1988): sec. 476(d)(2).

10. Ibid., 25 (1988) sec. 476(c)(3). The term "applicable laws" is defined to mean "any treaty, Executive Order or Act of Congress or any final decision of the Federal courts which are applicable to the tribe, and any other laws which are applicable to the tribe pursuant to an Act of Congress or by any final decision of the Federal Courts." Pub. L. 100–581 (1988): sec. 102(1).

11. Judith Resnik, "Dependent Sovereigns: Indian Tribes, States, and the Federal Courts," *University of Chicago Law Review* 56 (Spring, 1989): 672, 712.

12. Ibid. See also Curtis Berkey, "Implementation of the Indian Reorganization Act," *American Indian Journal* 2 (August, 1976): 2, 4. "In retrospect the Interior Department played a larger role than the tribes in drafting constitutions (p. 4)."

Tribal constitutions "were, in most instances, prepared in advance by the Bureau of Indian Affairs and reflected little, if any, tribal input and retained substantial review authority within the BIA." Frank Pommersheim and Terry Pechota, "Tribal Immunity, Tribal Courts, and the Federal System: Emerging Contours and Frontiers," *South Dakota Law Review* 31 (Summer, 1986): 553, 556.

13. *Kerr-McGee Corp. v. Navajo Tribe*, 471 US 195, 198 (1985).

14. For example, the very impetus for the adoption of the Indian Civil Rights Act of 1968, U.S., *U.S.C.* 25 (1983): sec. 1301–03, came from the federal government's perception and findings concerning the absence of these protections in Indian country. See Donald L. Burnett, Jr., "An Historical Analysis of the 1968

'Indian Civil Rights Act,'" *Harvard Journal on Legislation* 9 (May, 1972): 557–626; Comment, "The Indian Bill of Rights and the Constitutional Status of Tribal Governments," *Harvard Law Review* 82 (April, 1969): 1343–73. Tribal support was less than enthusiastic. See Robert T. Coulter, "Federal Law and Indian Tribal Law: The Right to Civil Counsel and the 1968 Indian Bill of Rights," *Columbia Survey Human Rights Law* 3 (January, 1971): 49–93.

Much of the current critique of tribal courts relates to the separation of powers question. See Pommersheim, "Legitimacy in Tribal Courts," p. 60. This critique continues to surface in almost any discussion of tribal courts with members of the practicing bar in South Dakota. There is little evidence in such conversations about the root of the problem resting with the BIA rather than the tribes.

15. Rosebud Sioux Tribe, Constitution, Art. X (1966). The Article specifically provides:

> Section 1. All members of the tribe and all Indians on the reservation shall enjoy without hindrance freedom of religion, speech, press, assembly, conscience and association.
>
> Section 2. Any Indian on the reservation accused of any offense shall have the right to a speedy and public trial and to be informed of the nature and cause of the accusation, and to be confronted with witnesses against him. Any Indian accused of any offense shall have the right to the assistance of counsel and to demand trial by jury. Excessive bail shall not be required, nor excessive fines imposed, nor cruel and unusual punishments inflicted.
>
> Section 3. No person shall be subject for the same offense to be twice put in jeopardy; nor be compelled in any criminal case to be a witness against himself; nor be deprived of life, liberty, or property, without due process of law; nor be denied equal protection of law. [Adopted by Amendment XI, effective May 21, 1966.]

16. U.S., *U.S.C.* 25 (1983): sec. 1301–03.

17. Article XVIII of the Rosebud Sioux Tribe Constitution effectively removed all prior review authority of the BIA to review tribal ordinances enacted by the Tribal Council pursuant to its enumerated and reserved powers set out in Article IV—Powers of the Rosebud Sioux Tribal Council. Rosebud Sioux Tribe, Constitution, Art. XVIII (1985).

18. Rosebud Sioux Tribe, Constitution, Art. IX, sec. 2 (1985). Other kinds of possible tribal constitutional amendments include such things as separation of powers, increased accountability through recall, initiative and referendum provisions, and decentralization with more authority accorded to local communities.

19. Perry, *Morality, Politics, and Law*, p. 142.

20. Frank Pommersheim, "The Reservation as Place: A South Dakota Essay," *South Dakota Law Review* 34 (Issue 2, 1989): 246, 252–53. The quality of those treaty "exchanges" varied significantly. Many tribes were forced to agree to small reservations in regions removed from their aboriginal territories because the federal government had the strong military upper hand. Yet in other cases, particularly involving the Lakota of the Great Sioux Nation in South Dakota, there was a virtual military standoff and the reservations were established in the heart of the traditional Sioux homeland in the Dakota Territory.

21. Ibid., pp. 252–53.

22. Peter John Powell, "The Sacred Treaty," quoted in Roxanne Dunbar Ortiz, *The Great Sioux Nation: Sitting in Judgment on America* (Berkeley, CA: Moon Books, 1977), p. 106.

23. U.S. Const. Art. III, sec. 2.

24. See notes 63–78 and accompanying text.

25. See John H. Garvey and T. Alexander Aleinikoff, *Modern Constitutional Theory*, 2d ed. (St. Paul, MN: West Publishing Co., 1993), for a discussion of the broad range of possibilities such as interpretism/non-interpretism, the role of the text, original intent, neutral principles, and balancing.

26. Perry, *Morality, Politics, and Law*, p. 132.

27. See Robert H. Bork, "The Constitution, Original Intent, and Economic Rights," *San Diego Law Review* 23 (July-August, 1986): 823–32; Edwin Meese III, "Toward a Jurisprudence of Original Intention," *Benchmark* 2 (January-February, 1986): 1–10; and Antonin Scalia, "Originalism: The Lesser Evil," *University of Cincinnati Law Review* 57 (Number 3, 1989): 849–65.

28. Perry, *Morality, Politics, and Law*, p. 133.

29. Ibid.

30. For example, basic legislative authority in the areas of tax and the regulation of land use.

31. See notes 64–78 and accompanying text.

32. *Johnson v. McIntosh*, 21 US 543 (1823).

33. *Cherokee Nation v. Georgia*, 30 US 1 (1831).

34. *Worcester v. Georgia*, 31 US 515 (1832).

35. Indian tribes are only mentioned once in the Constitution, and that is in the Commerce Clause, which states that Congress shall have the power to "regulate Commerce with foreign Nations, and among the several States, and with the Indian Tribes." U.S., Const., Art. I, sec. 8. Indian tribes are implicitly subjects of the treaty making power. U.S., Const., Art. II, sec. 2. Individual Indians are mentioned as "Indians not taxed." U.S., Const., Art. I, sec. 2.

36. *Worcester v. Georgia*, 31 US at 559–63.

37. See sources in notes 33–34.

38. See the cases and discussion in Getches and Wilkinson, *Federal Indian Law*, pp. 269–336, 416–547.

39. See Robert A. Williams, Jr., *The American Indian in Western Legal Thought* (New York: Oxford University Press, 1990), pp. 233–328.

40. See *United States v. Kagama*, 118 US 375 (1886); and especially, *Lone Wolf v. Hitchcock*, 187 US 553 (1903).

41. Perry, *Morality, Politics, and Law*, p. 137.

42. Ibid.

43. Ibid., p. 139.

44. Ibid., p. 137.

45. *Poe v. Ullman*, 367 US 497, 540 (1961), (Harlan, J., dissenting).

46. Ibid., at 540; citing *McCulloch v. Maryland*, 17 US 316 (1819).

47. Pommersheim, "The Reservation as Place," pp. 268–70.

48. Perry, *Morality, Politics, and Law*, p. 138.

49. Vine Deloria, Jr., and Clifford Lytle, *The Nations Within: The Past and Future of American Indian Sovereignty* (New York: Pantheon Books, 1984), p. 245.

50. Robert M. Cover, "The Supreme Court, 1982 Term—Forward: Nomos and Narrative," *Harvard Law Review* 97 (November, 1983): 4–5.

51. See Pommersheim, "The Crucible of Sovereignty," p. 333.

52. See Vine Deloria, Jr.'s observations that because federal courts seem to be operating on an *ad hoc* basis, Indian law does not really exist as a theoretical discipline. He said that the study of different disciplines such as culture, religion, education, economics, history, language, and logic all have important lessons for a lawyer looking for new strategies to practice law. "NARF Celebrates Its 20th Anniversary," *NARF Legal Review* 15 (Summer, 1990): 3.

53. See Cover, "Nomos and Narrative," pp. 4–11.

54. Robert N. Bellah et al., *The Good Society* (New York: Knopf, 1991). The authors also point out that "in surveying our present institutions we need to discern what is healthy in them and what needs to be altered, particularly where we have begun to destroy the non-renewable natural and nearly non-renewable human resources upon which all our institutions depend." Ibid., p. 5.

55. For example, no law review article in the past five years discusses tribal sovereignty in the context of local institution building. See also sources cited in notes 2–3.

56. See cases in note 1.

57. Chief Justice Marshall is a bilingual, bicultural member of the Rosebud Sioux Tribe. He is also a 1984 graduate of the University of South Dakota School of Law and a member of the South Dakota Bar.

58. Interview by author with Sherman Marshall, Chief Justice of the Rosebud Sioux Tribal Court, July, 1990.

59. Additional plans include the administration of a tribal bar examination. See generally, Pommersheim, "The Contextual Legitimacy."

60. See Resnik, "Dependent Sovereigns."

61. Charles F. Wilkinson, *American Indians, Time, and the Law: Native Societies in a Modern Constitutional Democracy* (New Haven, CT: Yale University Press, 1987), pp. 14–19. See also Pommersheim, "Reservation as Place," pp. 254–58.

62. See Justice Potter Stewart's declaration that "the sovereignty that the Indian tribes retain is of a unique and limited character. It exists only at the sufferance of Congress and is subject to complete defeasance." *United States v. Wheeler*, 435 US 323 (1978).

63. "Modern" tribal institutions, such as tribal courts, particularly those that have their origins in the Indian Reorganization Act of 1934, face the problem of

being seen as "the imposition of white man's law and standards." Pommersheim and Pechota, "Tribal Immunity, Tribal Courts," p. 556.

64. Pommersheim, "Crucible of Sovereignty," pp. 360–62.

65. *National Farmers Union Insurance Company v. Crow Tribe of Indians*, 471 US 845 (1985).

66. *Iowa Mutual Insurance Company v. LaPlante*, 480 US 9 (1987).

67. Ibid., at pp. 15–16; *National Farmers Union*, 471 US 856–57 (1985).

68. *National Farmers Union*, 471 US 856–57; see also *FMC v. Shoreline-Bannock Tribes*, 905 F.2d 1311, 1313–14 (9th Cir. 1990), cert. denied, 111 S. Ct. 1404 (1991).

69. Pommersheim, "Crucible of Sovereignty," pp. 354–55, discussing *Twin Cities Const. Co. v. Turtle Mountain Board of Chippewa Indians*, 857 F.2d 1177 (8th Cir. 1988). The alleged mistake of tribal law may or may not involve an alleged mistake of tribal constitutional law. In *Twin Cities*, the alleged mistake of tribal law involved an interpretation of a tribal ordinance.

70. See Robert F. Williams, "State Constitutional Law: Teaching & Scholarship," *Journal of Legal Education* 41 (June, 1991): 243.

71. Ibid., p. 245.

72. Ibid.

73. Ibid., p. 247.

74. For example, any number of seminal Indian law cases such as *Lone Wolf v. Hitchcock*, 187 US 553 (1903) (identifying Congress' unreviewable plenary power in Indian affairs and the unilateral right to abrogate treaties) do not even merit any meaningful attention in standard constitutional law texts.

75. See Rosebud Sioux Constitution, Art. X.

76. Williams, "State Constitutional Law," p. 246.

77. See Appendix A.

78. Robert A. Williams, Jr., "Encounters on the Frontiers of International Human Rights Law: Redefining the Terms of Indigenous Peoples' Survival in the World," *Duke Law Journal* 1990 (Number 4): 660, 684–85.

79. See the excellent discussion in Robert N. Clinton's "Tribal Courts and the Federal Union," *Williamette Law Review* 26 (Fall, 1990): 873–97.

80. See *Lone Wolf v. Hitchcock*, 187 US 553 (1903).

81. U.S., *U.S.C.* 25 (1984): sec. 1301–03.

82. Ibid., sec. 1303.

83. *Santa Clara Pueblo v. Martinez*, 436 US 49 (1978).

84. Ibid., pp. 66–67.

85. Ibid., p. 65.

86. See Appendix B.

87. See *Smith v. Confederated Tribes of the Warm Springs Reservation*, 783 F2d 1409 (9th Cir. 1986) where the procedures that tribal courts choose to adopt are not necessarily the same procedures that the federal courts follow; *Tom v. Sutton*, 533 F2d 1101 (9th Cir. 1976) where due process and equal protection

under the Indian Civil Rights Act of 1968 are not necessarily defined in the same way as they are under the Fourteenth Amendment.

88. Cover, "Nomos and Narrative," p. 40.

89. Resnik, "Dependent Sovereigns," pp. 754–56.

90. Ibid., p. 733.

91. Cover, "Nomos and Narrative," p. 5.

92. Kim Lane Schepple, "Forward: Telling Stories," *Michigan Law Review* 87 (August 1989) 2073, 2098.

Appendix A

Article IV—Powers of the Rosebud Sioux Tribal Council

Section 1. Enumerated powers.—The council of the Rosebud Sioux Tribe shall exercise the following powers, subject to any limitations imposed by the statutes or the Constitution of the United States, and subject further to all express restriction upon such powers contained in this constitution and attached bylaws. [Amendment No. 1, effective June 19, 1962.]

(a) To negotiate with the Federal, State, and local Governments on behalf of the tribe and to advise and consult with the representatives of the Interior Department on all activities of the Department that may affect the Rosebud Sioux Reservation.

(b) To employ legal counsel for the protection and advancement of the rights of the tribe and its members, the choice of council and fixing of fees to be subject to the approval of the Secretary of the Interior.

(c) To purchase and to otherwise acquire lands and other property for or on behalf of the Tribe and manage, permit, assign, lease, sell, exchange, encumber, or otherwise deal with tribal lands and property as authorized by law; provided that there shall be no sales of Tribal or T.L.E. managed lands and no land trades to any non-Indians within the original boundaries of the 1868 Treaty without the consent of Tribal members, and to prevent the sale, disposition, lease or encumbrance of tribal lands, interests in tribal lands or tribal assets without the consent of the Tribe; provided, that in leasing tribal land for grazing or agricultural purposes preference shall be given to any member of the Tribe who is the economic head of the family. [Amendment No. II, effective June 19, 1962.] [Amendment No. XXI, effective September 23, 1985.]

(d) To advise the Secretary of the Interior with regard to all appropriation estimates or Federal projects for the benefit of the tribe prior to the submission of such estimates to any Departments of the United States Government, and to Congress. [Amendment No. XVIII, effective September 23, 1985.]

(e) To make assignments of tribal land to members of the tribe in conformity with Article VIII of this constitution.

(f) To manage all economic affairs and enterprises of the tribe in accordance with the terms of a charter which may be issued to the tribe by the Secretary of the Interior.

(g) To appropriate for public purposes of the Rosebud Sioux Tribe available tribal council funds. [Amendment No. XVIII, effective September 23, 1985.]

(h) To levy taxes upon members of the tribe and to require the performance of reservation labor in lieu thereof, and to levy taxes or license fees upon non-members doing business within the reservation. [Amendment No. XVIII, effective September 23, 1985.]

(i) To exclude by ordinance from the restricted lands of the reservation persons not legally entitled to reside therein. [Amendment No. XVIII, effective September 23, 1985].

(j) To enact resolutions or ordinances not inconsistent with Article II of this constitution governing the adoption and abandonment of membership.

(k) To promulgate and enforce ordinances providing for the maintenance of law and order and the administration of justice by establishing a reservation court and defining its duties and powers. [Amendment No. XVIII, effective September 23, 1985.]

(l) To purchase lands of members of the tribe for public purposes, under condemnation proceedings in courts of competent jurisdiction.

(m) To safeguard and promote the peace, safety, morals, and general welfare of the tribe by regulating the conduct of trade and the use and disposition of property upon the reservation and provided further that non-restricted property of members which was obtained without any help or assistance of the Government or the tribe may be disposed of without restrictions. [Amendment No. XVIII, effective September 23, 1985.]

(n) To charter subordinate organizations for economic purposes and to regulate the activities of all cooperative associations of members of the tribe.

(o) To regulate the inheritance of property, real and personal, other than allotted lands, within the territory of the reservation. [Amendment No. XVIII, effective September 23, 1985.]

(p) To regulate the domestic relations of members of the tribe.

(q) To provide for the appointment of guardians for minors and mental incompetents by ordinance or resolution. [Amendment No. XVIII, effective September 23, 1985.]

(r) To exchange and foster the arts, crafts, traditions, and culture of the Sioux.

(s) To regulate the manner of making nominations and holding elections for tribal offices.

(t) To adopt resolutions regulating the procedure of the council itself and of other tribal agencies and tribal officials.

(u) To delegate to subordinate boards or tribal officials, to the several communities, or to cooperative associations which are open to all members of the tribe any of the foregoing powers, reserving the right to review any action taken by virtue of such delegated power. [Former Section 2 repealed by Amendment No. XVIII, effective September 23, 1985.]

Section 2. Future Powers.—The tribal council may exercise such further powers as may in the future be delegated to the tribe by the Secretary of the Interior or, by any duly authorized official or agency of the State or Federal Government.

Section 3. Reserved Powers.—Any rights and powers heretofore vested in the Rosebud Sioux Tribe but not expressly referred to in this constitution shall not be abridged by this article, but may be exercised by the people of the Rosebud Sioux Tribe through the adoption of appropriate by-laws and constitutional amendments.

Appendix B

S.517 (101st Congress) provides:

BE IT ENACTED BY THE SENATE AND HOUSE OF REPRESENTATIVES OF THE UNITED STATES OF AMERICA IN CONGRESS ASSEMBLED, that this Act may be cited as the Indian Civil Rights Act Amendments of 1989. Sec. 2. Title II of the Civil Rights Act of 1968 (Public Law 90–284, 25 U.S.C. 1301 et seq. (1988), commonly called the Indian Civil Rights Act or the Indian Bill of Rights, is amended by adding at the end thereof the following new section: CIVIL ACTIONS

Sec. 204. (a) Compliance With Section 202.—Federal district courts shall have jurisdiction of civil rights action alleging a failure to comply with rights secured by this Act. Sovereign immunity shall not constitute a defense to such an action. (b) Any aggrieved individual, following the exhaustion of such tribal remedies as may be both timely and reasonable under the circumstances, or the Attorney General on behalf of the United States, may initiate an action in Federal district court for declaratory, injunctive or other equitable relief against an Indian tribe, tribal organization, or official thereof, alleging a failure to comply with rights secured by this Act. (c) In any civil action brought by an aggrieved individual, or by the Attorney General, the Federal district court shall adopt the findings of fact of the tribal court, if such findings have been made, unless the district court determines that:

(1) the tribal court was not fully independent from the tribal legislative or executive authority;
(2) the tribal court was not authorized to or did not finally determine matters of law and fact;
(3) the tribal court permitted those subject to the Act, on issues of declaratory, injunctive or other equitable relief, to interpose a defense of immunity;
(4) the tribal court failed to resolve the merits of the factual dispute;
(5) the tribal court employed a factfinding procedure not adequate to afford a full and fair hearing;
(6) the tribal court did not adequately develop material facts;
(7) the tribal court failed to provide a full, fair, and adequate hearing; or
(8) the factual determinations of the tribal court are not fairly supported by the record, in which event the district court shall conduct a de novo review of the allegations contained in the complaint.

(d) In any civil actions brought under this Act the Federal court shall, whenever a question of tribal law is at issue, accord due deference to the interpretation of the tribal laws and customs.

Senator Hatch's proposed legislation initially was introduced in a different form as S.2747 in the 100th Congress and was reintroduced in the 101st Congress as S.517 and sent to the Judiciary Committee for review.

Index

About the Contributors

JAMES W. ELY, JR. is Professor of Law at Vanderbilt University. He is the author of *The Guardian of Every Other Right: A Constitutional History of Property Rights* (1991), co-editor of *The Uncertain Tradition: Constitutionalism and the History of the South* (1989), and numerous other books and articles.

PAUL FINKELMAN is visiting Professor of Law at Chicago-Kent College of Law and Hamline School of Law in 1995–96. He is the author of *An Imperfect Union: Slavery, Federalism, and Comity* (1981) and numerous scholarly articles, and he is co-editor of *American Legal History: Cases and Materials* (1991).

KERMIT L. HALL is Professor of History and Law and Dean of the College of Humanities at The Ohio State University. He is the author of *The Magic Mirror: Law in American History* (1989), *The Politics of Justice: Lower Judicial Selection and the Second American Party System, 1829–1861* (1979), and numerous edited books and articles.

ANDREW B. KOSZEWSKI is judicial law clerk for Judge David S. Doty of the U.S. District Court of Minnesota. He holds a law degree from the

University of Iowa and an M.A. in history from the University of Nebraska–Lincoln, having written the thesis, "William Jennings Bryan's Law Practice in Nebraska, 1887–1891." He is the author of "Career Differentiation: The Legal Community in Lincoln, Nebraska, 1880–1891," *Great Plains Research* 2 (August 1992): 281–300.

SCOTT LANDERS received his Ph.D in philosophy from Duke University. His research focuses on the nature of legal and moral rules, the work of Ludwig Wittgenstein, and epistemological and metaphysical problems in the social sciences. He has taught at Duke University and San Diego State University and currently teaches at the University of San Diego.

LAWRENCE H. LARSEN is Professor of History at the University of Missouri at Kansas City. He is the author of *Federal Justice in Western Missouri: The Judges, the Cases, the Times* (1994), *The Urban South: A History* (1990), and *The Urban West at the End of the Frontier* (1978).

MICHAEL S. MAYER is Associate Professor of History at the University of Montana. He is the author of *Merrill Proudfoot, Diary of a Sit-In* (1990) and numerous articles on civil rights during the Eisenhower administration.

FRANK POMMERSHEIM is Professor of Law at the University of South Dakota. He is the author of *Braid of Feathers: American Indian Law and Contemporary Tribal Life* (1995) and numerous articles on Indian courts and federal Indian law. He is also a judge on the tribal court of the Cheyenne River Sioux Reservation.

JOHN R. WUNDER is Professor of History and Director of the Center for Great Plains Studies at the University of Nebraska–Lincoln. He is the author of *"Retained by The People": A History of American Indians and the Bill of Rights* (1994), *Inferior Courts, Superior Justice: Justices of the Peace on the Northwest Frontier, 1853–1889* (Westport, CT: Greenwood Press, 1979), and other edited books and articles.

ISBN 0-313-29680-4

90000>

EAN

9 780313 296802

HARDCOVER BAR CODE